ELEMENTS OF CHANGE
IN
EASTERN EUROPE

ELEMENTS OF CHANGE IN EASTERN EUROPE
PROSPECTS FOR FREEDOM

Edited by

DAVID S. COLLIER

and

KURT GLASER

Published in cooperation with
Foundation for Foreign Affairs, Inc.

HENRY REGNERY COMPANY
CHICAGO

FOUNDATION FOR FOREIGN AFFAIRS SERIES, NUMBER 12

The Foundation for Foreign Affairs, 154 East Superior Street, Chicago, Illinois 60611, is a non-profit corporation devoted to the promotion of a wider understanding of international relations—political, economic and cultural. Books in the Foundation for Foreign Affairs Series are published in the interest of public information and debate. They represent the free expression of their authors and do not necessarily indicate the judgment and opinions of the Foundation.

Contents

Part One

EASTERN EUROPE IN THE INTERPLAY OF WORLD POLITICAL FORCES

Part Two

CHRISTIAN CHURCHES AND TOTALITARIAN RULE

Part Four

CULTURAL ASPECTS OF THE CHANGE IN EASTERN EUROPE

Part Five

IN SUMMARY

Introduction

THE ESSAYS IN this book, the fourth of a series, are based on the papers presented at the Fourth International Congress on the problems of Eastern Europe, held in Wiesbaden, September 6–9, 1966, under the joint sponsorship of the Foundation for Foreign Affairs of Chicago and the Studiengesellschaft für Fragen mittel- und osteuropäischer Partnerschaft of Wiesbaden. At a time when informed opinion seems to agree that there is a détente in East-West relations in Europe but is divided and uncertain as to its depth and meaning, these essays may contribute toward an intellectual foundation for rational foreign policy, despite their analytical rather than operational emphasis.

The first of the joint conferences, held, so to speak, in the shadow of the recently erected Berlin Wall, was among other things an initial meeting of minds across the Atlantic. Distinctive European and American approaches to the structural problems of European politics were quite evident, as was a need for intellectual as well as linguistic translation. The common experiences of a more or less permanent nucleus of scholars representing several countries including the United States and Canada have by now yielded clear evidences of an Atlantic approach to problems. Such an approach is the gateway to an Atlantic policy based on community of national interests and ethical convictions.

Successive conferences have dealt with the changing political, economic, and social situation on both sides of the Iron Curtain. The second conference, in 1963, took as its point of departure the premise that European integration, in the form of the Coal and Steel Community and the then evolving Common Market, could not fail to exercise an attractive force on communist countries in East Europe. The reaction of East Europeans, including party and government officials as well as a skeptical younger generation, was a major factor in producing the changes that were the subject of the conference that gave rise to this book. The third meeting, held in Chicago in 1965, undertook to focus attention on the morphology of communist systems, on the long-range objectives of communist plans, and on those communist tactics that constitute problems for Western policy. That conference also made clear, however, that there are natural limitations to totalitarian intellectual control, and that freedom is an existential reality, even, and perhaps precisely, when it has to struggle against political oppression. In so doing, the Chicago conference laid the groundwork for the most recent conference.

In selecting the Wiesbaden conference speakers and hence the contributors to this volume, the international committee tapped a wide range of political and scholarly experience and authority. It was thus possible to assure fair consideration for the legitimate interests of all nations and ethnic groups concerned in the unraveling of the complex problems that stand in the way of a viable European settlement.

Senator Thomas J. Dodd of Connecticut, who introduces the discussion with a survey in depth of the foreign policy problems facing the United States with respect to its European and Asian relationships, acquired familiarity with Europe as chief trial counsel at Nuremberg, but he is better known for his work as a member of the Senate's Foreign Relations Committee and Internal Security Subcommittee. Supplementing hearings and documentary study with fact-finding trips, occasionally at some personal risk, the Senator has established a reputation for constructive criticism of contemporary American foreign policy, which he insists should be based on facts, not illusions.

Professor Boris Meissner of the University of Cologne, who reports on political developments in the Soviet Union under Brezhnev and Kosygin, is a former diplomat who served for a time as First Secretary of the West German embassy in Moscow. Presently, he is chairman of the executive committee of the German Federal Institute for the Study of Marxism-Leninism. Besides his numerous contributions to scholarly journals, he has written a number of books and monographs on East European affairs, dealing with subjects such as *Russia, The Western Powers, and Germany* (1953), *Russia Under Khrushchev* (1960), and *The Soviet Union and International Law* (1963).*

* Titles by European authors have been translated into English.—*Eds.*

Professor Philip E. Mosely of Columbia University, who analyzes the effect of world power politics on East Europe, is director of studies of the Council on Foreign Relations and one of America's best known area specialists. He has served as political advisor to the United States delegations at a number of international conferences and is the author of *The Kremlin and World Politics* (1960).

Professor Wu Chen-tsai, Director of the Institute for International Affairs at Taipei, Republic of China, is well known for his active participation in international discussions on Far Eastern affairs and for his generous assistance to American scholars.

Dr. Richard Walker, who writes on European involvement in Asia, has traveled extensively in the Far East and is the author of a number of books on China. He is James F. Byrnes professor of international relations and head of the Department of International Studies at the University of South Carolina.

Of the two authors who deal with problems of German reunification and the European Center, Professor Willi Brundert is a former high official of the Sachsen-Anhalt government in the Soviet Zone and professor of administration and economics at the University of Halle. In 1949 he was arrested by the communist authorities and sentenced to fifteen years' imprisonment for "sabotage" in a notorious propaganda trial. After friends in West Germany secured his release in 1957, he re-entered public service, this time in the state of Hesse, and is now Lord Mayor of the city of Frankfurt am Main. Karl Theodor Freiherr zu Guttenberg, active in Bavarian politics since 1946, has been a member of the German *Bundestag* and its foreign affairs committee since 1957. His book *If the West Has the Will* (1964) is now being translated into English.

Dr. Wenzel Jaksch, who deals with "Germany and Russia's European Policy" in terms of contemporary political realities, was a member of the Czechoslovak parliament from 1929 to 1938, rising to the leadership of his party. In exile in England during World War II he was the leading democratic representative of the Sudeten Germans and sought vainly to dissuade Dr. Beneš from his plan to expel the German-speaking inhabitants of Czechoslovakia. Upon his return to Germany he assumed the demanding position of ministerial director in charge of expellee affairs in Hesse, leaving that post upon his election to the *Bundestag* in 1957. As a member of the foreign affairs committee, he sponsored the preparation of a series of parliamentary reports dealing with the normalization of relations between the

German Federal Republic and East European countries. His book *Europe's Road to Potsdam* appeared in English translation in 1963. Dr. Jaksch's sudden death on November 27, 1966, shortly after his seventieth birthday, was a tragic loss to all concerned with the betterment of relations within the Atlantic Community and with the search for just and permanent solutions to the problems of a divided Europe.

Will Herberg, who analyzes the dilemmas faced by Christians confronting totalitarianism, is one of America's best known Jewish theologians and graduate professor of philosophy and culture at Drew University. His many books include *Judaism and Modern Man* (1951) and *Community, State and Church* (1960).

Those liberals who are inclined to dismiss the phrase "atheistic communism" as a superpatriotic cliché would do well to ponder the experiences of Paolo Hnilica, who provides a firsthand account of the tribulations of the Roman Catholic Church under totalitarian rule. A member of the Jesuit Order who had not quite completed his studies for the priesthood, Hnilica was arrested in April, 1950, and confined in a forced labor camp along with all other members of religious orders in Czechoslovakia. After his release he was secretly ordained a priest and later a bishop in the underground Church, the members of which undertake at great personal risk to fill the vacuum left by state restriction and corruption of the visible Church. When the communist political police learned of his activities, Hnilica was forced to escape to the West, where he has since played a leading role in the religious affairs of Slovak exiles and emigrants. His critical analysis of communist religious policies at the Vatican Council on September 26, 1965, attracted considerable attention in both parts of Europe. His pamphlet, *Religious Problems in a Communist-ruled Country*, has appeared in nine languages.

In the symposium on "Recent Developments in East-Central Europe" five area experts analyze the contemporary situation in individual countries. Dr. Jerzy Hauptmann, who planned and organized this part of the program, is a former member of the Polish underground who fought in the Warsaw Uprising of 1944. Taken prisoner by the Germans, he decided to remain in the West when it became apparent that his country would be ruled by the Communists. After obtaining his doctorate at the University of Innsbruck, he came to the United States, where he is now professor of political science at Park College, Parkville, Missouri.

Dr. Heinrich Kuhn, who contributes the section on Czechoslovakia, is director of the Sudeten German Archives in Munich and author of several books, including *Communism in Czechoslovakia* (1965), *Governmental Handbook of Czechoslovakia* (1966), and several geographical and biographical reference works. The author of the Hungarian section, Dr. Helmut Klocke, is a career civil servant who has engaged in research on Hungarian problems and written extensively on economics and society in southeast Europe. Dr. Richard Staar, who provides the information on Poland, is professor of political science at Emory University, Atlanta, Georgia. He has lived in Poland and has written extensively on Polish affairs. Dr. Otto R. Liess, of Vienna, who deals with Rumania in his part of the symposium, is a well-known research scholar whose works include *Planned Economy and Socialism in Rumania* (1962), *Hungary Between East and West* (1965), and *WFTU vs. IFFTU: Trade Union Confrontation and East-West Conversations* (1966). The author of the section on Yugoslavia, Johann Hawlowitsch, is a graduate economist and research associate at the Seminar for Southeast European Economy and Society at the University of Munich.

Dr. Eugen Lemberg, who analyzes the recent evolution of Marxism-Leninism in East-Central Europe, has occupied various important positions in the fields of teacher training and school administration. Since 1957 he has been professor of history at the Academy for International Education in Frankfurt and a member of the board of directors of the J. G. Herder Research Council and Institute of Marburg. He has written a large number of books and monographs, including *People and Ethnic Groups in Exile* (1953), *Historical Awareness in East-Central Europe* (1962), and *Nationalism* (two volumes, 1964).

Eugene Davidson, whose essay, "The Wave of the Past," places the contemporary European situation in historical perspective, was for many years editor of the Yale University Press. Currently, he is President of the Foundation for Foreign Affairs and author of *The Death and Life of Germany* (1959) and *The Trial of the Germans* (1967).

Kurt Glaser, whose concluding essay summarizes and interprets the findings of the contributors, is professor of government at Southern Illinois University, Edwardsville, Illinois. His publications include *The Iron Curtain and American Policy* (1953) and *Czecho-Slovakia: A Critical History* (1961).

In conclusion, the editors would like to thank the many people who assisted in the assembly, preparation, and review of the manuscripts, in particular Misses Heike Krüger and Ursula Pontz, of the Studiengesellschaft für Fragen mittel- und osteuropäischer Partnerschaft, Mr. Terry Pickett, American exchange student at Kiel, and Miss Elisabeth Halasz, of the Foundation for Foreign Affairs.

David S. Collier
Foundation for Foreign Affairs, Inc.

Kurt Glaser
Southern Illinois University

March, 1968

CHAPTER I

The United States Between Europe and Asia

THOMAS J. DODD

ALTHOUGH THERE are a number of points on which issue might be taken with contemporary United States foreign policy—and the present writer has not hesitated to criticize when criticism seemed to fulfill a constructive purpose—there are nevertheless a greater number of aspects in which Americans can take pride. Among these may be enumerated the wisdom and generosity of our foreign aid program, through which we have thus far spent a total of $116 billion in promoting the security and the welfare of other nations. Despite occasional errors of judgment and the failures that are inevitable in any far-flung enterprise, there is no denying the miracles that this program has wrought in postwar Europe and Japan, in Formosa and Korea and Thailand, and in an ever-increasing number of emerging countries.

Americans can also take pride in the steadfastness displayed by successive Administrations and by the people as a whole in times of crisis. In three polls, one taken at the time of the Berlin blockade and the other two after Khrushchev's 1958 Berlin ultimatum, the American people were asked whether they believed their government should risk war to defend Berlin. By a margin of approximately ten to one, in each case, they replied that Berlin should be defended, even at the cost of war. And in the present crisis in Vietnam, all the indications are that the Administration enjoys the same overwhelming measure of popular support for its policy of firmness. There are, to be sure, widespread differences of opinion on what to do about Vietnam. But these differences are mainly a matter of tactics and degree.

1

In Vietnam the United States has demonstrated a willingness to face up to the fact that the struggle for freedom is indivisible—although some of our European friends, regrettably, still harbor the illusion that freedom can be defended in Europe while it is abandoned in Asia. Our Vietnam policy, moreover, should serve as a warning to our enemies and an assurance to our allies that we are prepared to pay whatever price may be demanded to defend freedom and resist communist aggression in any part of the world.

American foreign policy has with some justice been described as an extension of our own Declaration of Independence into the field of foreign affairs. Our European friends, with their centuries-long tradition of power politics, may consider this starry-eyed and unrealistic. But the American political tradition is profoundly different from the European tradition in several major respects.

Because our history begins with our own struggle for independence, anti-imperialism has from the beginning had the force of a credo with the American people. We have sympathized, spontaneously and genuinely, with every subject people aspiring to independence—sometimes, to be sure, even when they have not been culturally prepared for independence. We have sought—almost with missionary zeal—to internationalize our own concept of democracy and our commitment to the belief that all men are created equal. Sometimes, in our own idealism, we have been disposed to ignore those important differences that make paternalistic or authoritarian governments more natural and effective, at least for a transitional period, in the case of some newly emerging nations. But whatever mistakes of judgment may have been made, American policy has been right more often than wrong, both morally and in terms of the requirements of practical politics.

European Doubts About America

Before considering what concrete measures can be taken to strengthen NATO and reinvigorate the Western alliance, it is desirable to consider in complete frankness some doubts our European allies have about us and a few doubts we have about them. There has, for example, been widespread suspicion in Europe, especially in West Germany, regarding our negotiations for a treaty banning the proliferation of nuclear weapons. Some critics of American policy have suggested that America would be prepared to sacrifice NATO in return for a nonproliferation treaty.

Political realists need have no illusions about Soviet goals in seeking a nonproliferation treaty. The Soviets have sought from the beginning to bring about the dissolution of NATO and the withdrawal of American armed forces from Europe. The kind of treaty they have been demanding in Geneva is in essential harmony with this basic objective. Nor would a nonproliferation treaty bring many concrete benefits to the free world. It would not, for one thing, deter Red China from developing its own nuclear weapons. Nor would it discourage Nasser or any other extremist dictator who decided to acquire nuclear weapons to advance his imperialist ambitions and could afford them. It might not, in the long run, deter even the government of India, despite its present antinuclear posture, from embarking on a nuclear weapons program of its own as a measure of self-defense against Red China. To the extent that such a treaty might exercise any restraining influence, it would deter only those democratic nations that least require deterring because they have no present intention of trying to develop a nuclear capability of their own.

This is not a categorical condemnation of limited agreements in the field of nuclear armaments. On the contrary, every *realistic* agreement we can reach with the Soviet Union in this vital area serves the cause of peace. Nuclear weapons are so frightening, however, that our thinking on the subject tends to be fraught with emotion—with the result that we have sometimes pursued completely unrealistic and unobtainable objectives. It is obvious, for instance, that American efforts to achieve a comprehensive test-ban treaty were doomed to failure from the beginning, because the Soviet Union was never going to agree to a meaningful system of inspection and control. A limited agreement banning atmospheric tests, on the other hand, such as we now have, was realistic for the simple reason that it was self-monitoring.

These facts being taken into consideration and despite certain legitimate reservations that may be expressed about the nonproliferation treaty, the fears entertained in certain European quarters have little substance. It is true that the Soviet Union has demanded the permanent renunciation of any joint nuclear command involving West European nations as the condition of a nonproliferation treaty. But the United States, with the staunch support of Great Britain, has just as adamantly taken the stand that a nonproliferation treaty should not foreclose the possibility of creating some kind of NATO or European nuclear force. It is on this issue that the current talks in Geneva have remained deadlocked from the beginning.

On the subject of NATO, there is another complaint that our European allies frequently make—much more frequently in private than in public. They believe that the United States has been too insistent on having its own way and cavalier in disregarding the opinions of its allies. On this point, there is some merit to European criticism of American attitudes. The House Committee on Foreign Affairs recently commented:

> Our efforts to bring the other members of NATO into a meaningful partnership have been sporadic, inadequate, and marked by inconsistencies. We made unilateral declarations and entered into bilateral agreements instead of trying to arrive at joint decisions on issues which affect the security of the entire North Atlantic Community. And we have devoted less than our best effort to the task of promoting the mutual understanding which is vital to the achievement of unity within the North Atlantic Community.[1]

This criticism by the House Committee is admittedly harsh, but there is much truth to it. All the members of NATO, however, share the responsibility for the appalling deterioration that has taken place, in particular over the past year. Moreover, the United States, as the most powerful member of the alliance, is obliged to exercise certain prerogatives of leadership, despite the fact that this is bound to result in some resentment.

Another charge, bruited about by some of our more severe critics in France and Germany, has been that the United States is responsible for undermining the Franco-German alliance by means of a mixture of pressure on and inducements to the Bonn government. This charge, unlike the others, has no basis whatever in fact. The recent deterioration in German-French relations, which the Kiesinger cabinet is having some success in repairing, is to be regretted, as is the parallel deterioration in French-American relations. But in both cases General de Gaulle must bear a large portion of the responsibility.

In November, 1965, for instance, Henry Tanner of *The New York Times* reported from France that "French diplomacy . . . has been seeking to convince the State Department that an improvement of

American-Soviet relations hinges mostly on Washington's willingness to be tough with the West Germans. . . . So deep is this new French distrust of Bonn," said Mr. Tanner, "that the German leaders are accused here of seeking access to nuclear weapons for use as a lever to force the reunification of Germany and to reconquer the eastern provinces lost to Poland after World War II."[2]

The United States has, no doubt, erred in several respects in its dealings with General de Gaulle, and there is much to be said for an all-out effort to reestablish relations with him and to seek that "grand concert of policy" of which he was once the principal advocate. But, whatever our errors and failings, it is self-evident that the United States commitment to European unity has in no way been weakened or diluted.

THE VIETNAM WAR

Widespread doubts have also been expressed in the NATO countries about our Vietnam policy. Significantly, there is far more support for our policy in Germany than in any other NATO country. This support is rooted in the fact that the German people live in daily confrontation with the meaning of communism, both inside their own country and on their own borders; this experience enables them to understand the American confrontation with communism in Vietnam far better than do some of their neighbors.

European doubts about our Vietnam policy are of several different kinds. First of all, there are doubts based on a kind of European isolationism that is the counterpart of the neo-isolationism that has sprung up in recent years in the United States. Like the American isolationists who talked about a "Fortress America," the European isolationists of today apparently believe it possible to maintain a "Fortress Europa" that will be able to survive, no matter how many countries succumb to communist aggression in other parts of the world.

It is extremely difficult to reason with neo-isolationists, of either the European or the American variety, since they manifest a deep-seated psychological desire to escape from reality. One might recommend to these escapists that they read Marshal Lin Piao's now famous statement on how the Communists, as a prelude to the final assault on the bastions of capitalism, must seek to surround and isolate these bastions by taking over the underdeveloped world, just as the Communists triumphed in China by surrounding and isolating the cities from the countryside.

Other Europeans doubt our policy because they have learned nothing from the tragic experience of Munich. Like their predecessors of the thirties, these modern-day appeasers believe that the appetite of totalitarian aggressors can somehow be sated by making concessions to their expansionist ambitions, and in this deluded quest for peace at any price they close their eyes to the inhumanity of turning other human beings over to totalitarian rule.

The essential weakness of appeasers is not that they are evil but that they yield to the all-too-common human penchant for wishful thinking. At the time of Munich, for example, the spirit of appeasement was not confined to Chamberlain and a handful of Tory M.P.'s. On the contrary, it represented the mood of the country—and when Chamberlain reported to Parliament on the agreement he brought back from his meeting with Hitler, his efforts to preserve the peace were praised even by left-wing Laborites like James Maxton and Fenner Brockway. Today's appeasers are, in all probability, as sincerely devoted to peace as were Chamberlain and the Tory and Labor appeasers of 1939. They are also just as blind to the nature of totalitarianism and to the consequences of the policy they advocate.

More reasonable Europeans, while expressing some sympathy for our Vietnam policy, are nevertheless worried about it because they fear that we are overcommitted in Vietnam and that our current emphasis on the Vietnam war will inevitably lead to a de-emphasis of our European commitments.

These fears are without foundation. Indeed, properly understood, our Vietnam policy constitutes the best possible proof both of our determination to honor our commitments and resist communist aggression and of our ability to sustain the burden. The United States now (1966) has 300,000 men in Vietnam. But the Vietnam war is absorbing less than 1.5 per cent of our gross national product. To top off this remarkable record, we have thus far been able to honor our commitments in Europe and other parts of the world and to meet the demands of the Vietnam war without general conscription—even without calling up our reserves. In fact, because the strength of American armed forces has risen from 2,600,000 to 3,100,000 since January, 1965, there are actually more men available to meet our other international commitments than there were before our major Vietnam buildup. And the Vietnam war has had the further effect of raising the level of training throughout the American armed forces, providing us with a corps of battle-hardened officers and completely renewing and further modernizing our military equipment.

Although the members of the Democratic Policy Committee and certain other members of Congress consider a minor reduction of American forces in Europe compatible with the requirements of Western security, it is clear that Congress as a whole—including those who favor a reduction of forces—understands the critical importance of NATO and the importance of maintaining American forces in forward positions in Europe. Secretary McNamara has recently confirmed that the United States has no intention of withdrawing any major units from Germany. While a limited withdrawal is not inconceivable at some future date, such a decision would only be made after consultation with our NATO partners and upon the assurance that the move would in no way imperil European security.

Still other Europeans, though generally sympathetic to our policy, are fearful that the United States does not have the moral resources and the staying power to see the Vietnam war through to the point of final victory. Their fears are based on the impression that the great majority of informed Americans are opposed to our Vietnam policy, that the opposition is mounting, and that the Administration, for political reasons, will ultimately have to yield to this domestic opposition.

It is true that a vociferous minority in the United States opposes our Vietnam policy. But repeated public opinion polls have established that up to September, 1966, this domestic opposition has at no point exceeded 15 per cent of the people, while the true degree of popular support for the Administration's Vietnam policy may be gauged from the fact that 80 per cent of the American people approved our resumption of the bombing of North Vietnam.

Qualitatively, the domestic opposition to the Vietnam war is even less impressive than it is quantitatively. An analysis of some of the petitions against the war signed by intellectuals and academicians reveals that an overwhelming majority of the petitioners are people whose disciplines are remote from the field of politics and world affairs—doctors of medicine and dentists, psychologists and obstetricians, philosophers and mathematicians, bacteriologists, biochemists, astronomers, and so on. The recognized U.S. scholars in the fields of political science, foreign policy, communism, and American security problems are, as a recent study points out, conspicuously absent from the roster of critics. Of some 6,000 academicians and professionals who signed a three-page advertisement in *The New York Times* of June 5, 1966, attacking United States policy in Vietnam, only four were international relations specialists, only nine were economists, and only fifteen were historians.

Because the opposition to our Vietnam policy has millions of dollars at its disposal and is noisy and provocative, it has been able to foster the impression that it represents far more than it actually does. This false impression has been further assisted by the fact that the press tends to regard opposition to the war as news, while manifestations of support for the war are not considered news. Recently, some high school students in Wolcott, Connecticut, organized a national campaign which they called Project SAVE: Students Approve Our Vietnam Effort. Over several months they gathered some 325,000 signatures from high school students which they presented to the Vice-President. But they had no funds with which to purchase full-page ads in *The New York Times*. And, since the press virtually ignored the story, very little is known about the episode outside the state of Connecticut.

This point deserves particular emphasis because the Communists and many West Europeans have been sadly misled by the exaggerated reports about the domestic opposition to our Vietnam policy. Indeed, Viet Cong representatives have publicly declared their conviction that the Johnson Administration will be compelled by popular pressure to pull out of Vietnam.

Let there be no mistake about it: the overwhelming majority of the American people and the overwhelming majority of those Americans who have special knowledge of the problem support the Administration's policy to the hilt. The Administration is aware of this. And for these reasons there is *absolutely no danger* that President Johnson will capitulate before the domestic opposition and abandon the people of South Vietnam to the tender mercies of Viet Cong terrorists.

AMERICAN DOUBTS ABOUT EUROPE

The various doubts that Europeans have expressed about American policy are counterbalanced by certain doubts voiced in the United States from time to time about the steadfastness and wisdom of our European allies. There is, first of all, a continuing and widespread resentment over the failure of the NATO nations, with the notable exception of Germany, to meet the quota of forces to which they agreed in the early days of NATO. American friends and critics of Europe share the conviction that, apart from the German Federal Republic, our European allies are not bearing their share of the burden of European defense.

The general tendency in Europe is, apparently, to resist any larger military commitment because of the conviction that the so-called balance of nuclear terror and the purported moderation of Soviet policy have reduced the danger of Soviet aggression to the vanishing point. Carried to its logical conclusion, this attitude would lead to the complete abandonment of NATO. If NATO ever were abandoned, our European allies would soon learn to their own dismay that the danger of Soviet aggression is not a thing of the past. Indeed, our European allies should today be asking themselves why the Soviets continue to seek the dissolution of NATO through a thousand different artifices if they harbor no aggressive intentions toward West Europe.

The relatively widespread European conviction that the Soviet regime, in direct contrast to the Red Chinese regime, has outgrown the subversive and aggressive tendencies of earlier decades is not shared by the American people. While our policy has at times been ambiguous and contradictory, we have, on the whole, a different view of Soviet intentions in the world today. This is so in the first place because the Soviet Union is, according to its own boasts, the chief supplier of arms and ammunition to North Vietnam, because American flyers are being shot down by Soviet guns and missiles and planes, and because thousands of Americans have already given their lives to resist this Soviet-supported aggression.

We also have a different view of Soviet intentions because of our proximity to Cuba, because of our continuing concern with Castro-communist subversion in the Americas, and because of the commanding role which Moscow played in the so-called Tri-Continental Conference in Havana, held in January, 1966. Under the leadership of Moscow, the delegates to this conference first openly committed themselves to the violent overthrow of all those governments that did not meet with their approval and then seᵗ up a tri-continental apparatus of subversion with headquarters in Havana.

Those who have found comfort in the belief that Soviet policy has undergone significant moderation would do well to read the speech of Mr. Sharaf Rashidov, the leader of the Soviet delegation in Havana:

"The Soviet delegation has arrived at this conference with the aim of giving all-round assistance to the unification of the anti-imperialist forces of the three continents in order to provide greater impetus to our common struggle against imperialism, colonialism and neocolonialism—led by the U.S. capitalists.

"The Soviet Union," Mr. Rashidov continued, "is supplying the fraternal people of Vietnam with the most modern weapons for meeting U.S. aggression. We are doing everything in order that deliveries of Soviet military equipment—aircraft, rockets, artillery, ammunition, and so on—will get into the hands of the Vietnamese freedom fighters as rapidly as possible." Saluting the communist-dominated guerrillas in South America, Mr. Rashidov declared: "We express our fraternal solidarity with the armed struggle being waged by the Venezuelan, Peruvian, Colombian, and Guatemalan patriots for freedom against the stooges of imperialism."

Rashidov's statement led to vigorous protests by more than 20 Latin-American governments. It also led the Special Consultative Committee on Security of the Organization of American States to condemn communist intervention and aggression and to describe the Havana Conference as "the most serious and dangerous threat that international Communism has yet made against the inter-American system."

These are some of the reasons why American estimates of Soviet intentions differ radically from the prevailing estimates in most of West Europe. This difference in appraisal lies at the root of the widespread European failure to understand American policy vis-à-vis Cuba and the Dominican Republic. It also explains why virtually every European government, including that of Franco's Spain, has refused to cooperate with the United States in imposing restrictions on trade with Castro's Cuba. But, whatever the explanation may be, our European friends should know that Americans in general are resentful over the lack of cooperation from Europe in dealing with the problem of Castro subversion in the Americas, over their business-as-usual attitude toward Havana and Hanoi and Peking, and over the credits that are now being extended to Cuba to help Castro finance his purchases of equipment from Europe.

Americans are also greatly disturbed by the plans of an international industrial consortium to build a major steel producing plant for Communist China, financed by a generous five-year credit from the German government. The protest registered by the Department of

State enjoyed the virtually unanimous endorsement of the American people. This entire situation is all the more regrettable because it has created the impression that West Germany is playing a leading role in the trend toward an unconditional relaxation of East-West trade and credits, whereas in fact West Germany probably has the best overall record of cooperation with the United States in this area.

THE COMING COLLAPSE OF COMMUNISM

Whatever differences we may have, there are four basic objectives on which Europeans and Americans should be able to agree:

First, to hold the line against communist aggression.

Second, to arrest the process of erosion in the Western alliance.

Third, to preserve peace where peace exists and to limit the area of conflict where peace does not exist.

Fourth, to find ways to encourage the peaceful opening up of the moribund communist system.

In pursuing these objectives, it is essential that we study the weaknesses of communism as well as its strong points.

The economic failure of the communist system is dramatically demonstrated by the continuing crisis in agricultural production which the communist governments of Europe and Asia have been unable to solve. As an economic system, communism simply does not work because it destroys the leaven of human incentive.

That the system has failed to win the support of the peoples subjected to its rule has been demonstrated many times over in many different ways. It was demonstrated in the mid-fifties by the massive popular revolts that took place in rapid succession in Soviet Zone Germany, Poland, Hungary, in the Vorkuta slave-labor complex in Soviet Siberia, and in Tibet. It has been demonstrated by the popular revolt against an incipient communist regime in Ghana as well as by the popular revolts against threatened communist take-overs in Indonesia and Brazil. And it is being demonstrated again by the intellectual ferment that in recent years has been sweeping like an unchecked epidemic through every communist country, including the Soviet Union and Red China.

This intellectual ferment, viewed against the background of the

economic failure of communism, constitutes the chief justification for
optimism about the future. What it signifies is that youth and the intellectuals have turned en masse against communist tyranny. Their revolt has been marked by a revival of national sentiment, by a quest for
truth, by a passionate reassertion of interest in the simple enjoyment
of life, and by an uncontrollable and friendly curiosity about Western
culture. It has expressed itself in poetry and essays that have pentrated
official literary publications, in the clandestine circulation of banned
books and mimeographed bulletins, in mass meetings devoted to the
reading of the poems of Yevtushenko and other rebel poets.

The spirit and purpose of this revolt were concisely expressed by a
young Soviet engineer in a letter recently published by the newspaper
Sovyetskaya Kultura. "Do not creep into my soul," he wrote. "Do not
spit in my face when my view is different from yours . . . I want to
have my own tastes, my own opinions of art . . . I want to think for myself, examine things myself, appreciate them myself. And I believe this
is my right."

The tyranny of communism is crumbling before the pent-up hatred
of its subjects. The process is inexorable. Communist regimes may
imprison the Djilases, the Mihajlovs, the Sinyavskys, and the Daniels,
and they may send others like Valery Tarsis to the insane asylums that
have now replaced concentration camps, but they will not succeed in
repressing this ferment because it has gone too far. Nor can they retard this process for very long by granting a carefully measured quota
of freedom. One of the wisest political thinkers, Alexis de Tocque-
ville, put the matter in these words:

> Experience suggests that the most dangerous moment for an
> evil government is usually when it begins to reform itself . . . The
> sufferings that are endured patiently, as being inevitable, become
> intolerable the moment it appears that there might be an escape.
> Reform then only serves to reveal more clearly what still remains
> oppressive and now all the more unbearable; the suffering, it is
> true, has been reduced, but one's sensitivity has become more
> acute.[3]

There are, however, two ways in which the communist rulers can
arrest the erosion of their control. They can retard the process if they
are able, with Western assistance, to make certain economic concessions to their subjects, so that the material conditions of life become

less arduous. And they can retard the process in even more significant measure by scoring victories against the free world. This explains why the apparent relaxation of intellectual controls has been accompanied, not by a true relaxation of tensions, but by an intensification of the Cold War. Communist rulers seek to distract the attention of their subjects by fanning suspicion and hatred of the West, by encouraging North Vietnam to prolong the war, and by constantly probing for new possibilities of expansion.

We are confronted, therefore, with a race against time. The fateful question is: Will the process of intellectual ferment and "opening up" develop rapidly enough to head off the possibility of a major collision between the communist world and the free world? Or will the communist leaders, in an effort to cope with mounting popular discontent, probe once too often or engage in one too many adventures, thus touching off the global conflict that even they have every reason to avoid? The outcome of this race is not preordained. It can be affected, for better or worse, by what we of the free world do or fail to do.

MULTICENTRISM AND ITS LIMITATIONS

While there is no doubt that the Sino-Soviet rift is genuine as far as it goes, it would be foolish to overestimate it to the point where we relax our own vigilance. The rift between Moscow and Peking is a two-edged sword. Under certain circumstances it may redound to the benefit of the free world. But its immediate consequence has been an intensification of the tempo of subversion, because the two great communist power centers now compete in order to be the first to take over in various parts of the world. The concrete results of the Soviet-Chinese split so far point to the need for a more vigilant defense against communist subversion.

There has also been a loosening of ties between the European satellites and Moscow. But the relationship remains ambivalent. On the one hand, the communist regimes in East-Central Europe are under pressure to meet certain demands of their people. Since these demands cannot possibly be met with Soviet help, they have no alternative but to seek improved ties and increased trade with the West. On the other hand, East European communist leaders know from the experience of Hungary and Soviet Zone Germany that they cannot possibly remain in power without Soviet support. Despite their desire for a greater degree of independence, therefore, they remain largely subservient to Soviet foreign policy. Despite varying degrees of partial autonomy, the communist states still continue to act as a bloc and to vote as a bloc in the United Nations—on Vietnam as well as on every other basic issue of the Cold War.

The erosion of communist control and the centrifugal forces within the communist world are phenomena that have both internal and external origins. It would be an exaggeration to give NATO the prime credit for the revolt of the youth and the intellectuals against communist dictatorship. But the general success of the containment policy since the fall of China has unquestionably played a role in strengthening the forces of moderation and the voices of dissent within the communist bloc and in encouraging the lesser communist countries to seek at least a limited measure of independence.

Experience teaches that when the free world permits communist aggression to succeed, this success strengthens the hands of the more extreme elements in communist power centers. Conversely, each defeat inflicted on communism has the effect of compromising the more extreme elements, strengthening the more moderate elements, and encouraging the voices of dissent in their relentless, erosive attack on the totalitarian regime.

The United States, NATO, and Vietnam

The foregoing considerations point the way to certain specific conclusions on the policy the free world can most profitably adopt. These conclusions may be grouped under ten headings:

1. The prime objective of our diplomacy should be to encourage the opening up of communist society and the further loosening of bonds between communist nations. No nonaggression pact can ever completely assure the free world against the possibility of surprise attack. The only real assurance is "openness." In the age of the thermonuclear missile the closed totalitarian society has become an anachronism that civilization can no longer tolerate.

2. To encourage this opening up, we must pursue the policy of "positive containment." The line must be held against communist expansion and subversion, whether the prime aggressor is Moscow or Peking or Hanoi or Havana.

3. We should also seek to encourage the opening up of communist

society through the expansion of existing exchange programs and by a greater insistence than we have heretofore displayed on complete reciprocity in such programs.

4. The Western intellectuals who manifested their solidarity with Sinyavsky and Daniel, with Djilas and Mihajlov, and with the other courageous dissenters who have been persecuted for speaking their beliefs have already made a signal contribution, as private citizens, to the opening up of communist society. But the protests thus far have been weakly organized and poorly publicized, and they have therefore had only a small fraction of their potential impact on the other side of the Iron Curtain.

The Communists, however, with fully sufficient funds at their disposal, have shown great organizational genius in the international campaigns they have mounted against the executions of Julius and Ethel Rosenberg, against American policy in Vietnam, and for other fraudulent causes. With proper techniques and adequate funds it should be possible for free men to organize an international campaign on behalf of the intellectual martyrs for freedom that will shake the very ramparts of communist society.

5. East-West trade, properly used, can be a real instrument for peace, stability, and prosperity, and a true means of building bridges between the peoples of Eastern and Western Europe. As matters stand now, however, each NATO country has its own East-West trade policy, and these policies are inconsistent in themselves. American policy and German policy, in general, are more restrictive; the policies of the other NATO countries generally less so.

There is a desperate need for a joint NATO policy governing East-West trade and long term credits to communist nations. If such a policy could be agreed upon at a special NATO conference, it would not only serve to reverse the growing trend toward bilateralism that has afflicted NATO in recent years, but it would also enormously enhance our diplomatic leverage and ability to exercise a moderating and "opening" influence on the communist regimes themselves.

The communist nations urgently require Western grain and equipment and the credits with which to purchase them, perhaps even for survival. Because of their desperate need, it is entirely realistic to require them to pay for such trade and credit in the form of political concessions. By giving these things to them on a platter, without conditions of any kind—as most Western nations are doing—we deprive ourselves of all serious diplomatic leverage, we strengthen the power elite in the communist countries, and we encourage them to persist in their present aggressive and subversive policies.

The NATO nations should gear the scale of East-West trade and supporting credits to the actions and policies of communist governments. Every positive action or development should be rewarded by an expansion of trade and a liberalization of conditions. If the Communists are prepared to assist in settling the Vietnam war, to accept a true abatement of the Cold War, to tear down the Berlin Wall, or to grant significant new concessions to their own people, the NATO nations should be prepared to pay very high prices in terms of trade and credits for such items. Conversely, very retrogressive or aggressive action should be punished by restrictions on trade and credit and in certain cases by joint sanctions.

6. NATO was created to contain Soviet aggression. The sacrifices necessary to maintain it can only be justified by NATO governments on the ground that the danger of Soviet aggression still exists. The tendency to belittle this danger and indeed to pretend that it has gone away is one of the main factors contributing to the erosion of NATO unity and morale. Conversely, realistic recognition and psychological acceptance of this continued danger are the essential first steps in the rehabilitation of NATO.

7. The United States and the other members of NATO should continue to seek reconciliation with General de Gaulle, insofar as this is possible without compromising the principle of NATO integration. America has a particular responsibility for holding open the door of NATO to its oldest ally, France.

8. Americans have the further duty to reaffirm repeatedly their determination to press for German reunification by every peaceful means. They should always answer proposals to freeze the status quo by pointing out, as Secretary of State Rusk has already done, that there can be no true relaxation of tension while Germany remains forcibly divided, since this division is the greatest single cause of tension with the Soviet Union.

9. NATO governments must seek to explain the American position in Vietnam to their own peoples and to win support for far larger Vietnam aid programs than those to which they are now committed. Opposition to American policy in Vietnam militates in the final analysis against NATO itself. For if America fails in its commitment to defend the freedom of Vietnam, what NATO nation could thereafter repose confidence in the American commitment to defend Europe?

10. A solution for the problem of nuclear sharing in NATO must be found. There has been too much emphasis on sharing control of strategic weapons targeted on Soviet population centers. It would be more realistic politically and more meaningful militarily if a formula could be found for sharing control of tactical nuclear weapons of stated maximum tonnage and range so that there could be no doubt about their clearly defensive nature, especially as tactical nuclear weapons designed for combat situations now exist in a form that makes it possible to use them with great discrimination, without fear of atmospheric contamination, and without significant danger to civilian life in nearby communities.

Such a solution would fit in with the concept of a graduated response to Soviet aggression, while providing NATO with an effective means of meeting the contingency of aggression by superior communist forces.

Conclusion

The political philosophy expressed in this essay may be summed up briefly as follows:

The key to enduring peace is the nonviolent transformation or opening up of communist society.

The key to such an opening up is containment.

The key to containment is NATO.

The key to NATO's survival is the guarantee inherent in the continued maintenance of United States divisions in Germany and in the reform of NATO into a somewhat more meaningful structure. If we fail in this last task, we face a cloudy and uncertain future. If we succeed, the possibilities are limitless.

This philosophy is clearly understood by President Johnson, who declared on May 2, 1966:

It remains our conviction that an integrated Atlantic Defense is the first necessity—not the last result—of the building of unity in Western Europe—for expanding partnership across the Atlantic—and for reconciling differences with the East.[4]

This is not only a formula for survival but a foundation for a constructive policy designed to achieve permanent conditions of peace and freedom.

NOTES TO CHAPTER ONE

1. *The Crisis in NATO,* House Committee on Foreign Affairs Report.

2. Henry Tanner, "Paris and Moscow, Focus on Bonn," *The New York Times,* November 7, 1965.

3. Quoted in *Le Monde,* Paris, October 30, 1956.

4. Speech of President Lyndon B. Johnson during signing ceremony in the White House, May 2, 1966.

Part One

Eastern Europe in the Interplay of
World Political Forces

CHAPTER II

The Soviet Union Under Brezhnev and Kosygin— Its Role Today

BORIS MEISSNER

SOVIET POLITICS UNDER THE PRINCIPLE OF "THE PRIMACY OF INTERNATIONAL POLITICS"

KHRUSHCHEV'S OVERTHROW brought into clear relief the Soviet Union's struggle, not only with a crisis of leadership and difficulties in economic development, but also with a structural crisis that has its roots in the totalitarian system itself. The history of economic growth in the Soviet Union has shown that state power can be employed to accelerate economic development within definable limits, but not to eliminate social underdevelopment completely. Once a certain level of development has been achieved, the totalitarian system of government and thus the unlimited power of the state cannot operate other than as obstacles blocking further economic and social progress.

The Soviet Union reached this level some time ago. Its contemporary internal situation is therefore shaped decisively by a basic conflict between the demand of the Communist party (CPSU) for total control in matters of ideology and organization and the developmental needs of a modern industrial society. The only way in which the party can alleviate this acute contradiction is to relax its permanent dictatorship, freeing important areas of social and intellectual life from its control. The latter is particularly urgent for the humanities and social sciences, as well as for literature and the arts.

21

The professional bureaucrats of the party are not ready, however, to make such a decisive break with established practice. They prefer to continue and escalate the struggle with progressive social forces, having necessary recourse to the repressive weapons of the police state that remain at their disposal. The new general line adopted at the Twenty-third Congress of the CPSU (March 29–April 8, 1966) is a unique attempt to satisfy more completely the economic needs of a modern industrial society while at the same time drawing the reins tighter in the cultural field. The party leadership refuses to admit that progress in material production cannot be achieved without greater intellectual freedom. This fundamental reactionary attitude results in a paradox. Modern ideas are permissible in the economic field, but political and cultural life is subjected to the domination of ideas which obstruct social progress in every possible way. The party's insistence on unlimited rule thus prevents a basic reform of the economy and society—a reform essential if the stagnation that pervades all areas in which progress depends on social spontaneity and personal initiative is to be overcome.

A second fundamental conflict, which affects internal and foreign policy in equal measure, results from the contradiction between the position of the Soviet Union as a world power—a position achieved far too rapidly—and its lack of sufficient economic resources and social maturity to maintain and develop this position. While the triumphs achieved under Khrushchev in rocket weaponry and space travel increased the prestige and military power of the Soviet Union, they did so at the cost of overstraining the limited financial power of the Soviet state.

The hesitancy manifested by Khrushchev's successors in the field of foreign policy is dictated mainly by their efforts to build up the economic support that must underpin Soviet power. They hope at the same time to reduce further the weapons gap in relation to the United States, to take the wind out of the sails of oppositional forces in Soviet society, and to achieve the prerequisites for a more active policy in world affairs. Success in these undertakings would have a profound impact in East-Central Europe, since Brezhnev and Kosygin have never abandoned the imperialist goals pursued by Stalin and Khrushchev. Even if Soviet Russia were to enter a posttotalitarian stage of development, the immediate effect in foreign policy would most probably be a limitation but not an abandonment of communist expansionism.

CHANGES IN THE STRUCTURE OF SOVIET RULE
AND IN THE KREMLIN LEADERSHIP

An understanding of the contemporary role played by the USSR in world politics, particularly in East-Central Europe, is dependent on a knowledge of its internal structural and political evolution. The post-Khrushchev leadership's stress on domestic policy makes this especially true.

The unlimited autocratic rule exercised by Stalin rested on a balance among several sources of authority: the party apparatus, the state apparatus (including the economic administration), the state police, and the armed forces. The coordination of these four pillars of power, among which MGB-MVD* occupied a key position, was accomplished through the private secretariat of the "Vozhd" (leader), which, more than the party secretariat, constituted the central fulcrum of power.[1] After Stalin's death in 1953 Khrushchev managed to reestablish the control of the party, and hence of the professional party apparatus, over the other sources of power, one after the other.[2] Through his administrative reforms of 1957 and 1962, which abolished for practical purposes the dual chain of command that had previously characterized the Soviet system of control, he expanded considerably the party's opportunity to influence and guide the economy. In so doing, however, he assigned the party a task for which it lacked the necessary professional competence and which distracted it from its proper political functions. The reforms had the further effect of liberating within the party apparatus pluralist forces, which obstructed the execution of directives issued by the central party authorities in Moscow.

The reform of 1962 abolished the National Economic Councils established in 1957 in each oblast and bifurcated the party apparatus up to the Union Republic level into industrial and agricultural branches. The Supreme Economic Council of the USSR was simultaneously liquidated and the Council of Ministers reduced from a hierarchical structure with almost one hundred members to a more normal size. These changes led to a strengthening of the state, as opposed to the party, apparatus. The economic administration has again been tied closely to the state apparatus. At the same time the

---

* Ministries of Internal Security and the Interior, in charge of political police operations, forced labor camps, and the like.–*Eds.*

state police and the armed forces have recovered considerable political influence since the fall of Khrushchev. The balance of power among the four pillars of authority has been more or less reestablished, with the party apparatus enjoying a certain primacy.

There are, however, important differences between the present system of control and that which existed during the Stalin era. First, the state police is no longer a "state within the state." Second, the four pillars of power are now coordinated, not by an autocratic "Vozhd" with his own power apparatus in the form of a private secretariat, but by a "leadership collective" that exercises its power through constitutional machinery. This "leadership collective" consists of the eleven full members of the Politbureau, called the Presidium between 1952 and 1956. The restoration of the Politbureau and the office of Secretary-General at the Twenty-third Party Congress served to consolidate the unlimited autocracy of the party through the use of institutions that were typical of the Stalin era.[3]

As happened after Stalin's death, the actual power within the "leadership collective" after Khrushchev's overthrow was assumed by an inner circle of five individuals. In the immediate post-Stalin situation, Prime Minister Malenkov shared power with his first deputy Beria (until the latter's fall in June, 1953), and with Molotov, Kaganovich, and Bulganin. In addition to First Party Secretary (now Secretary-General) Brezhnev and Prime Minister Kosygin, the new "oligarchs" initially were the nominal head of state Mikoyan and the two party secretaries Suslov and Podgorny. This inner circle usually appeared together at official ceremonies. Its membership was reduced by the retirement of Mikoyan in late 1965, after Podgorny has succeeded him as nominal head of state. The "oligarchs," whose average age is 62, are currently listed in this order: Brezhnev, Kosygin, Podgorny, and Suslov. The top position shared by Brezhnev and Kosygin is emphasized by the practice of listing the chief of government ahead of the "chief of state," contrary to official protocol.

Among second-rank leaders who seem likely candidates for promotion, mention may be made of the Central Committee secretaries Shelyepin and Kirilyenko, as well as the two First Deputy Prime Ministers of the USSR, Polyansky and Mazurov. Significantly, none of the three "Young Turks" (Shelyepin, Polyansky, and Mazurov), whose average age is fifty years, has been taken into the top leadership group, although at least the first two would qualify in terms of seniority. Shvernik, who retired for reasons of age at the same time as Mikoyan, has been replaced as chairman of the reorganized Committee for Party Control by a new member of the Politbureau, the former Latvian party chief Pelshe. New faces among the eight candidate members of the Politbureau are those of the Kazak party leader Kunayev, a follower of Brezhnev, and the Byelorussian party leader Masherov, Mazurov's successor. Meanwhile, L. N. Yefremov, whose position had already been undermined, has been dropped as a Politbureau candidate. A number of the full members and candidate members of the Politbureau may be regarded, among other things, as representative of certain important Union Republics.

The concentration of power at the top has been combined with a renewed enlargement of the Central Committee and the Central Auditing Commission. Comprised of 195 full members (1961:175) and 165 candidates (1961:155), the Central Committee is larger than ever before. The Central Auditing Commission has been increased to 79 members; in 1961 it had 65 members.

There is a striking continuity among the full members of the Central Committee, 80 per cent of whom were reelected in 1966, as compared with a "survival ratio" of only 50 per cent in 1956. This continuity indicates that the deposition of Khrushchev was approved by the overwhelming majority of the top-rank functionaries. But it also indicates that the present leadership in the Kremlin is strongly dependent on its personal supporters. The tightening of leadership controls, one phase of which was the dissolution of the Central Committee's Bureau for the RSFSR, and the reestablishment of an All-Union Party Conference are measures intended to reduce this dependency.

Inasmuch as the Politbureau has undertaken to assure a certain balance of power, not only among the several institutions of authority, but between the party and state bureaucracies as well, it has achieved importance in relation to the Central Committee secretariat. This balance of power, symbolized by the duumvirate of Brezhnev and Kosygin, is of vital concern to those Politbureau members who do not belong to the secretariat, as well as to party secretaries, such as Suslov and Shelyepin, who prefer collegial management to one-man leadership. Careful efforts to maintain the balance between Brezhnev and Kosygin were apparent during the Twenty-third Party Congress and thereafter. Upon this balance rests the viability of the "collective leadership."

As a result of the party's achievement of primacy over the other institutions of power, the Secretary-General, whose office is now for the first time anchored in the party constitution (Article 39), naturally enjoys a preponderant authority. Historical experience, furthermore, shows that the tendency toward one-man rule is inherent in autocratic-totalitarian systems of government. In the absence of constitutional safeguards the chances of avoiding it are not very great. Such rule can, of course, be exercised in very different ways, as the examples of Lenin, Stalin, and Khrushchev have shown.

Brezhnev clearly does not possess the characteristics of a second Lenin or Stalin. The question is only whether he will be able to secure a dominating position analogous to that of Khrushchev. Should he fail in his struggle for sole authority, the falling robe will surely be grasped—perhaps by one of the younger Politbureau members, who were so ostentatiously silent at the Twenty-third Party Congress. From time to time incidents occur that illustrate the continuing power struggle in the Kremlin. The lack of mobility evident in Soviet policy is mainly a reflection of the fact that a clear solution of the leadership crisis has not yet been found.

THE BREZHNEV-KOSYGIN ECONOMIC POLICY

The Economic Development Plan of the USSR was approved at the Twenty-third Congress as an integral part of the new general party line.[4] The new Five-Year Plan is more sensible in conception than the Seven-Year Plan, not to mention the utopian Twenty-Year Plan, which has been quietly dropped.[5] The new Plan perpetuates the primacy of heavy industry but gives greater consideration to the consumer goods industry and agriculture. The military potential of the Soviet Union is, on the other hand, to be considerably strengthened. The "rockets or butter" dilemma thus remains: the same dilemma that finally led to Khrushchev's downfall. On the basis of previous experience it appears entirely impossible for Brezhnev and Kosygin to come anywhere near realizing the tremendous planned investment of 310 billion rubles (47 per cent more than in recent years) without a decisive reduction in armament expenditure.

The actual economic policy decisions had already been taken at the plenary meetings of the Central Committee in March and September, 1965. They were recorded in the Brezhnev plan for agriculture,[6] as well as in Kosygin's economic report.[7] In justifying the economic reform, Kosygin admitted openly the decreased rate of growth of the Soviet economy since 1959, a decline hitherto consistently denied by Soviet spokesmen. He failed, however, to mention that not only the rates of growth of the national income, of industrial production, and of labor productivity, but also that of investment had declined severely in recent years. The rate of growth in industrial gross production dropped from 11 per cent in 1959 to 7.5 per cent in 1964, thereby reaching the lowest level since World War II. The actual net growth was approximately 5 per cent, a rate lower than that of the United States or the German Federal Republic. The most unfavorable trends during the period were shown by the consumer goods industry, the growth rate of which declined from 10.3 per cent to 5 per cent, and by light industry, which registered an analogous decline from 8 to 2 per cent. For the first time the Soviet Union fell back, not only in absolute figures, but also in relative growth in comparison with the United States.

The spread between the two world powers' Gross National Products increased from $276 billion in 1961 to $336 billion in 1964 in favor of the United States. But during the same period Soviet population, 229.1 million in 1965, grew faster than that of the United States. And this increase in population made an expansion of agricultural production, the principal hindrance to which is the collective farm system, a matter of particular urgency. In this light the crop failures of 1963, which forced Khrushchev to dip into the gold reserves and scarce foreign currency of the Soviet Union to import between 11 and 12 million tons of grain—the same quantity that Czarist Russia exported in 1913—and of 1965, which forced the new rulers to make foreign purchases of 8.5 million tons of grain, mostly wheat, were severe blows.

The reform proposals that Brezhnev submitted to the March plenum in 1965 show awareness of the connection between the backward development of agriculture, the Achilles' heel of the Soviet economy, and, in particular, the unsatisfactory development of the consumer goods industry. Khrushchev's successors do not seem, however, to have faced the fact that the Soviet economy cannot achieve full maturity unless agriculture is developed at a much faster rate than the other branches of the economy for the next few years. This requires a very different concentration of resources than that provided in the new Five-Year Plan.

To achieve the decisive breakthrough, Brezhnev and Kosygin

would have to mobilize the tremendous resources needed for the concentrated development of agriculture, the consumer goods industry, and the service industries, combined with simultaneous development of the related infrastructure. In view of the limited financial resources of the Soviet Union such an economic policy could only be realized at the expense of heavy industry and of arms production. This is what Malenkov tried to do with his "new course" policy in 1953 and 1954 and what Khrushchev failed to do, though he made an attempt to resume Malenkov's policy after the Twenty-second Party Congress. As advocates of an intermediate policy, Brezhnev and Kosygin have avoided this decision, but it cannot be postponed indefinitely. The new leaders have instead concentrated their attention on improving the productivity of the Soviet economic system through rationalization of the planning and administrative apparatus and through the employment of efficient methods of control. In so doing they are attempting to combine administrative practices from the Stalin era with modern concepts, partly those of the reformers surrounding Professors Liberman and Trapeznikov and partly those of their more conservative colleagues, who hope to achieve the perfection of total economic planning with the aid of a network of calculators.

The basic idea of Kosygin's economic reform, which is mainly concerned with the industrial field, is the policy of using highly centralized planning and control and individual enterprises enjoying greater autonomy as the basic units of the state-owned economy. Planning and performance evaluation are to be based in the future on turnover and solvency and therefore on profit, and not as hitherto on gross production alone. To accomplish this, the autonomy of individual enterprises is to be expanded within the framework of a decentralization far more limited than that demanded by the reformers, but corresponding to the model bylaws for a "state socialist productive enterprise" issued on October 4, 1965.

The principal indices, including productive capacities desired, amounts to be invested, the wage fund, prices, and procurement of materials, are to be determined centrally as heretofore. The individual enterprises, on the other hand, will be able to plan independently their production costs, their labor productivity, their average wages, and, most importantly, their worker requirements. They will also be able to dispose freely of a greater part of the profits realized (approximately 4 per cent) on expanding productive facilities, improving working and living conditions, and rewarding employees. A similar expansion of the autonomy of collective farms is being developed by a commission under Brezhnev.

The Kosygin reform also undertakes to give practical application to Professor Liberman's proposal to coordinate demand and production within a centrally-controlled planned economy. The planning of the entire consumer goods industry and possibly later of other branches of the economy as well is to be based on incoming orders received by enterprises and trade organizations. On the basis of experience gained in suitable experimental enterprises, particularly within the textile and shoe industries, consumer goods are now to be produced according to orders from the market and no longer according to command. The attempt to combine central control with decentralized decision making cannot, however, achieve any genuine success until the overcentralization and overbureaucratization that plague the Soviet economic system are eliminated and the influence of the party on planning decisions is measurably reduced.

But the elimination of bureaucratic controls is precisely what the Kosygin economic reform fails to accomplish. Its half-way measures stand in marked contrast to the Yugoslav reform of July, 1965, which provides for almost universal usage of economically determined prices and values and for a high degree of decentralization in economic planning.

SOCIAL POLICY UNDER BREZHNEV AND KOSYGIN

The sociological importance of the Kosygin economic reform lies mainly in the fact that it strengthens considerably the power position of the state and economic bureaucracies relative to the party apparatus, thereby restoring the state of affairs that existed before the economic reform of 1957. The benefits it affords to the actual economic managers, the directors of enterprises, are secondary in character. In view of the predominant authority of the GOSPLAN and the largely restored technical ministries, the total number of which now stands at forty-seven, and in view of the organizational principles of "democratic centralism," "unified command" ("Yedinonatshaliye"), and planned supervision, the new bylaws for enterprises can hardly be expected to prove a Magna Charta for business managers. Then, again, economic experts, who belong to an elite along with the scientists, literati, and artists, are unlikely to be content with the results of the reform. Kosygin was correct in taking issue with those foreign voices who greeted the economic reform with remarks about the introduction of a market economy in the Soviet Union and its "return to the road of capitalist economic management." The decisive questions determining the nature of an economic system, he emphasized, were: In whose hands are the power of the state and the means of production? And "in whose class interests are investment funds and profits distributed?" There is no doubt that in Russia today these characteristics of a "ruling class" are found in the higher bureaucracy, and particularly in the party bureaucracy, which is the central force of totalitarian rule.[8]

The economic reform is therefore designed mainly to establish an improved balance within the higher bureaucracy, while at the same time consolidating the position of the ruling power elite as a whole. The mass of this power elite owes its ruling position primarily to party patronage dispensed under the "Nomenklatura system." For this reason the power elite is to an increasing degree regarded as parasitic by the genuine leadership elites: the economic managers and the prestige elite, whose social roles are based upon accomplishment and knowledge. Even within the power elite itself there are forces, particularly among state officials, that regard the party bureaucracy as an obstacle to the development of Russia along modern lines. The case of Colonel Penkovsky indicates that such ideas are also found among the higher military officers.

Ambiguous economic reforms, which serve the interests of the ruling elite rather than those of progressive forces, are hardly capable of eliminating this social contradiction, which is becoming increasingly acute and is assuming to some extent the character of a conflict between generations. Symptoms of this development include not only the propaganda trial of the Soviet writers Sinyavsky and Daniel but also the special honors paid to the late Party Secretary Zhdanov, whose death in 1948 concluded one of the darker chapters of Stalinism. The two Soviet writers, who had published abroad under the *nommes de plume* Terz and Arshak, were sentenced to seven and five years of forced labor, respectively.[9] Their colleague Valery Tarsis, the author of the *Legend of the Blue Fly* and the *Message from an Insane Asylum,* had better luck; he was deprived of his Soviet citizenship during a visit to England. In an interview he called attention to the fascist traits of the totalitarian communist system prevailing in

Russia, which he had characterized as a "prison socialism" in his writings.

The political importance of the antitotalitarian Soviet literati is to be seen mainly in the fact that they express the unarticulated opinion of wide strata of Soviet society, thus exercising a "quasi-parliamentary" function, since a genuine representative body does not exist in the Soviet Union. In the words of Yevtushenko, "In Russia, the poets always constitute an intellectual government—stable, not subject to dissolution, and invulnerable to violence and death."[10]

The unusual prestige enjoyed by the literati, artists, and scientists permits them to reach out beyond the social level to which they belong and to influence deeply the behavior of the entire society, at times in opposition to the group in power. The value judgments of Soviet society are sometimes more strongly determined by the intellectual influences emanating from this prestige elite than by the functional efficiency of economic managers or by the norms set for them by the ruling power elite and its dependent bureaucrats. This fact has been demonstrated clearly by Soviet sociological investigations conducted in Leningrad and Moscow, in which the value judgments, ideals, and aspirations of an elite group among Soviet youth were examined.[11]

In view of this situation the reticence of the new Kremlin leadership to grant greater rights to industrial enterprises and collective farms and the vacillations of its cultural policy are quite understandable. While a reinforced orthodoxy was manifest at the Twenty-third Party Congress, a threatened restalinization, against which twenty-seven well-known representatives of Soviet literature, art, and science warned the party leadership, did not take place.

The offensive of restorational forces, which was set in motion early in 1966, was soon blocked by the resistance, not only of the liberal, but also of the moderate conservative, opposition. The strength of the social groups interested in destalinization prohibited its repeal at the Twenty-third Congress, but, even so, it was appreciably reduced in scope. Khrushchev's successors were anxious to reestablish full control over the intellectual forces released by the 1956 and 1961 waves of destalinization. And the limited departure from destalinization they desired was most noticeable in the fields of literature and art. Antistalinist, muckraking literature had threatened to undermine totalitarian one-party rule and destroy the positions of the functionaries who had grown up under Stalin, particularly the party organizers, who predominate in the present party leadership. Such literature also helped to reveal the close connection between Soviet totalitarianism and militarism, a tendency not agreeable even to those military officers who had disapproved of Stalin. Finally, even the party ideologues who do not share the ultraconservative views of Suslov are nevertheless interested in more intensive control of the social sciences and the fields of literature and art. As party clergy, they need a function that justifies not only their own activities but also the right of the party to exist.

The restorational tendency therefore found its strongest expression in those parts of the Central Committee report dealing with cultural policy and the party.[12] The reins were again pulled tighter in the areas of literature, art, the social sciences, and the humanities. The role of ideology, however, the importance of which has been especially emphasized by Brezhnev, is conceived differently than it was under Khrushchev. While Marxist-Leninist utopianism was evident in the 1961 party program, theory gave way to practice in the section on "building the material-technical basis of Communism." Nowadays, the main stress is laid on those parts of ideology having to do with the social sciences. The individual disciplines within the social sciences and the humanities, which have been upgraded in comparison with the natural sciences, are to be developed within the borders set for them by ideology. Theory (as an ideology of motives) is again to be placed ahead of practice. It is to guide practice, not to justify it after the fact.

In his concluding remarks at the Congress Brezhnev observed that the party had gathered wide experience "in the guidance of society." From this he derived its claim to continued total control over society. The question remains how long Soviet society, which has developed into an industrial society based on performance, will consent to endure the tutelage of a ruling organization that has no intention of recognizing that this society has come of age.

BREZHNEV'S AND KOSYGIN'S DEFENSE POLICY

Defense policy under Khrushchev was determined by the military-strategic conception of massive retaliation and based on the possibility of an initial attack by the Soviets.[13] In replacing the weapons of the Soviet armed forces since 1959, therefore, the main emphasis was laid upon strategic rockets.[14] While he built up the stock of modern atomic armaments, Khrushchev simultaneously attempted to resume Malenkov's "new course" policy under his own slogan of "welfare Communism." As in 1953 and 1954, such a policy could only be carried into effect at the expense of heavy industry and of armament production. It necessarily collided with the same forces that had overthrown Malenkov in his day. This time these forces were headed by Second Party Secretary Frol Koslov, who was closely associated with the military, and by Chief Ideologist Suslov. Khrushchev was forced to retreat before his enemies at the plenary session of the Central Committee in March, 1962. At the close of the Central Committee plenum he admitted the priority of armaments and repudiated his intention "to transfer funds to agriculture at the expense of industrial development and the strengthening of the national defense."

Khrushchev's attempt to undermine the defense position of the United States by constructing intermediate-range bases on Cuba may very well have been motivated by the hope that success in this venture would improve his chances of putting through economies in the military sector. Following the Cuba crisis, Khrushchev attempted to obtain the funds he needed for intensified development of agriculture, the consumer goods industry, and "heavy chemistry" through a further reduction of conventional armed forces. The army and the air force were particular targets for retrenchment. Not only traditionalist military officers must have regarded this policy as a threat to the military power position of the Soviet Union. There was also increasing realization that massive retaliation à la Khrushchev no longer satisfied fully the requirements of a changed situation in world politics. The change of leadership in the Kremlin was therefore welcomed by the Soviet High Command, particularly since Brezhnev and Kosygin were more ready than Khrushchev had been to favor the interests of the military sector of the power elite.

The decision taken by the "leadership collective" in May, 1965, to strengthen further the military potential of the Soviet Union led to an increase in the 1966 defense budget from 12.8 to 13.4 billion rubles, that is, by fully 5 per cent.[15] According to the estimates of Western specialists, total Soviet military expenditures (including military research) amounted to $40 billion in 1965; in comparison, the United States defense budget was $52.2 billion.[16] By increasing the total number of intercontinental rockets from 200 to 270, Brezhnev and Kosygin succeeded in reducing the gap in relation to the United States from 4:1 in 1964 to 3:1 in 1965, and they have also expanded the submarine arm to more than 40 atomic-powered vessels.[17] Defense Minister Marshal Malinovsky's remark about a "blue belt" at the Twenty-third Party Conference was obviously a reference to the strategic sea defense he had constructed around the Soviet Union.[18]

The writings of Soviet theoreticians, among whom Marshal Sokolovsky and Major-General Tsherednichenko have played the leading roles since 1962, now demand a Soviet and socialist-bloc capability to fight local wars with conventional weapons. While the danger of escalation is emphasized, the thesis advanced by Major-General Talensky in 1958—that a local conflict must necessarily escalate into a worldwide war of rockets and nuclear weapons—does not find much support. The question may be left open whether this changed attitude toward local war, particularly when international in character, reflects the beginnings of a Soviet strategy of graduated retaliation. In any case it makes necessary a stronger emphasis on conventional forces, which Khrushchev was not ready to accept. In order to make available the necessary funds for the modernization and qualitative improvement of the army, Brezhnev and Kosygin were forced to undertake a further reduction, not only in the air force (10 per cent), but in the army and other branches of the armed forces as well.[19] The total strength of the army has been reduced from 2.2 to 2 million, that of the airborne infantry from 70,000 to 60,000. The total personnel of the Soviet armed forces is 3,150,000. The intensified efforts of the Kremlin to compensate for these reductions through expanded defense efforts on the part of the East-Central European satellites will be dealt with later.

Soviet military doctrine since the overthrow of Khrushchev once more reflects the belief that a world war would result only in the end of the capitalist world, and not in that of world civilization as a whole. This thesis seems to serve to raise the morale of the troops, who are being conditioned to accept the possibility of a thermonuclear war with all its terrors.

THE FOREIGN POLICY OF BREZHNEV AND KOSYGIN

In the field of foreign policy, the efforts of the new Kremlin leadership are directed toward a continuation of the strategy of long-range "peaceful coexistence," which is based on the assumption that an atomic world war can be avoided. The strategy is expressed in a primarily defensive status quo policy. The concrete goals of this foreign policy do not exhibit any appreciable difference from those of Khrushchev, but there is a noticeable contrast in style. Special emphasis is placed upon a "responsible approach to the most important questions of world policy," a formula that clearly rejects any adventurist policy such as Khrushchev's operation in Cuba.

There is, on the other hand, no evidence of willingness to make foreign-policy concessions that might lead to a genuine reduction of world tensions. On the contrary, emphasis of the class-war aspects of "peaceful coexistence" at the Twenty-third Congress of the CPSU points to an evident hardening of policy.[20] Peaceful conditions for internal construction are to be achieved both by maintenance of the status quo and by intensified efforts to exploit disagreements in the Western world for Soviet purposes.[21]

The Kremlin's main efforts are directed toward strengthening Moscow's hegemony in the European sector of the Eastern bloc and toward preserving the formal unity of world communism while repressing Chinese influence. Relations with the Western states and with the developing countries take second and third priority respectively. In Europe, the Soviet Union hopes to secure the western flank of its sphere of hegemony through legitimizing the partition of Germany in international law and through the disintegration of the Atlantic Alliance system, which would remove the United States from the center of Europe. These objectives are to be realized through a European security conference, a nonaggression pact between the two power groups, and an all-European security pact, such as that first proposed by Molotov at the Berlin Four-Power Conference in February, 1954. Underlying this plan, which at the time did not exclude the possibility of restoring the unified German state under conditions of armed neutrality, was the concept of a continental European bloc directed against the Anglo-Saxon states, in which Soviet Russia would play the predominant role. With this background it is easy to understand why General de Gaulle's Greater European conception is received favorably by the Soviets, even though it assumes the participation of an all-German state and greater independence on the part of the Soviet satellites. The Soviet willingness to dissolve the Warsaw Pact organization as a *quid pro quo* for the abandonment of NATO is likewise not a new development. Nor does it involve any greater risk for the Kremlin, since the Soviet bilateral pact system in East Europe, which has no counterpart in West Europe, would remain intact.[22]

So long as an all-European solution in the Soviet sense remains out of reach, the Kremlin's German policy is to mark time. To avoid jeopardizing Soviet hegemony in East-Central Europe, Brezhnev and Kosygin are nervously concerned to avoid any movement in the German question. One positive factor is that they do not aggravate the Berlin problem.

The deterioration of Soviet relations with the United States is not a result of the Vietnam conflict alone. Brezhnev's and Kosygin's attempts to exploit the special aspirations of European states in order to force the United States out of Europe indicate that they are far less interested than Khrushchev was in bilateral talks. They appear to consider such conversations useful only when they can be conducted from a position of strength. The cool Soviet-British relationship is mainly a consequence of Great Britain's support of United States policy. The Soviet Union and the Anglo-Saxon powers are both interested in atomic nonproliferation. The Kremlin is particularly anxious to prevent the German Federal Republic from sharing control of atomic weapons. As became evident during General de Gaulle's visit in the Soviet Union, the Soviet attitude on this point is very close to that of the French.

In the Near and Middle East, Brezhnev and Kosygin are combining traditional Soviet policy, which was directed toward a neutralization of this region, with efforts to maintain and consolidate further positions achieved in North Africa. Relations with Turkey and Iran, and with Pakistan in connection with mediation of the Kashmir conflict—that is, with states that belong to Western alliance systems— have been considerably improved. Turkey is the first NATO state to receive a Soviet credit. The Soviet engagement in Egypt has been intensified. Although relations with Algeria have been cooler since the downfall of Ben Bella, the Soviet Union is second only to France in providing development aid to that country. In the wake of recent developments the Soviet Union is also making efforts to achieve closer relations with Syria and Iraq. In Black Africa, on the other hand, a reduction of Soviet activity can be observed.

A similar development is to be noted in the Latin American area, although Cuba's ties to the Soviet Union have been strengthened since Castro's break with Peking. Concentration on areas closer to the Soviet Union may very well reflect the fact that Brezhnev and Kosygin pursue less far-flown revolutionary goals than did Khrushchev and are interested in ensuring a more efficient use of funds in developing countries. A corresponding localization of effort may be observed in South and Southeast Asia, where—aside from North Vietnam—India is the chief beneficiary of the considerable Soviet aid program.

The primary object of Brezhnev's and Kosygin's policy in Asia is containment of the Chinese People's Republic. They also seek to restore Moscow's former influence over Asian communism. Through development of its relations with India and Japan the Kremlin hopes to avail itself of these two Asian great powers as a counterweight against China. A rapprochement with the Soviet Union is to be observed in both North Vietnam and North Korea. Mongolia's close ties to the Soviet Union were emphasized by renewal of their alliance on January 15, 1964.

The dispute between Peking and Moscow has become further aggravated under Brezhnev and Kosygin.[23] The Chinese accuse the new Kremlin leadership of using Khrushchev's overthrow merely to change scenery and of actually pursuing Khrushchevite revisionism as before.[24] On September 3, 1965, Marshal Lin Piao expanded Mao Tse-tung's doctrine of the two middle worlds by adding the thesis of the antagonistic contradiction between world cities and world villages—a thesis clearly directed, not only against the United States, but also against the Soviet Union.

The CPSU made its own accusations against the Chinese leadership in a secret letter to a number of communist parties in early 1966, charging the Chinese with their own brand of revisionism and with following an anti-Soviet policy. The latter, the Soviet party declared, was apparent in continued border conflicts and efforts to exploit the Vietnam war to provoke a military conflict between the USSR and the USA. According to the CPSU: "The conception of the revolution as a struggle of the world village against the world city is nothing other than a rejection of the leading role of the working class. It implies the total revision of Marxist-Leninist teachings concerning the world historic mission of the working class."[25]

At the Twenty-third Congress, which the Chinese boycotted, Brezhnev attempted to belittle Soviet-Chinese differences of opinion, but he still called for "unity of action" in a closed front against Peking. The new leadership in the Kremlin is evidently not prepared to make concessions to Communist China. It intends to avoid an official break if possible. It would not hesitate, however, to make this break at a juncture favorable to the Soviet side, should the Chinese leadership continue to deepen the fissure in world communism.

The dispute with China and the desire to restore the unity and solidarity of the world communist movement may very well have been the main reasons Brezhnev and Kosygin engaged themselves more deeply in Vietnam, even before the war there reached full intensity. It was possible, with relatively modest resources, to give the North Vietnam leadership moral support and to tie down a very large American armed force in Southeast Asia, as well as to provoke a further deterioration in relations between the United States and the Chinese People's Republic. This situation affords the Soviet Union greater mobility in Europe and relieves the pressure on its long border with China.

There is on the other hand a danger, for the Soviet Union no less than for Communist China, that increasing American military effort may cause them to lose face in their inner sphere of power and interests as well as in the uncommitted Third World. Furthermore, experimentation with modern military technology in Vietnam is forcing the Soviet Union to step up its armament efforts, jeopardizing the internal development that was supposed to benefit from a "more realistic foreign policy." The same internal development is also considerably hampered by Soviet military strategy, which remains based on the concept of an initial attack, so that the Soviet Union cannot be satisfied with a limited potential for retaliation but feels constrained to catch up with and overtake the United States in the military field. This strategy, which dictates an excessive expansion of the armament burden, justifies the suspicion that the Kremlin has never abandoned its expansionist objectives, particularly not in Europe, and that it regards the present phase of détente merely as a period of transition.

The Soviet Union and East-Central Europe

The internal and external political situations confronting the Soviet Union, as they have been pictured, form the background against which Soviet relations with the countries of East-Central Europe may be projected. The tendency toward polycentrism within the Eastern bloc, which has been considerably stimulated by the Peking-Moscow conflict, and the success of West European economic integration through the Common Market have induced the Soviet Union to make haste with the integration of Eastern Europe. Stalin's old objective, the creation within East-Central Europe of a proto-imperial Muscovite hegemony, was followed by Khrushchev with different methods.[26] The 1961 party program of the CPSU and remarks made by Khrushchev in 1962 suggested a federation of the communist-ruled area, from the Elbe-Werra line to Vladivostok, as an economic, political, and governmental unity under Moscow's leadership. In a programmatic article published during the fall of 1962 Khrushchev expressed the opinion that it was time to consolidate the individual national economies gradually into a "unified production organization."[27]

Acceptance of the new party program of the CPSU—with the exception of the Twenty-Year Plan—by Khrushchev's successors indicates their intention of maintaining these imperialist goals. The only difference is that they intend to use greater caution in achieving them.

The principal instrument of Khrushchev's integration plans was the Council for Mutual Economic Aid (COMECON); Brezhnev and Kosygin, however, are according greater importance to the Warsaw Pact organization for the time being. In its early years the Warsaw Pact served primarily as an organizational device to permit Soviet military presence in East-Central Europe and to unify the policies of the Soviet satellites.[28] The Political Advisory Committee, the highest organ of the Pact organization, served as a forum for explaining the current goals of Soviet foreign policy and for securing coordination of foreign-policy operations. The upheaval in Soviet military-strategic thought and the conversion of the Soviet armed forces since 1959–60 to atomic weapons systems, of which rockets form the principal element, resulted in a military upgrading of the Warsaw Pact.[29] The East-Central European armed forces, with a total strength of about one million, have been provided with new weapons since 1961, including tactical rockets with ranges up to slightly less than 250 kilometers. The atomic warheads remain in Soviet hands. Standardization of weaponry and common training programs were carried further. A permanent conference of the Warsaw Pact defense ministers has been established, and nine major common maneuvers have been held since October, 1961.

The greater the reductions that financial reasons compelled

Khrushchev to make in Soviet conventional armed forces, the greater the importance that East-Central European armies necessarily assumed for the Soviet High Command. The necessity for adequate forces in case of atomic war and to an even greater extent the requirements of a possible local war—a contingency given increasing attention by Soviet military doctrine—enhanced further the military importance of the Soviet satellites.

Immediately after assuming the leadership, Brezhnev and Kosygin called for a further expansion of East-Central European armed forces. They also undertook to promote closer integration of these forces and their fuller subordination to Soviet military leadership. In addition, they insisted that their allies pay a larger share of the high cost of arms conversion. But even beyond these military problems the Warsaw Pact organization seemed to Brezhnev and Kosygin a more suitable instrument than COMECON for consolidating the hegemony of the Soviet Union and assuring greater discipline and unity among its satellites.

At a meeting of the Political Advisory Committee in Warsaw on January 17 and 18, 1965, the participants declared themselves in favor of a European security conference, a worldwide summit conference on the prohibition of atomic weapons, and a world disarmament conference. They also urged realization of the Gomulka and Rapacki plans and of a German peace treaty according to the Soviet recipe. Countermeasures were threatened in case a multilateral atomic force should be established under NATO. Failure to mention the Soviet reform proposals in the communiqué suggests the probability that the Soviet demarche met with resistance.[30]

After this meeting Brezhnev, in particular, made a number of speeches urging the improvement of the Warsaw Pact organization and the creation of appropriate administrative machinery.[31] His ideas found greatest support in the Soviet Zone and Czechoslovakia. Remarks made by Novotný indicated that a strengthening of the Political Advisory Committee had been proposed. It very soon became evident that Rumania was again the leader of resistance to Soviet integration plans, this time in the military field. After the Warsaw meeting Rumania reduced its term of military service from two years to sixteen months and withheld its armed forces from participation in joint maneuvers.[32] It has been reported that the Rumanians, in a note to the other Warsaw Pact powers, demanded participation in the planning and engagement of Soviet atomic weapons, a fuller participation of all member states in the combined High Command, and relief from payments for Soviet troops in other countries.[33] In contrast to the Rumanian attitude, the Czechoslovak defense minister General Lomský, writing in the Soviet army newspaper *Kraznaya Zvezda* on the anniversary of the Warsaw Pact, urged a strengthening of the Pact organization and a "certain centralization in the military field."[34] He emphasized the leadership function of the Soviet Union, but at the same time he demanded a "greater responsibility for the defense of the entire coalition" for the individual member states.

In a programmatic speech on May 7, 1966, the new Rumanian party leader Ceausescu urged the dissolution of existing military blocs. He asserted that military blocs, military bases, and the stationing of armed forces on the territories of other states were anachronisms, "incompatible with the national independence and sovereignty of peoples and with normal international relations."[35] Citing experience with the Cominform, Ceausescu rejected centralized leadership of world communism and emphasized the right of each party to determine its own political line.[36] He declared that the Rumanian Communists had struggled to secure the national existence of the Rumanian people, and he criticized indirectly the annexation of Bessarabia by the Soviet Union.

Brezhnev's attempt to change Ceausescu's mind during a three-day visit in Bucharest was unsuccessful.[37] At the secret meeting of the Warsaw Pact defense ministers in Moscow on May 27 and the subsequent two-week conference of foreign ministers on June 6, 1966, it became evident that Rumania sought a transformation of the Warsaw Pact into a classical alliance and planned to reduce its cooperation to the indispensable minimum.[38]

At the subsequent eighth meeting of the Political Advisory Committee in Bucharest (July 4–6, 1966), held after General de Gaulle's visit in the Soviet Union, a declaration "On the Consolidation of Peace and Security in Europe" was adopted, the compromise character of which was apparent.[39] Revival of the Soviet proposals of 1954 and 1955, which envisioned the conclusion of an all-European security pact and the dissolution of the two military blocs, and the pronounced bilateralism associated with these proposals were concessions to Rumanian conceptions. In dealing with the German question, the declaration followed the rigid Soviet line, omitting the Rumanian proposals to overcome the division of Europe. The declaration also included a more exact statement of most points already considered at the Warsaw meeting the year before. A resolution was adopted commenting on the Vietnam conflict and indicating possible support with "volunteers," even though the jurisdiction of the Warsaw Pact does not extend to Asia.[40] A fact of decisive importance is that the Soviet plans for reform of the Warsaw Pact organization received no mention whatsoever.

Brezhnev and Kosygin thus enjoyed no more success in overcoming Rumanian obstructionism than Khrushchev, a few years earlier, had scored within the Council for Mutual Economic Aid. Under Khrushchev, there had been rapid initial progress in the organizational and legal consolidation of COMECON.[41] As an executive organ in place of the national representatives, a new Executive Committee had been established, consisting of the appropriate deputy prime ministers of the member states and vested with considerably greater powers. The previous secretaries of the individual permanent commissions were transformed into divisions of the central secretariat in Moscow. The Executive Committee was provided with a planning bureau, an institution that, according to Khrushchev's intentions, would later undertake production planning for the entire economic area of COMECON.

The first resistance to Khrushchev's plans for unified "collective planning" and his concepts of an "international socialist division of labor"—which amounted to discrimination against less developed partners—became apparent toward the end of 1962. Rumania took the lead in demanding that priority be given the development of national economies. It was unwilling either to postpone construction of the combined iron works at Galatz or to concentrate as hitherto on delivering raw materials to the more highly industrialized COMECON states. At the sixth meeting of the COMECON Executive Committee in Warsaw in May, 1963, the Rumanian delegation rejected categorically a proposal for joint economic planning within the framework of COMECON.

A resolution passed by the Central Committee of the Rumanian Workers' party, meanwhile renamed the Communist party, in April, 1964, may be regarded as a Rumanian declaration of independence. In part, it states:

> The idea of a common unified planning organ for all COMECON countries involves the most serious economic and

political complications. The planned management of the economy is one of the most fundamental, important, and inalienable attributes of the sovereignty of a socialist state, since the state plan is the principal instrument through which the state accomplishes its political and social-economic goals.[42]

A proposal made by the Soviet geographer Valev in February, 1964, calling for the establishment of an international economic complex on the lower reaches of the Danube on territory belonging to the Soviet Union, Rumania, and Bulgaria, the riparian states, provoked a violent reaction among the Rumanians. It is evident that they interpreted this suggestion as a revival of the plans for partial federation announced by Stalin in 1948 and of the Soviet annexation goals inherent therein.[43]

When he arraigned Khrushchev before the Central Committee of the CPSU, Suslov accused him of attempting to dictate the economic policy of individual COMECON countries and of starting a personal quarrel with Gheorghiu-Dej while attempting to force his agricultural concepts upon the Rumanians. Furthermore, Suslov charged, he had launched a war of competition between Soviet and Rumanian oil with his "Friendship" pipeline, thereby forcing Rumania to orient itself more strongly toward the West in its trade relations.[44]

The more recent meetings of the Council for Mutual Economic Aid and its executive committee have been overshadowed by the meetings of the Warsaw Pact organization. In the meantime, the burden carried by the Soviet Union in supplying raw materials, fuels, and semi-finished goods to the COMECON countries is becoming increasingly noticeable.[45] Soviet economic analysts accuse socialist "brother countries" of importing cheap Soviet raw materials that require high investment in exchange for goods that are often of low value and of exporting finished products made from the Soviet raw materials to the West in exchange for hard currency.[46] The Soviet Union is therefore demanding increases in the prices of raw materials and fuels, as well as long-term credits from the COMECON partners for the development of Soviet raw-material industries. This demand, addressed particularly to the industrial members—Czechoslovakia, the "German Democratic Republic," and to a lesser extent Hungary —could easily provoke a new conflict, especially with Czechoslovakia.

Rumania's rebellion is an indication of the limits faced by the Soviet hegemonical power in East-Central Europe. It would nevertheless be wrong to conclude from the growing strength of centrifugal forces, especially in southeast Europe, that the Soviet hegemonical league is in a process of dissolution. Rumania, which is well aware of the danger of its geopolitical situation, has never considered withdrawing from the Warsaw Pact organization or COMECON during its dispute with the Soviet Union. The Kremlin has been able to accept its setbacks so far without great concern, since it holds the northern flank of its sphere of power and interests in firm hands and Hungary is occupied by Soviet troops. According to reliable information, it was mainly pressure from Moscow that caused Gomulka to raise objections to the Polish bishops' invitation of the Pope in connection with the thousandth anniversary of the Christianization of Poland. The Kremlin is able to count on his loyalty just as much as on that of Ulbricht or Novotný.

A federation of Poland, Czechoslovakia, and the "GDR," which is one of Gomulka's objectives,[47] would certainly not meet with the approval of Brezhnev and Kosygin, who have their own goal of tying the three countries more closely to the Soviet Union, both militarily and economically. The region the countries occupy recently received military emphasis as the "first strategic line of defense" of the Warsaw Pact.[48] It is surely no coincidence that, while the foreign ministers of the Warsaw Pact states were preparing the Bucharest meeting, a session of the defense ministers of the Group of Four was held in East Berlin with highest-ranking Soviet military officers in attendance.[49] The emphasis on regional differentiation within the Soviet hegemonical league indicates the Kremlin's intention to intensify its efforts toward integration of the northern area. Whether these efforts will have more success than the integration plans designed to coordinate the entire European sector of the Eastern bloc, it is difficult to predict at present. In any case, either success or failure of these integration efforts promises to produce decisive changes in the situation in East-Central Europe.

NOTES TO CHAPTER TWO

1. On Stalin's methods of rule, see Fainsod, M., *How Russia is Ruled* (Cambridge, Mass.: 1953); Meissner, B., *Rußland im Umbruch*—Der Wandel in der Herrschaftsordnung und sozialen Struktur der Sowjetunion (Frankfurt a. M.: 1951).

2. *See* Meissner, B., "Die Wandlungen im Herrschaftssystem und Verfassungsrecht der Sowjetunion," in Böttcher-Lieber-Meissner (eds.), *Bilanz der Ära Chruschtschow* (Stutt-

gart: 1966), pp. 141 ff.; Meissner, "Party and Government Reforms, Russia since Khrushchev," *Survey*, July, 1965, pp. 31 ff.

3. *See* the report by the author in the special issue, "Der XXIII. Parteikongreβ der KPdSU," *Osteuropa*, 1966.

4. Text of the Kosygin Report: *Izvestia*, April 6, 1966.

5. For a critical analysis of the Seven- and Twenty-Year plans *see* Meissner, B., Ruβland unter Chruschtschow (Munich: 1960), pp. 203 ff.; *Das Parteiprogramm der KPdSU 1903–1961* (3d ed., Cologne: 1965), pp. 72 ff.

6. Text of Brezhnev's report: *Pravda*, March 26, 1965.

7. Text of Kosygin's report: *Pravda*, September 28, 1965.

8. Meissner, B. (ed.), *Sowjetgesellschaft im Wandel* (Cologne: 1966), pp. 115 ff.

9. *Neue Zürcher Zeitung*, February 16 and 26, 1966.

10. Interview, *Borba*, September 5, 1965.

11. Meissner, *op. cit.*, p. 109.

12. Text of Brezhnev report: *Pravda*, March 30, 1966.

13. Dinerstein, H. S., *Der Krieg und die Sowjetunion* (Cologne: 1960); Wolfe, T. W., *Soviet Strategy at the Crossroads* (Cambridge, Mass.: 1964).

14. Sokolovsky, V. and Čerednićenko, M., "Nekotorye voprosy sovetskogo vennogo stroytel ́stva v poslevenny period" [Some Questions of Soviet Military Development in the Postwar Period], in *Vennoistoriceskij zurnal* [Journal of Military History], 1965, No. 3, pp. 3–16.

15. Meissner, B., "Sowjetruβland zwischen Restauration und Reform," *Osteuropa*, Vol. XVI, 1966, pp. 87 ff. The official rate of exchange, which does not necessarily reflect purchasing power, is 1 ruble = $1.10 U.S.

16. Institute for Strategic Studies, *The Military Balance 1965–1966* (London: 1966), p. 2.

17. *Ibid.*, p. 2.

18. Marshal Sokolovsky's press conference of February 17, 1965 (TASS report of February 17, 1965).

19. *Pravda*, April 3, 1966.

20. Sokolovski, V. D. (ed.), *Vennaja Strategiya* [Military Strategy] (Moscow: 1962; 2d ed. Moscow: 1964); Sokolovsky, V., Čerednićenko, M., "O sovremennoy vennoj strategii" [Concerning Modern Military Strategy], in *Kommunist Vooruzennych Sil* [The Communist in the Armed Forces], 1966, No. 7, pp. 59–66; also *The Military Balance 1965–66*, *op. cit.*, pp. 3–6.

21. *See* foreign policy section of the Brezhnev report, *Pravda*, March 30, 1966.

22. Meissner, B., "Das bilaterale Paktsystem der Sowjetunion in Osteuropa," in *Recht im Wandel* (Cologne: 1965), pp. 497–512.

23. Brahm, H., *Pekings Griff nach der Vormacht* (Cologne: 1966).

24. "Rejection of the Gossip of the New CPSU Leaders About 'Common Actions,'" in *Peking Rundschau*, November 23, 1965, No. 47, p. 12.

25. *Ost-Probleme*, Vol. XII, 1966, p. 234.

26. Meissner, B., "Sowjetische Hegemonie und osteuropäische Föderation," in Ziebura, G., *Nationale Souveränität oder übernationale Integration* (Berlin: 1966), pp. 64 ff.

27. Khrushchev, N. S., "Wesentliche Fragen des sozialistischen Weltsystems," in *Einheit*, 1962, No. 9, p. 6.

28. Meissner, B. (ed.), *Der Warschauer Pakt* (Cologne: 1961).

29. Wolfe, T. W., "Die Entwicklungen im System des Warschauer Paktes," *Osteuropa*, Vol. XVI, 1966, pp. 209–226; Hacker, J., "Der Warschauer Pakt 1961–1965," in Hacker-Uschakow, *Die Integration Osteuropas 1961–1965* (Cologne: 1966).

30. Text in Hacker-Uschakow, *op. cit.*, p. 74.

31. *Pravda*, September 15 and 30 and October 24, 1965, and March 30, 1966.

32. *Die Welt,* April 18, 1966.

33. *Die Zeit,* April 3, 1966, p. 23.

34. *Christ und Welt,* June 24, 1966, p. 7.

35. *Neue Zürcher Zeitung,* May 16, 1966, p. 2.

36. Ströhm, C. G., "Rumänien gefährdet den Warschauer Pakt," *Christ und Welt,* May 20, 1966, p. 3.

37. *Neue Zürcher Zeitung,* May 16, 1966.

38. "Warsaw Pact Muddle," *Radio Free Europe Research,* Communist Area, June 14, 1966.

39. Text in *Pravda,* July 9, 1966.

40. Text in *Pravda,* July 8, 1966.

41. Uschakow, A., "Der Rat für gegenseitige Wirtschaftshilfe 1961–1965," in Hacker-Uschakow, *op. cit.*

42. Hacker-Uschakow, *op. cit.,* p. 230.

43. *Ibid.,* p. 109. The Rumanian journal, *Viata Economica,* June 12, 1964, rejected the Valev proposals as "nonsense."

44. Meissner, B., "Chruschtschowismus ohne Chruschtschow," *Osteuropa,* Vol. XV, 1965, p. 145.

45. *Neue Zürcher Zeitung,* July 11, 1966, p. 2.

46. Ströhm, C. G., "Die ausgebeuteten Sowjets: COMECON-Konferenz mit dramatischem Akzent," *Christ und Welt,* July 1, 1966, p. 6.

47. This objective was pointed out by the former chief of the Polish military mission in Berlin, Colonel Tykocinski, in "Gomulkas Rückkehr zur Orthodoxie," *Neue Zürcher Zeitung,* July 30, 1966, p. 3.

48. *See* remarks of Zonal Defense Minister Heinz Hoffman in *Neues Deutschland,* April 22, 1966.

49. *See* listing in *Neues Deutschland,* July 13, 1966.

CHAPTER III

Eastern Europe
in World Power Politics

PHILIP E. MOSELY

BY THE TIME of Stalin's death in March, 1953, the fate of the proud nations of East-Central Europe appeared, in the eyes of both the Kremlin and most Western observers, to have been sealed, if not irrevocably, then at least for many decades to come. The passage of time, it seemed, could only serve to confirm the harsh twin realities of external Soviet overlordship and domestic Stalinist rule. Dissidence had been pressed into silence, and the oncoming generation was being subjected to a massive molding of thought and action.

Today the situation in East-Central Europe is much more complex and diverse. No single or simple term, whether it be "satellite" or "former satellite," is adequate to describe the varieties and nuances of communist rule that have emerged. Only one true satellite remains today: the abjectly subservient Ulbricht regime. Other communist-ruled countries of East-Central Europe can appeal, within certain limits of discretion, to a national identity and can even, again within limits, defend the national interests of their peoples. That appeal and those interests are denied the Ulbricht regime, and this factor tends to make it both lonely and disreputable among the supposedly "fraternal" regimes of the communist grouping.

The signs of burgeoning autonomy are both numerous and well reported, even overreported, in the West. The communist regimes in Hungary and Czechoslovakia are experimenting much more freely than is their Soviet "protector" in their attempts to promote enterprise efficiency and develop a communist variant of a competitive market economy. Rumania has declined to subordinate its own economic future to the regional planning of COMECON or to take part in the joint maneuvers of the Warsaw Pact. The moviemakers of Poland, and more recently of Czechoslovakia, have struck out on new lines of innovation, far exceeding the timid loosening of the rigid canons of "socialist realism" in the Soviet Union. Again, in cautious dissent from Moscow, none of the regimes is willing to foreclose the possibility of a future accommodation with the growing economic power of the European Economic Community. Nor have they shown any zeal for the efforts of Khrushchev, and now of Brezhnev and Kosygin, to reestablish an authoritative center of international communist orthodoxy and leadership.

These obvious signs of autonomous thinking and aspirations have tended, in Western eyes, to obscure the equally clear limitations on the freedom of action to which these regimes are likely to aspire in any near future. In terms of strategic power, both nuclear and conventional, they recognize an overarching Soviet hegemony. They must constantly affirm and reaffirm their loyal support of Moscow's supreme security interests, and the rulers would be the last to repeat the mistake of attempting, as Imre Nágy did in October, 1956, to opt out of the Warsaw Pact, however they may twist and turn in their efforts to minimize its burdens. Similarly, in the political field the regimes must constantly assert and reassert their unfailing loyalty to basic communist doctrine. Indeed, it is their insistence on that loyalty that enables them to claim the right to interpret the dogma each in its own way, rather than in Moscow's way. This basic loyalty makes it possible for them to seek willing support among their own people and to pursue their own advantage, even when this pursuit runs counter to Soviet dogma or interests. Finally, even if the communist regimes believe that they can now rely on support at home, as opposed to having to rely on Moscow's fiat, to assure the continuity of their rule, they see no advantage in carrying defiance of Soviet leadership beyond the increasingly flexible and deliberately undefined limits of the autonomy that they now enjoy.

The new and complex situation in Eastern Europe poses novel and difficult problems to Western policy making. Can the Soviet hegemony be dissolved, as President Charles de Gaulle maintains, and can Europe be reunited "from the Atlantic to the Urals"? Or will economic cooperation and relaxation of political tensions simply consolidate antipopular, unrepresentative regimes and thus enable the international forces of communism to accumulate new strength and resources? Does the West possess sufficient leverage to strengthen the autonomy of those regimes against Soviet hegemony? Or will friendly Western initiatives simply enable them to camouflage their fundamental dependence on Soviet power? Should the West try to formulate a common policy toward the "East"?

The issues, for the West, are complex. The auguries are obscure, and the stakes are momentous. Yet neither the new situation in East-Central Europe nor the problem of defining new policies toward it can be understood or resolved in isolation. The recent and continuing changes in East-Central Europe must be examined in the light of the profound shifts that, since 1956, have been remolding the contours of world politics. Among these new factors are the ever spreading impact of destalinization within and outside Russia, the profound antagonism between Moscow and the Mao regime in China, a widely held belief in the reality and durability of the strategic stalemate, the renewed vitality and attraction of Western Europe, and the revival of nationalism in East-Central Europe—even if now in communist trappings.

Destalinization and Its Consequences

The process of destalinization, once Nikita Khrushchev launched it in February, 1956, was the first and mild tremor of a seismic convulsion with ultimate consequences that cannot be fully measured or foretold even now. When Khrushchev embarked on this revolutionary policy, he did so for reasons that were deeply relevant to Soviet urgencies. He saw that this was the only way to shake the Soviet economy and ways of thinking out of their deadening routine of fear-stricken conformity. Despite, or because of, his long and faithful apprenticeship to Stalin, Khrushchev recognized that something startling and dramatic was desperately needed to launch the Soviet system on a more dynamic path of development. When thwarted by obstacles to his own desires, however, when he failed to elicit spontaneous conformity, Khrushchev regularly exposed his own Stalinist training, as in his hardfisted treatment of creative writers and painters in 1962 and 1963. Yet even while thundering his Stalinist threats of exasperation, Khrushchev hesitated, where Stalin would not have hesitated, and he usually stayed his hand from executing his own worst threats. When the chips were down, Khrushchev wanted to be known in Russian history as the man who released his country from the madness of Stalinism and thereby unlocked its great human reserves of talent and energy.

Even within the Soviet system, which he knew so intimately, Khrushchev was often unable to foresee the continuing impact of the forces being released by the process of destalinization, once it had been officially launched. He was sincerely puzzled and personally aggrieved when many of the ablest writers insisted, out of a deep national and party patriotism, that even a circumscribed freedom to depict Soviet realities in literary form would not always lead to automatic hosannas to the leader's competence and wisdom. Khrushchev wanted the economists to come to grips with real problems and thus give good advice to the policy makers. But he was impatient of the new "freedom" when it led to criticism of his own "achievements." By his personal insistence Khrushchev opened the "window to the West" a substantial crack, for he saw the need to promote fuller utilization of the cultural and scientific achievements of the outside world and to revivify Soviet cultural and educational life. Yet he continually insisted that there could be no "coexistence of ideologies" even while urging the West to accept the sincerity of his appeals for political coexistence.

Within the Soviet Union with its massive heritage of Stalinist centralism and conformity, destalinization has inaugurated a prolonged, incomplete, and uneven process of change. It has unleashed strivings for truth and individual freedom and responsibility that, if they are to be increasingly satisfied over several decades, will eventually require a profound reshaping of Soviet society. So far this satisfaction has been granted in relatively modest doses. It has, of course, not been the intention of Khrushchev or his successors to bring about any fundamental reshaping of the system, and in any case the Kremlin is confident of its power to guide, direct, and, if necessary, limit the process of change so as to enhance Russia's prestige and its leaders' power.

The process of change within Russia is proceeding almost entirely in response to deepening inner needs of the Soviet system, and it can be influenced only marginally from without. Increased trade and sharing of managerial and technological skills by the West, a trickle of cultural and scientific exchanges, an agreement on airline privileges, a consular agreement, the extension of the nuclear test ban to underground tests—all these contribute something to atmospherics. These small steps make it easier for Moscow to draw a sharp contrast between its own moderation and Peking's extremism. They also weaken the memory of the Stalinist garrison state. All such external steps are symbols of change and the possibility of further changes and therefore have some value. But none of them reaches very far into Soviet society or substantially affects the direction of change or its pace.

For the dependent communist regimes in East-Central Europe, destalinization, once initiated in Moscow, has had and continues to have far more drastic and dramatic consequences than within the Soviet Union. For one thing, these nations did not experience Stalinism as a phenomenon that had evolved through a process of national development, whereas it had some deep roots in Russia. To them the Stalinist system was an external that had been imposed on them in its full panoply of terror. It was brought to them in its full Russian flavor, which contrasted sharply with their own historic experiences as participants for centuries in the complex flow of European civilization. Stalinization suppressed, but could not completely destroy, values that they held deeply.

One factor that is often overlooked is that the period of all-out Stalinism was a relatively brief one in East-Central Europe, where it lasted from 1947 or 1948 to 1953 or 1956. In many essentials the people who emerged from this tunnel of horrors blinking at the unexpected daylight had not been "remolded." In the Soviet Union the upper and nether grindstones of Stalinism had turned long and inexorably over several decades. In the satellites they ground cruelly but for a relatively short period of time. As Moscow's pressure began to be relaxed in 1956, older and deeper values of basic humanism gradually reemerged from the psychological substratum. Very many people, among them even some satellite Communists, had discovered that pure Stalinism was intolerable and unworkable. Many of them made this clear by their role in the abortive liberalization and popular uprisings of 1953 in the Ulbricht-ruled part of Germany and by the attempt of the first Imre Nágy government in Hungary to escape from the burden of Rákosi's "Muscovite Communism." And in 1956 it was the "national" Communists who led the struggle against Moscow's direct control, this time quoting the Khrushchev destalinization speech against the local "Muscovites."

It was thus natural for the impact of Khrushchev's destalinization policy to be far more explosive in the dependent but restive regimes of East-Central Europe than it was in the Soviet Union. Khrushchev's soul-searing speech of February, 1956, which to this day remains unpublished within the Soviet Union, was widely distributed, perhaps in an expurgated version, among the satellite parties. Quite possibly Khrushchev at that time welcomed the support of satellite communist allies against his domestic Stalinist enemies. In taking this adventurous step, Khrushchev again showed a lack of sensitivity and foresight in the handling of peoples and problems that lay outside his sphere of direct experience. Apparently he expected the satellite parties to carry out an orderly and gradual "correction" of Stalinist "excesses" within their own regimes, just as he proposed to do within the Soviet Union, and had no concept of the accumulated forces of wrath that he was unleashing. Only this can explain the rage with which he denounced Gomulka at the Warsaw airport in October, 1956, or make clear why he decided, apparently after a good deal of hesitation, to reconquer Budapest by Soviet tanks and artillery.

A Decade of Change

The ten years since the crucial events of October, 1956, have confirmed the first impression of many observers, namely, that the launching of destalinization set in motion ever widening waves of change in East-Central Europe, and that neither the Kremlin, nor the communist rulers in that part of Europe, nor the most astute analysts in the West can predict exactly how far these processes will lead. What is clear is that change is proceeding there more rapidly than in the Soviet Union, is probably restrained but certainly not deterred by Soviet criticisms, and, unlike what is happening in the Soviet Union, is influenced substantially by a growing interaction between the former satellites and the nations of the West.

The growth of diversity has had an unexpected influence on the evolution of Soviet Russia. As a by-product of their differing rates and paths of change, the former satellites have, in a sense, become proving-grounds for economic and cultural innovations, some of which are studied and later copied in the Soviet Union. Thus to a significant degree the formerly subservient satellites have reversed the flow of ideas and influences between their own systems and those of the Soviet Union. In the fields of managerial techniques, the arts, the cinema, and literature they sometimes "acclimatize" Western ideas and then pass them on to help Soviet innovators understand and meet the needs of their own evolving society.

Destalinization has had numerous other consequences. It lies at the root of the bitter clash between Moscow and the Maoist regime in Peking. It tends to isolate the Ulbricht regime, which has shown that it cannot accept the risks of destalinization and be sure of surviving. Indeed, the contrasting attitudes to destalinization have left the Pankow leadership a rather lonely outsider among the former or partial satellites in East-Central Europe. Above all, the repudiation of Stalin and monolithic Stalinism has undermined the artificial but formerly powerful faith of Communists in the omniscience and omnipotence of a single communist center of doctrine and policy. Destalinization has undercut the belief, long taken for granted by Communists, in the "infallibility" and the "inevitability" of communism. It is no longer easy to say what constitutes the canon of "true" communism, and quarrels over communist doctrines now parallel the conflicts of power interests.

If communism can mean so many different things in different settings, then its followers must resort to some test of logic or empirical experience—to a measure of validity that exists outside the dogma and independent of it—in order to appraise conflicting interpretations of doctrine. In other words, communism, like other political beliefs in the modern world, is beginning to be judged by its own adherents in pragmatic terms, in terms of what it achieves or fails to achieve for its people. This evolution toward an empirical application of dogma has apparently not begun in Maoist China, though the clashes within Chinese communism may eventually introduce a process of reevaluation. Within the Soviet Union the movement from a teleological to an instrumental interpretation of the doctrine is gaining momentum. But it is much further advanced, with many intellectual and practical consequences, within the communist parties of East-Central Europe. It has moved even further and faster in the Yugoslav, Italian, and Swedish Communist parties.

Once deprived of their faith in an omniscient communist Mecca, the ruling cadres in Eastern Europe have had to resort to empirical arguments to justify, in the eyes of their own peoples, their right to a monopoly of rule. One argument they use is that they are now prepared to improve their economies through experimentation and aim thus to provide their peoples with a rising standard of living. Another is that their management of economic and cultural life is more efficient and more tolerant than the Soviet pattern. Still another argument holds that, in view of Russia's strategic power and needs, their peoples have no realistic choice other than that between direct Soviet domination or a local communist regime, the latter both tolerated and kept in power by Moscow. To curry favor with their own subjects, the satellite Communists criticize Russia as "backward," but they still rely on the Soviet guarantee of their power over their own people.

Both historians and contemporaries often underestimate the span of time that is required for major changes to unfold. They forget, for example, that serfdom, as a political, social, and economic system, developed over several centuries, and that its elimination has usually taken at least a century. Even in the world of today, with its recent and kaleidoscopic changes, historians must be chary of predicting "inevitable" processes of change. It is presumptuous to assume that the communist-ruled countries of East-Central Europe will evolve "inevitably" toward a predetermined and predictable goal of freedom and full independence. Nor should either the Soviet Union or the West assume that the system of one of them provides the "inevitable" pattern of the future for this major part of Europe.

The slowness and uncertainty of change are illustrated in the experience of Yugoslav communism. Almost nineteen years after the break with Stalin, the Yugoslav leadership, which is in some ways the least dogmatic and the most experimental in its approach, is still groping for new ways to cope with the basic problem of developing an effective economy. Neither has it resolved several of its political dilemmas. If, for example, the economic system is now to operate according to the new ground-rules of plant autonomy, competition, and efficiency, which in turn are to be measured in the domestic and international market-place, just how big a role remains for a monopolistic political party? If the power of the political police must be restrained in order to secure greater political, cultural, and economic efficiency, can the ruling party in practice refuse to allow the formation of loyal factions that will debate, from within the party, the wisdom and desirability of this or that new policy? In the end the processes through which national interests, popular demands, and communist dogma are reconciled or compromised may prove to be more prolonged and uncertain in other countries of East-Central Europe than they have been in Yugoslavia.

THE SOVIET-CHINESE CONFLICT AND THE SATELLITES

The repudiation of Stalin, which has led by many paths to polycentrism, also lies at the root of a second major new factor of world politics: the deep hostility that divides Soviet communism from Maoist extremism. Destalinization and Mao's declaration of political warfare against it have touched off a bitter conflict between the two strongest centers of communism. The struggle over "revisionism" has reached a peak of violence in the Maoist "great cultural revolution" (or "counterrevolution," as Moscow calls it), which burst into the public arena in mid-August, 1966. The conflict within China has shaken the very core of the Chinese Communist system of power. No longer satisfied to denounce Khrushchev and his successors root-and-branch, Mao has turned his "anti-revisionist" rage against large segments of his own party, government apparatus, secret police, and army—the pillars of his rule since 1949. It is too early to predict what kind of a regime will emerge from this vast turmoil. Yet it is clear that for a long time to come it will have little or nothing in common with the Soviet policy of "Khrushchevism without Khrushchev" or the striving of East-European Communists to "Europeanize" or "de-Russianize" poststalinist communism in their countries.

For the communist regimes in Eastern Europe the top-to-bottom clash between Moscow and Peking has brought several advantages and some risks. Peking has loudly accused the Kremlin rulers of attempting, like Stalin, to dictate policies to, and to choose leaders for, all other parties. Even before the two major communist powers publicly admitted the reality of their rupture, the Chinese Communist taunts had stung Khrushchev to reaffirm ever more vehemently the twin principles of the complete independence of each communist party and the "equality" of all parties.

Khrushchev's actions in 1956 certainly did not demonstrate any great attachment on his part to these "sacred" and "immutable" principles, but by 1960 and in later years his claims had become more convincing to him as well as to the satellite leaders. Almost overnight many of the formerly subservient rulers came to believe in these newly proclaimed "eternal" verities and to act on them, even to the point of chipping away at Moscow's own prestige. Today each state party claims the right to govern its own people and define its own interests within a rather loose pledge of allegiance to Marxism-Leninism and to "proletarian internationalism." In this way destalinization and the Sino-Soviet conflict have resolved in practice the long-unsolved problem of the "correct" relationship between the Moscow center of communist power and the lesser communist regimes.

In order to rally the majority of foreign communist regimes and parties around the anti-Mao banner, Khrushchev and his successors have had to woo and cajole their fellow Communists. This has not yet resulted, as Khrushchev intended, in a united front of communist parties. Two of the complaints raised against Khrushchev at the time of his dismissal in October, 1964, were that he had been pushing prematurely for a general condemnation of the Maoist heresy, and that new efforts should first have been made to restore unity of action, if not of trust, between Moscow and Peking. In this effort Khrushchev's successors have been no more successful, but their patience and long periods of reticence, together with the setbacks administered to Peking's prestige by its own actions, have enabled Brezhnev and Kosygin to rally a wider range of parties behind their banner and thus to press forward with their campaign to isolate the new, extreme, Maoist version of communism.

In this bitter struggle between the two communist "greats," the communist leaders of East-Central Europe have kept a close eye on their own jealously guarded interests. On the one hand, the excesses of the new Maoism remind them of the Stalinist vise from which they are now free. As Poles say to Poles, "Thank God, Poland has Russia as a buffer-state between it and China!" On the other, communist leaders in East-Central Europe are reassured by Kremlin's attack on the new Maoism, for the attack strengthens its own rejection of Stalinism, both at home and in its relations with the former satellites.

At several earlier stages in the conflict that has arisen since 1956, various satellite regimes toyed with the idea of enlarging their own independence from Moscow through strengthening their direct relations with Peking. One satellite, Rumania, even flirted publicly, until brutally rebuffed by Mao, with the notion of serving as mediator between Moscow and Peking. All of the East-Central Europe regimes, except the Ulbricht, have taken advantage of Moscow's unexpected need for their public support to secure various gains for themselves.

None has been eager to foregather in a public international conference convened to expel Maoist China from the communist fold.

The leaders of the former satellites instinctively prefer the present situation of "neither peace nor war" (in the political sense). On the one hand, all-out political warfare between Moscow and Peking might force the smaller communist regimes to accept a larger measure of Moscow leadership, and this they do not want. In addition, since any new precedent for the expulsion of an "heretical" party from the fold of orthodoxy might at some later time be used against one or another of them, the satellites are extremely reluctant to join in anathematizing the Maoists. On the other hand, they fear that a reconciliation between Moscow and Peking would reduce their bargaining power in Moscow and might in turn lead a reunited bloc to undertake a more adventurous policy in the world. Either development would cut across the desire to achieve greater comfort at home and to pursue continuing relaxation abroad. Either all-out conflict or effective reconciliation would reduce their expanding freedom of decision at home and their arena of maneuver in regional and European politics.

NUCLEAR STALEMATE AND ITS UNCERTAINTIES

Still another major factor in the new situation of the countries of East-Central Europe has been the emergence, since the Cuban missile crisis of October, 1962, of a firm belief, widely held in East and West, that the world has now entered a prolonged, perhaps permanent, phase of nuclear balance or stalemate. If this belief is well founded, and if this strategic situation is likely to persist into an indefinite future, its consequences will involve important and favorable advantages for the former satellite regimes in East-Central Europe. A permanent stalemate would mean that they are now protected by Soviet nuclear power against any military or political pressures from the West, and that, similarly, they are safeguarded against sudden Soviet pressures by the strategic might of the West.

In addition to a greatly diminished fear of nuclear war, even the possibility of a conventional war in Europe seems greatly reduced. Since neither Russia nor America can expect to be a "victor" in a nuclear war, even a conventional war in Europe seems less and less possible, for it would almost certainly quickly involve both the reluctant nuclear powers in a struggle to the death—for both. If this conjecture is accurate, then in turn it hardly behooves the former satellites, anymore than France, to exert themselves to maintain large conventional forces. Indeed, the main purpose of maintaining such forces would seem to be the necessity for assuring the Soviet leadership of their loyal backing. Since the East European, like the West European, regimes now believe that any major war anywhere in the world is unlikely, and that any war, even a small one, in Europe is impossible, they feel increasingly free to maneuver under the umbrella of nuclear stalemate in pursuit of many small interests of their own.

It is perhaps useful to examine more closely the assumptions and experiences out of which this atmosphere of carefree optimism has grown so quickly. The "lessons" of the Cuban missile crisis may be more complex and less reassuring than those briefly outlined above. Because that crisis constituted the first nuclear confrontation in history, and because the consequences of a different outcome would have brought unparalleled disaster on much of mankind, people generally have been eager to believe that this was not only the first but also the last such crisis. This craving to assume that the nature of the power contest has been radically changed by a single crisis has led swiftly to the wishful belief that no such crisis can conceivably occur in the future, even to the end of time.

Unfortunately for this craving, the lessons of the October, 1962, crisis are not so clear and simple as that. For one thing, the outcome of that crisis was determined to a major degree by the fact that at that time one of the two contestants, the United States, had far more numerous and varied means of delivery available than its adversary had. That situation of imbalance may now be passing from the scene as both sides strive to improve and protect their strategic forces. A second factor of great importance was that the United States could have overwhelmed Khrushchev's exposed nuclear salient in Cuba by using its conventional land, sea, and air forces. The brutal choice—whether or not to initiate the use of its then inferior nuclear arsenal—would then have fallen squarely to the Kremlin. In the third place, Khrushchev underestimated the electrifying effect his attempt to bring about a clandestine and drastic change in the world balance of power would have on the United States' European and Latin American allies.

Because the Kremlin then had no choice but to terminate its adventurous thrust as quickly as possible, and because the United States government was determined to act with or without the support of its allies, the stability of the Western alliance was not exposed to a prolonged crisis. Finally, Khrushchev believed in his own ability, as leader of a dictatorial regime, to parlay his nuclear power into political gains—first in the Caribbean, then in Berlin, and perhaps later in the Aegean and Iran. His worst blunder was to underestimate American willpower. Khrushchev refused to believe, until it was almost too late, that a democracy could muster its strength of will and the support of its allies to face the prospect of nuclear war. Later Soviet leaders may not be immune to similar failures of judgment.

From a hasty reading of the Cuban missile crisis, which like most crises has many unique facets, two opposite and equally misleading conclusions have been drawn. One conclusion, which was at first widely held in Europe and America, was that the pattern of Soviet advance and retreat might be repeated elsewhere; that the United States had only to brandish its nuclear arsenal to ensure Soviet acquiescence to U.S. purposes so long as those purposes did not menace any direct Soviet interest. The fallacy, of course, lies in assuming that the course, nature, and scope of any future crisis would be a copy of the conditions that accompanied the October, 1962, crisis. A second and contradicting conclusion, sketched above, holds that both sides in the nuclear balance will henceforth be permanently inhibited by a real or apparent stalemate from having recourse to nuclear weapons or threats, and that a situation of mutual deterrence makes all wars, even the smallest conventional wars, less and less likely.

The basic assumption underlying both these conclusions may well prove unsound. An entirely new situation, the opposite of nuclear stalemate, may emerge from the continuing arms race. Both major powers are working very hard to achieve various forms of technological superiority. These efforts include the development of hardened and dispersed bases, improved missile-bearing submarines and elaborate antisubmarine systems, multiple warhead launchers, and anti-ballistic-missile systems. It is not likely that any single major breakthrough, such as the post-1945 development of the nuclear warhead and the intercontinental missile, will give decisive advantage to one side or the other. Nevertheless, the accumulation of a series of important systems advantages might lead one side to calculate that the strategic balance had been tipped significantly in its favor and to insist on receiving political gains commensurate with its heightened power.

If the Soviet Union should achieve a recognized strategic advantage, its leadership might again feel duty bound to exploit it to the full politically. In that event the most valuable—and, in some ways, a still vulnerable—target for Soviet ambitions remains Western Europe. If the Kremlin should revert to a menacing policy toward Western Europe, it would insist on receiving full political and military support from the East European regimes, even though the management of the crisis would remain tightly held in Soviet hands. Such a return to an aggressive policy would place in question the survival of the governments in East-Central Europe or would at least undermine the degree of autonomy and initiative they now exercise. It is inevitable, therefore, that East Europeans, regimes and nations alike, feel a strong preference for the alternative of a lasting nuclear stalemate. It is natural for them, as for the majority of West Europeans and, indeed, for all other people, to feel an irresistible urge to believe that that desirable state of permanent balance and stability has already been achieved and will last forever. These assumptions may or may not prove sound over the next ten years or so.

East-Central Europe and the West

Still another new factor that has strongly influenced the position and expectations of the peoples of East-Central Europe in the decade of destalinization has been the renewed economic and cultural vitality and the political stability of Western Europe. Having claimed, unwisely, that the communist system would out-invest and out-perform the modified free-enterprise system that prevails in Western Europe and North America, the Leninist-style ideologues have been confounded by the dynamism that has been demonstrated by most of Western Europe. Since their economic planners began a serious examination of the lagging rate of growth that has afflicted Eastern Europe since 1960, the smaller communist regimes have had to admit that they have a good deal to learn from the West with regard to the rational use of capital and labor resources, the provision of incentives, the achievement of a balance between investment and consumption, and the effective use of the international division of labor. Even their heavy dependence on the Soviet economy, which was long viewed by their dogmatists as an advantage, has been called into question. Recently some Soviet economists have wondered aloud whether the Soviet Union can afford to make the large capital investments that will still be needed in 1970 or 1980 to enable it to supply the very large requirements of the former satellites for raw materials such as coal, steel, oil, cotton, lumber, manganese, and so forth. They have asked whether it would not be more profitable, to both the countries of East-Central Europe and the Soviet Union, for the satellite countries to produce more goods that can be sold outside the COMECON group, so as to be able to import more raw materials and minerals from the developing countries. The idea that integration through COMECON can match the economic power and gains of the European Community has less and less reality or attraction.

Instead, despite their heavy dependence on the Soviet economy, the former satellites are trying to expand their commercial dealings with the West, open new outlets there, and thus acquire more modern equipment. Unlike the Soviet government, which still pursues its dogmatic attacks on the European Community, the smaller regimes are working hard to develop closer economic relations with the Community and Western countries in general. They feel no ideological shudders when they contemplate either the advantages of such trade or the eventual necessity of recognizing the Community and negotiating trade agreements with it. Indeed, East Europeans are more optimistic than many West Europeans in believing that the Community will continue to grow markedly in economic strength, will expand by adding Britain and several other countries to its membership, and will eventually take on some significant political functions. In a quiet way many East Europeans hope that an integrated Western Europe will become, not only a profitable and considerate trading partner, but also an economic and political counterweight to the Soviet Union. They hope that the remarkable economic upsurge in Western Europe will enable them to achieve a wider measure of independence in their dealings with both East and West.

Last in order but not least, East-Central Europe has witnessed over the past ten years a strong revival of national pride, no longer subordinated to an overriding subservience to Soviet policy. In Poland and Czechoslovakia the governments claim that they alone are capable of assuring the national existence and territorial integrity, and these claims carry great weight with their peoples. National rivalries have reemerged in Yugoslavia, where the Communist party had long boasted of having created for the first time a nationwide patriotism, capable of submerging the particularist nationalisms of Serbs, Croats, Slovenes, Montenegrins, and Macedonians. Taking advantage of Soviet distrust of Hungarian nationalism in and since 1956, the Rumanian leadership has reminded the Kremlin, not too loudly, that the "Moldavians" of the adjacent Soviet Union Republic are really Rumanians in language and tradition.

In Czechoslovakia the Slovaks, inspired by their memorable uprising of 1944 against Hitler's oppression, have constantly taken the lead in the process of modernizing the regime, while the Czechs have, until recently, been more cautious or more lethargic. In Poland the year of the millennium saw the communist regime and the Roman Catholic Church locked in a bitter rivalry to determine which better represents the continuity of the national tradition. Everywhere in East-Central Europe communist regimes have reestablished the cult of precommunist and even "feudal" heroes, and "democratic" patriots of the past have begun to receive fresh tribute after some twenty years of oblivion. One striking manifestation of revived national pride is the strong reaction against all forms of Russian cultural influence; paradoxically, the communist regimes take pride in pointing to evidences of Russian backwardness in the arts and in the comforts of daily life.

Despite these important changes of the past ten years, East-Central Europe remains a basically passive participant within the conflicting pressures of world politics. On the one hand, while the local communist leaders can and must assert their autonomy from Moscow's leading-strings, they cannot escape from their geographical predicament. On the other hand, they need the military protection of the Warsaw Pact, ostensibly against Western and particularly German "aggression," but actually against their own citizens, and they know, moreover, that the Kremlin would not tolerate the Pact's breakup. They also need the political protection that they derive from Moscow's guarantee of the survival of their regimes. Therefore, they must assure the Kremlin of their allegiance to the basic tenets of Marxism-Leninism, if only to gain the right to apply its doctrines in a more flexible and autonomous way. They seek at the same time to give their people a partial or symbolic satisfaction of their deepset longing to "rejoin Europe" through promoting more active economic and cultural relations with the West. They believe that the decline in the solidarity of NATO makes it safe for them to deal more actively with the West without arousing dangerous suspicions in Moscow. They believe that they can execute these not very complicated maneuvers in safety because of the growing uncertainties that beset Soviet policy in an unforeseen environment of nuclear stalemate and communist polycentrism. This changing situation of East-Central Europe in turn presents the nations of the West with new perplexities, as well as new opportunities, and requires them to reexamine many of the comfortable certainties on which they have based their policies over the past two decades.

CHAPTER IV

The Moscow-Peking Dispute And Its Impact on Eastern Europe

WU CHEN-TSAI

THE RUSSIAN and Chinese Communists are commonly said to be locked in an ideological dispute. It would be more correct, however, to call the dispute doctrinal: a term that involves both ideology and strategy. Both are involved in the schism that has developed between Peking and Moscow in recent years, but the focus of the argument is concerned with strategy. Since scholars the world over have written about "ideological disputes," that term may appear in this article, but it should be understood in the broader sense to mean "doctrinal disputes," which also involves strategy.

According to the Russian Communist party: "The Chinese Communists made public their split with International Communism in 1960 when they published the article entitled 'Long Live Leninism.' "[1] The Chinese Communists maintain that "the theoretical schism dividing monolithic International Communism actually dates back to the 20th Congress of the Communist Party of the Soviet Union (CPSU) in 1956."[2] It is thus apparent that Peking and Moscow have been engaged in "secret struggle" for more than ten years.

Both sides limited themselves at the outset to indirect references and innuendoes in both public and behind-the-scenes controversy. This reserve and discretion made it difficult for the world to understand what was happening. Both sides later resorted to the familiar communist tactic of distortion and invention of lies. Peking charged, for instance, that the Soviets had entered into an anticommunist conspiracy with the United States.[3] And yet Soviet documents show that the Kremlin had in fact been making elaborate preparations for de-

63

feating the United States with methods even more realistic and direct than those adopted by Peking. On another occasion the Soviets called the Chinese Communists racists perpetuating the tradition of Genghis Khan.[4] Peking's documents, however, never failed to harp on China's orthodoxy and proletarian internationalism and to accuse the Russian comrades of violating the fundamental tenets of Marxism-Leninism. All this proved highly misleading to outside observers.

Through careful comparison and analysis of the earlier and later documents of both Russian and Chinese Communists, it can be shown that ideological and nonideological elements were often mixed up in the Sino-Soviet disputes to such an extent that they could not be separated. At the Twentieth Congress of the CPSU in 1956, for instance, Khrushchev launched his campaign of destalinization and denounced the personality cult. Shortly thereafter the Chinese Communists published an article entitled "On the Historical Experiences of the Dictatorship of the Proletariat"—obviously a defense of Joseph Stalin, who was now classified by the Russians as a tyrant. The mention of Stalin was brief: he was praised as having "made more contributions than mistakes." The motive for this article was not revealed until seven years later, when the Chinese charged that "Khrushchev's opposition to the cult of personality was only a mean political intrigue," and that its purpose was "to subvert willfully the leadership of a brother party and brother nation by meddling in their domestic affairs."[5] If we fail to recognize the nonideological elements and eliminate them as irrelevant, it will be difficult for us to make a judicious study of the ideological disputes between Peking and Moscow.

After the downfall of Khrushchev the Chinese Communists temporarily adopted a wait-and-see attitude. Facts proved, however, that the resolutions passed at the Twentieth and Twenty-second congresses of the CPSU did not represent Khrushchev's personal ideas. Instead, they signified a policy line the entire Soviet party considered imperative at the current stage of development. This line was not changed by the emergence of the Brezhnev-Kosygin duumvirate. The Chinese Communists therefore accused the new Soviet leaders of engaging in "Khrushchevism without Khrushchev"[6] and attacked them for "using two-faced tricks more hypocritical and calculated than those of Khrushchev."[7] In March, 1966, the Peking leaders made the unprecedented move of refusing to attend the Twenty-third Congress of the CPSU— a gesture that signified that the Peking-Moscow quarrel had gone beyond the point of no return. While both Brezhnev and Kosygin have repeatedly talked of communist unity, implying that they have also adopted a wait-and-see attitude, this tactic is not expected to produce miracles.

The tendency for doctrinal disputes to continue was indicated by the remarks of Liu Shao-chi and Chou En-lai at a party welcoming Premier Mehmet Shehu of Albania. Liu said: "The modern Russian revisionists have continued along the road of surrender to imperialism. They have fallen so low as to become rebels against Marxism-Leninism and lackeys of U.S. imperialism. To realize their dream of United States-Soviet co-operation for world conquest, they have conspired with the American imperialists to sabotage the revolutionary struggles of the peoples of various countries and to smash the solidarity of revolutionary forces . . . let us raise higher the banners of Marxism-Leninism and proletarian internationalism and raise higher the banners of opposition to American imperialism and modern Russian revisionism in order to advance the struggle."[8] Chou said on the same occasion: "At the 23rd Congress of the CPSU, the Soviet leaders continued to play the two-faced trick of pretending to be anti-imperialist while really surrendering to imperialism, of pretending to work for revolution while really betraying it, and of pretending to support unity while actually fomenting division . . . while talking eloquently about solidarity and anti-imperialism, they seek alliance with U.S. imperialists and their hired thugs in order to attack China, Albania, and all revolutionary peoples . . . the only way to fight American imperialism victoriously is to oppose firmly the modern revisionism propagated by the Soviet leaders."[9]

THE BONE OF CONTENTION OF THE PRESENT ERA

Lenin said: "We must first assess the various fundamental characters of different eras before we can formulate our own strategy." The doctrinal disputes between the Chinese and Russian Communists began with an argument about the attributes of the era in which we are living.

Until 1956 the policy of international communism was designed to conform to the fundamental character of the "era of imperialism," as defined by Lenin. According to Lenin: "The era of imperialism was the era dominated by capitalism." In other words, the capitalist class enjoyed total control of political power the world over. Three major contradictions existed during this era: (1) a contradiction between the workers and the capitalists, (2) a contradiction between conflicting imperialism, and (3) a contradiction between colonies or semicolonies and imperialism. All three contradictions centered around the capitalist class. In order to carry out their revolution, the proletariat must therefore exploit these contradictions—the basic policy of such exploitation is actually the fomenting of an international war. According to Lenin, all international wars in the era of imperialism are imperialist wars that can be used to whittle away the ruling power of the capitalist class. At the opportune time such international wars were to be changed into civil wars to make possible the take-over of political power by the proletariat through the process of national revolution and class struggle. That was what the Russian Communists did during World War I and what the Chinese Communists did during World War II.

At the Twentieth Congress of the CPSU Khrushchev pointed out that the "era of imperialism" described by Lenin had ended, and that the old strategy was therefore no longer applicable. The principal attribute of the earlier era, he contended, was an imperialism that was "an all-embracing world system," while the chief attribute of our era is "the socialism that has become another world system." Khrushchev went on to say that the "simultaneous existence of two opposite world economic systems, the capitalist and the socialist, developing according to different laws and in opposite directions, has become an indisputable fact." He urged that Leninism be considered a principle of "creative development" and that a new general policy for international communism be mapped out.[10]

Later, Khrushchev elaborated his point thusly: In the confrontation of the two world systems—capitalism and socialism—both have their centers of political power. "Wars are chiefly prepared by imperialists against Socialist countries, and in the first place against the Soviet Union as the most powerful of the Socialist states."[11] The Soviet Union would not be able to stay out of a conflict, and it would exploit an international war in order to undermine national ruling classes and seize political power. Khrushchev later observed that the production of missiles and nuclear weapons in mid-century has changed the character of war in general.[12] The Communists should try to manage things so that "during mortal struggle between the socialist and capitalist systems, the Communists would be able to achieve victory with minimum loss."[13] This is not the way the Chinese Communists look at it. They believe the establishment of the socialist system facilitates the implementation of Lenin's strategy. They contend: "The present world situation has obviously shown great changes as compared with Lenin's lifetime. Nevertheless, all these changes do not prove that Leninism is out of date; on the contrary, they serve to show with increasing clarity the truths Lenin revealed to us. The premise that our period is the period of imperialism versus proletarian revolution and also the period of triumph for socialism and Communism is the reason that such a premise fully and correctly grasps the basic attributes of this great epoch of ours."[14] "The main current of the world situation today is the formation and growth of the system of socialism and the continuous upheaval of the national liberation movements. These two historically important tides have shaken the system of capitalism."[15]

What the Chinese Communists mean is that national liberation movements can serve as spearheads while the socialist system can be relied upon as a bolster. They claim there is no reason to fear international war because the proletariat is waiting for the opportunity to seize political power within the enemy camp. According to Peking: "The appearance of nuclear weapons has not changed and cannot change the revolutionary truth of Marxism-Leninism. Despite the availability of nuclear weapons, class struggle remains the motor of historical progress and war is still the extension of politics."[16] In other words, the Chinese Communists still stand pat on Lenin's line and devote themselves to world revolution.

The Split in the International Communist Line

Since the Chinese and Russian Communists take different views on the characteristics of the times, they have incorporated different strategies into the general line of the international communist movement. The contents of these divergent strategies require analysis.

The Russian Communists favor "peaceful coexistence." The reasons for this choice they have made public concern the nature and effect of nuclear war. Their expressed views are: "Should imperialism start a new world war, the results would be far more disastrous than those of any other war in the past, no matter how cruel it was. Only the insane and the lunatic would call for a new world war at present."[17] "To carry out revolutionary work by means of a world war is an unacceptable proposition. The reason is that the proposition ignores the realistic results of a world war fought with missiles and nuclear weapons."[18] "A sober appraisal of the inevitable consequences of nuclear war is the indispensable condition for a persistent pursuance of a policy of preventing war, and of mobilizing the masses for the solution of this task."[19]

The Soviets, however, have a more important unpublished reason for their determined stand for "peaceful coexistence." This reason is hidden behind the concept of the "peace race." As the Soviets themselves point out, they are still in an inferior position in the struggle between world socialism and world imperialism. But they contend that "all facts prove that the socialist countries may be able to overtake the capitalist countries economically within a short period of history."[20]

Conceivably, the Soviets are interested in the "peace race" for only "a short period in history," which would afford them the time needed to overcome their inferior ratio of strength before launching their "struggle against world imperialism." Khrushchev once observed that "not everyone is aware that socialism is better than capitalism. The people judge their living conditions in terms of their level of welfare . . . we tell the capitalists: 'There are unemployed among you. We have no unemployment.' They reply: 'Our unemployed man gets more than your employed worker.' It is a pity that this is true."[21]

Politically, "It often happens that a man goes to work, without knowing whether he will be able to return home again, whether he will be able to see his wife again, whether he will be able to see his children again."[22] That such a conflict persists between the Soviets and their people indicates a risk the Soviets would have to run during any external struggle in which the Kremlin may engage. The slogan of the "peace race" is in fact aimed at covering up this unpleasant situation.

On the questions of the "ratio of strength" and "internal contradictions," Lenin's views are different from those the Soviets hold now. Lenin's premises for a strategy of struggle in the "era of imperialism" were that "the capitalist class monopolizes the political power of various countries," that all contradictions are centered in the capitalist class, and that the proletariat has nothing and therefore no internal contradictions. Thus, any international war would be an internecine struggle within the capitalist class. Regardless of the ratios of strength of the belligerents, the war would inevitably weaken the internal control of the capitalists, and they could be overthrown by exploiting the various contradictions.

But the situation has undergone a vast change since the emergence of the "socialist world system." Both the capitalists and the socialists have political power; both sides have internal contradictions. In fact, there are more contradictions under communist rule. Should international war occur, it is highly probable that it will be fought between "socialist countries" and "capitalist countries." An estimate of comparative military forces would therefore be most important. The side possessing superior military power will defeat the side possessing inferior military power. In the "socialist countries" that have more internal contradictions than "capitalist countries," war will weaken their internal control, and it will be the anti-Communists, not the Communists, who will transform the international war into internal wars. This is why the Soviets have raised the shield of "peaceful coexistence" to forestall their enemy's assault from strength, while using the pretext of the "peace race" to gain time for changing the ratio of strength in their favor and alleviating internal contradictions.

Another problem in the strategy of "peaceful coexistence" is the question of "peaceful transition." The Chinese Communists have accused the Soviets of "stressing the possibility of peaceful transition as a growing reality" while "opposing the war of national liberation and the people's revolutionary war."[23] This is typical of the traditional smearing tactic of the Chinese Communists and contrary to fact.

In Soviet eyes, "peaceful coexistence" is a form of struggle short of total war. The Soviets have clearly declared: "Peaceful co-existence does not imply a compromise between socialist ideology and capitalist ideology . . . or restrict the world movement of Communism or the national liberation movement."[24] The struggle of "peaceful coexistence" requires that the Soviets (1) develop and consolidate without interruption the defensive strength and the economy of the socialist countries; (2) maximize efforts to develop revolutionary forces throughout the world; (3) mobilize the masses to struggle for peace, the prevention of nuclear disaster, and the isolation of the capitalist class; (4) force imperialism to carry out disarmament measures so as to improve the climate for national liberation movements; and (5) extend greater economic and political assistance to countries already freed from colonial oppression so that they will develop along noncapitalist lines. It can be seen, therefore, that in implementing the "peaceful coexistence" strategy, drastic struggle must be carried out against imperialism, both in the economic field and in the political and ideological arena.[25] The pattern of transition to socialism can be peaceful or nonpeaceful depending on the conditions of struggle in the country concerned.

The Chinese and Russian Communists hold vastly different views on the "ratio of strength," on "internal contradictions," and on nuclear war. It is Peking's belief that "the ratio of strength in the whole world shows that it is socialism and revolutionary peoples, not imperialism and its lackeys, that enjoy supremacy."[26] In this comparison, the so-called revolutionary peoples in the free world were added to the "socialist countries" in order to achieve supremacy. The Chinese emphasized that "the wonderful revolutionary situation should be fully utilized for positive efforts to develop the revolutionary struggle and for preparing to win the victory of the revolution in accordance with the different concrete conditions in various countries."[27] This is tantamount to calling for a showdown with "imperialism" in order to conquer the whole world. The reasoning behind the Chinese concept of struggle is as follows:

> After the end of World War II, Mao Tse-tung, noting the new changes that had taken place in class relations and in the relative strength of nations, issued the call for an international anti-U.S. United Front. This united front, with the international proletariat as its core and based on unification of the international proletariat and the oppressed peoples of the world, was designed to exploit all contradictions that could be exploited to isolate and attack as extensively as possible the arch enemy of the people of the whole world, American imperialism. In this way, all positive factors conducive to world revolution could thus be mobilized for achieving the victory of people's revolutions in various countries. This is a most important concept of strategy for world revolution set forth by Mao Tse-tung under new historical conditions.[28]

It is the firm belief of the Chinese Communists that a force readily usable by this anti-U.S. united front will be provided by "the revolutionary struggle of the oppressed nations and peoples in Asia, Africa, and Latin America. . . . These areas constitute the weakest link of the chain of imperialism and represent the main source of the storm of world revolution. . . . To render assistance and support to these areas in their struggle will have a decisive effect on the whole enterprise of the international proletariat."[29]

The Soviets said: "The Chinese Communist leaders have ranged the people's interests of the three big continents—Asia, Africa and Latin America—in direct opposition to the interests of the peoples of Soviet Russia and socialist countries of Europe and of the workers' class of Western Europe and North America."[30] They point out that in the Chinese Communist saying "the East wind defeats the West wind," the word "west" refers to white people and the word "east" to colored people. According to a Soviet newspaper: "The slogan of the Chinese Communist politicians is 'Down with the white people.' The slogan of American racists is 'Down with colored people.' Both constitute racism, with minor variations."[31] The comparison is, of course, not just; it is only another example of traditional communist smearing.

The Chinese Communists do not worry about the problem of "internal contradictions." They divide contradictions into two groups. The first group includes "contradictions between our enemy and ourselves, based on the conflict of interests between opposing classes." Such contradictions cannot and should not be compromised and must be placed under ruthless control. The second group is "internal contradictions of the people, which are not due to the fundamental conflict between class interests." Such contradictions can be "solved to achieve new consolidation under new conditions." "Internal contradictions of the people," however, can be transformed into "a part of the contradictions between our enemy and ourselves"; in that case, struggle should be continued. "Between 1918 and 1920, Soviet Russia was subjected to the attack of 14 capitalist countries . . . In the decisive period of World War II, Soviet Russia alone faced the offensive of several millions of Hitler's troops and defeated them." "Such tests did not overwhelm Soviet Russia," indicating that "under proletarian dictatorship," "internal contradictions" are not operative.[32] On the other hand, the "internal contradictions" in the democracies can be utilized.

With regard to nuclear war, the Chinese Communists have adopted the principle of "walking with two legs." The first leg is Soviet supremacy in military technology, which deprives U.S. imperialism of its monopoly in the manufacture of atomic and nuclear weapons. The second leg is the "masses of the people [who] are what decide the future of mankind. They can always find a new way to overcome the superior weaponry of the reactionaries and to win their own victory." Should American or other imperialists start an atomic war, the Chinese believe, Soviet Russia will deal with them with the same weapons, making them "beasts cornered by the people of the world and facing destruction. . . . The triumphant people, stepping over the debris of imperialism, will quickly create a civilization a thousand times better than the capitalist system and a truly beautiful future for themselves."[33] Since the deterioration of their relations with Soviet Russia, the Chinese Communists have been testing nuclear devices as well as preparing for the Peoples' War, obviously persisting in their insane policy of "walking with two legs."

CONFLICTS IN ECONOMIC THOUGHT

The Soviet strategy of "peaceful coexistence" was initially conceived in terms of rigid viewpoints and ideology. The Soviets said: "Although the relationship between countries of different social systems should be based on peaceful co-existence, we and the bloc under the domination of capitalist countries hold different views and we will never give up our viewpoints. . . . To apply the principle of possible peaceful co-existence between countries with different political and social systems to ideological affairs is an extremely harmful misinterpretation."[34] Certain technical measures later carried out by the Soviets nevertheless gave rise to problems of viewpoint and ideology.

The first question concerned economic measures. The Soviets seemed to have suddenly become enlightened when they undertook to alleviate their contradictions with the people, pointing out: "In this age of ours, the peoples of various countries judge Communism not by its formal slogans and ideology but rather by what welfare and benefits it has brought society and the people."[35] "The people judge socialism by what benefits it has given them, not by what it says and what it promises. Their judgment is based upon what living improvements have been made following the triumph of socialism. In other words, they judge by how much bread, meat, oil and other things they can get, how much clothing and of what material, how much time is at their own disposal, how they rest and how they can improve the satisfaction of spiritual needs. If socialism fails to provide these, and cannot give the people better things than capitalism does, then whoever speaks for socialism says nothing."[36] "If our life is no better than in pre-revolutionary days, people will wonder what Communism has been doing and they will ask why they have no pants under the socialist system while they had not only pants but even coats when under the capitalist system."[37]

The Soviets therefore took stock of their agriculture and industry and adopted a number of measures "to dispel old concepts and eliminate everything that was out of date and obstructed progress."[38] They adopted economic principles previously ignored or even opposed by communism and demanded that "socialist management and planning should have a strict scientific basis. The important thing is to learn the proper use of economic levers and economic computations, prices, credits, and profits and by using these factors to create effective incentives to increase production and speed technical improvement."[39] This shook the three pillars of socialist construction previously extolled by communism: equal distribution, collective benefit, and the planned economy.

Khrushchev said: "All manifestations of equalitarianism and implementations of the principle of reduced material benefit have no basis in economics and are harmful to the economy."[40] "Equalitarianism gives rise to inequitable distribution. When good and poor workers get equal rewards, it is the idle workers that stand to benefit from the arrangement. It is therefore impossible to increase labor productivity and step up production through material incentives."[41] The Soviets further pointed out that if "Communism is considered as a kind of asceticism, there will be no completely rich elements and all the people will have equal shares of misfortune and disaster."[42]

In reviewing past Soviet mistakes, Khrushchev said: "As is well known, in the past we had cases of deviation from the principle of material incentive, particularly in agriculture, which caused serious damage to agriculture production and to the Kolkhoz system. Contempt for the material requirements of the working people and the concentration of emphasis on enthusiasm and awareness, on social and moral forms of incentive and reward, hampered development of production and the raising of the living standards of the working people."[43]

In criticizing the mistakes of the Chinese Communists, the Soviets said: "To adopt widely the method of voluntarism is to overlook that of administrative management of economic principle."[44] Khrushchev declared at the Twenty-second Congress of the CPSU: "In the combination of the material with the moral stimulus, the Party sees the true road to the life of plenty and distribution according to needs which it will reach without fail . . . The working man's personal ownership of a large number of things, as a form of personal consumption, is not at variance with the principles of Communist construction as long as it keeps within reasonable bounds and does not become an end in itself . . . "[45]

Finally, the Soviets had this to say about economic planning: "Whether the production mission of an enterprise has been completed or not is not to be determined by weighing the total output of the enterprise. It should be determined by a study of the quality, distribution, and sales of the products. The quantity of a product to be manufactured should be decided by the purchase orders of stores."[46] And Kosygin said: "Experience shows that the general index can no longer serve as a guidepost for determining the total production of an enterprise. It is no longer what the national economy really needs and in some cases, it exercises a restraining effect upon the improvement of quality and the diversification of products. . . . Production plans for specific enterprises should be based upon the sales of products, not on a general production index. . . . With relationships between various enterprises properly organized and the contract system well developed, it is probable that the categories of products authorized for production in the national plan will be further reduced in number . . . by closely linking production with consumption, profits and the rate of profit constitute the best index of improvement in the productive efficiency of an enterprise."[47]

From the foregoing, we can see that the Soviets, in meeting urgent demands for increased production and alleviating internal contradictions, have found it necessary to face facts and to stress basic economic principles. In doing so, they have brushed aside the basic doctrine of communism: the elimination of production for sale and profit as a form of human exploitation. That doctrine is now called "obsolete," "ancient," and "an obstacle to progress." They still face major steps, however, if they are to break the chains of the past.

The Chinese Communists have taken upon themselves the mission of firmly defending the last stronghold of the economic theory of communism. Peking counterattacked thus: "[Khrushchev] considers Communism not as a system for total elimination of classes and class differences but rather as a 'dinner plate heaped with products of physical and spiritual labor and within reach of everyone.' To him, the struggle of the working class of Communist ideals is not a struggle for complete liberation of one's self and mankind as a whole. Instead, it becomes a struggle for 'a good dish of stewed beef with potatoes.' . . . When material incentive is promoted, human relationships become money relationships and individualism and the pursuit of selfish goals are encouraged. . . . The spread between the incomes of a small elite and those of workers, peasants, and ordinary intellectuals is increased rather than reduced . . . What he has learned from the management pattern of American capitalism and the life of the capitalist class has now been elevated to the status of national policy. . . . He particularly wants to learn the profit principle of American capitalist enterprise. . . . Socialist enterprise, now owned by all the people, is to be transformed by degrees into capitalist enterprise, and collective farms are gradually to be turned over to rich farmers. . . . Under the pretext of comprehensive Communist construction, the way has been paved for the revival of capitalism."[48]

The above quotations indicate clearly that the Chinese Communists intend to carry Marxist doctrine all the way to their graves.

THE CONFLICT OF POLITICAL PRINCIPLES

The Soviets are well aware that another contradiction with their people is political. The method of terror adopted under communist dictatorship has deepened the chasm between the ruler and the ruled and produced two sharply opposed factions in the country. The Russian Communists consider it essential to alleviate this contradiction, as well as the economic contradiction just discussed, in order to settle their internal crisis. Brushing aside the Marxist theory of the state and Lenin's theory of political parties, they have declared formally that Soviet Russia is a "state of all the people," and the Communist party of the Soviet Union is a "party of all the people."[49] They have explained: "Transformation of a country from proletarian dictatorship into a country of all the people does not weaken the power of the state. Instead, it will improve the effectiveness of this instrument for Communist struggle. . . . By becoming a party of all the people, the CPSU has strengthened its ties with the people and enhanced its strength."[50] In view of the Soviet system and the organization of the Russian Communist party, however, this move was tantamount to making out a check that cannot be honored. The so-called state and party of all the people will not cease to slave-drive the people toward the unattainable golden apple.

The Chinese Communists have taken strong exception to the Soviet concession to the people in the class struggle. They have said: "The state is the instrument of class struggle, the organization used by one class for the suppression of another. Every state in the world is run under a class dictatorship. As long as the state exists, it cannot be beyond class, so it cannot represent all people."[51] This is an idea based on the Marxist theory of the withering away of the state. The Chinese Communists also said: "All fundamental problems of revolution are problems of state power. . . . The problem of the revolution of the proletariat is the problem of proletarian dictatorship. Proletarian dictatorship established by smashing the state machine of the capitalist class through revolutionary means is the continuation of class struggle in another form under new conditions. It is a continuous evolutionary struggle to liquidate the resistance of the exploiting class, to defy foreign aggression, and to combat obsolete social influences and traditions. . . . There can be no socialism without proletarian dictatorship."[52] "The Communist Party should always support proletarian dictatorship. The leadership of the proletariat is realized through the leadership of the Communist Party."[53] These statements reflect the Leninist idea concerning proletarian dictatorship and the vanguard role of the proletariat.

How can "internal contradictions" be settled then? Chinese Communist documents use bloody terms, advocating employment of force and repression. The Chinese Communists have declared: "The state is a kind of violent force. The principal part of a state machine consists of troops and police. Throughout history, all ruling classes have resorted to violent force to keep themselves in power."[54] "Dictatorship should be imposed on the reactionary class and those opposed to socialist reform and construction. . . . The armed forces and security organizations of a socialist country should always be placed under the leadership of the proletariat. . . . Rebellion must be suppressed, errors must be corrected."[55] In a word, the Chinese Communists firmly believe that all "internal contradictions," whether political or economic, should be solved by means of violent repression. On the basis of this principle, they have carried out bloodbaths to repress various anti-starvation, fight-for-freedom movements conducted by youths and intellectuals on the Chinese mainland over the years. When, therefore, will they stop using repressive measures? The answer is: not until they have conquered the whole world. The reason is: the Chinese Communists have given foremost emphasis to the theory that "under the circumstances in which imperialism exists, the international class struggle is inevitably reflected inside socialist countries."[56]

Soviet criticism of the Chinese position ran in this vein: "The brand of socialism embraced by the Chinese Communists is most unique, for it is not in favor of democracy, the rule of law, or respect for human dignity. . . . In the words of Mao Tse-tung, they treat the masses as they do 'a piece of white paper' and a leader can write on the paper anything he wants."[57] "What the Chinese Communists want their party organizations to do is to take charge of ascertaining and fixing the whole gamut of activities of local authorities, courts and procurators' offices. . . . The so-called proletarian dictatorship is becoming the dictatorship of a group of leaders."[58]

THE SCHISM IN PHILOSOPHICAL CONCEPTS

Communism is known as a theory derived from a philosophical concept. The disputes between Peking and Moscow concerning philosophical concepts have finally resulted in a schism. Although philosophical concepts have not yet become the main subject of the quarrel, it can be seen from the following that highly divergent philosophies are already developing.

According to the Chinese Communists: "The program of work passed at the 22d Congress of the CPSU indicates that the Soviets have adopted humanitarianism in place of the Marxist-Leninist theory of class struggle, and that they have substituted the capitalist slogan of 'liberty—equality—fraternity' for Communist ideals."[59] "Khrushchev speaks for capitalist ideology; promotes capitalist liberty, equality, and fraternity and humanism; and impregnates the minds of the Soviet people with idealism and metaphysics as well as the reactionary capitalist ideas of individualism, humanitarianism, and pacifism."[60]

The Soviets said: "We are realists, with healthy rationality."[61] "In building a new society, it is not considered proper to rely directly on enthusiasm alone. Dependence upon individual interest and individual benefit is imperative."[62] "In their propaganda, the Chinese Communists have used every vituperative to denounce humanitarianism and the struggle for human welfare. . . . To carry their slogan to its logical conclusion, what the Chinese Communist leaders need is 'a personality without personality.' . . . They are not interested in human expression in the relationship between the individual and society, nor do they care to explore the spiritual world of the individual. Instead, they call for manifestations of the masses that are without personality."[63] "The so-called 'Great Leap Forward' policy of the Chinese Communists was based on fundamental denial of the individual. An individual is considered as merely a screw in the huge state machine."[64]

One question calls for brief discussion here. When the Chinese Communists subjected Yang Hsien-chen, head of the senior party school, to inquisition, they branded his principle of "combination of two into one" as revisionism and demanded its elimination, declaring that the theory of "division of one into two" should be adhered to. As a matter of fact, the dialectical formula of positive-negative combination is the continuation of "division of one into two" and "combination of two into one." Chinese Communist opposition to "combination of two into one" resulted from a special psychological phenomenon, comparable to Stalin's refusal to discuss the "negation of negation." This phenomenon showed Peking's determination to remain at odds with the Soviets.

In sum, Marxist predictions of more than a century ago are historically untrue, as can be judged by what has happened since. This is the main reason for the dilemma in the communist movement. Strict adherence to communist doctrine results in loss of support of the people. It may be called "dogmatism" or "leftist opportunism"; it is in fact communist idealism. It is impossible to compromise with the masses without relinquishing communist principles. This is how "revisionism" or "rightist opportunism" originated; it is literally communist realism. Loss of mass support means loss of raison d'être. Relaxation of doctrinal control is tantamount to giving up the reason for domination. Both are ways to eventual collapse. The Communists, therefore, have resorted to "struggle on two fronts," attempting to vacillate between theory and fact, like a circus performer walking on a tightrope. The Chinese Communists have adopted the former, the Soviets the latter; hence they are moving in opposite directions. Recently, Brezhnev declared: "The Russian Communist Party and people wish sincerely to be friends with the People's Republic of China and the Chinese Communists. . . . We are ready to discuss the current schism with the Chinese Communist leaders at any time and to find ways to overcome the differences in accordance with Marxism-Leninism."[65] All signs, however, have shown that this was only a gesture, as the Chinese Communists have made amply clear: "It is impossible to stop our theoretical war. It is impossible even for a day, a month, or a year. It will be impossible even after 100 years, 1,000 years, or 10,000 years! If our criticism cannot be completed in 9,000 years, then we will criticize them for 10,000 years."[66] We must wait to see what the next step of their theoretical war will be.

THE EFFECT OF THE SCHISM ON EASTERN EUROPE

The communist empire established in Europe and Asia after the end of World War II, the so-called World System of Socialism, is disintegrating rapidly. This development in the wake of the Moscow-Peking schism is an incontrovertible fact.

The components of the communist empire in Asia are Soviet Russia, Communist China, North Korea, and North Vietnam. Recently, both the Korean and the Vietnamese Communists chose not to join Peking in declining invitations to the Twenty-third Congress of the CPSU. It can be seen, therefore, that their stubborn dogmatism has no theoretical basis and that they behave as they do mainly because of the leviathan, Communist China, behind their dogmatism. As long as the leviathan remains alive, the attitude of the Korean and Vietnamese Communists will not undergo any significant changes. It is the countries of Eastern Europe, which constitute the majority of individual components of the communist empire, that pose the most important problems and deserve our serious attention.

The future behavior of East European countries will to a large extent be determined by such nontheoretical factors as historical background, geographical location, external pressures, and internal crises. Some of the countries have been traditional enemies of Russia, some have seen parts of their territories annexed by the Russians, some have seen their people slaughtered by the Soviets. In some countries the communist parties have been severely purged by Moscow; in others Russian military occupation has continued; in still others the Soviet military is responsible for safeguarding their sovereignty. Analysis of these nontheoretical factors is not within the scope of our discussion, which is limited to the effects of the ideological conflicts between Peking and Moscow.

With the exception of the leaders of the Albanian Labor party, the dictatorial rulers of Eastern Europe including leaders of the Communist party of Bulgaria, the Communist party of Czechoslovakia, the Socialist Unity party of East Germany, the Hungarian Socialist Workers' party, the Polish Workers' party, the Rumanian Communist party, and the Communist League of Yugoslavia all attended the Twenty-third Congress of the CPSU, showing—in appearance at least —their theoretical tendency toward revisionism. As a result of the sectarian activities carried out by both Peking and Moscow in their ideological disputes, however, none of these Communist parties is undivided. According to the Soviets: "The Chinese Communists have recruited followers from among brother teams and used them for setting up sections and blocs."[67] "The Chinese Communist leaders have resorted to more and more ignominious methods to place parts of memberships of other countries under their wing, . . . generously giving these blocs such titles as 'real revolutionaries' and 'real Marxist-Leninists.' "[68]

Among the seven East European countries, Yugoslavia is the forerunner of revisionism. Its new program of 1958 provided more latitude for ideological relaxation than the 1961 new program of the Soviets. Poland and Hungary gave up collectivization of agriculture after the anticommunist campaign and revolution of 1956.* Czechoslovakia and East Germany, the prewar economic foundations of which were far more advanced than those of other East European countries, sank into economic straits under communist rule after the war and therefore urgently sought to carry out a number of new measures. Rumania and Bulgaria have initiated economic reforms. At the same time these countries, carrying the coexistence strategy into practice, have developed trade relations with Western countries and welcomed foreign investment. This does not mean, however, that they have given up their principles, since under no circumstances will their leaders voluntarily abandon their political power. Their purpose is to alleviate their own internal and external crises and reserve their strength for future struggle. So far as the deterioration of relations between Peking and Moscow is concerned, the main

---

* Hungarian agriculture was recollectivized by 1961. See "Hungary" in the chapter on "Recent Developments in East-Central Europe"–Eds.

concern of these countries has been reflected in their worry over "socialist enterprise."

These countries have followed Soviet Russia on the road of revisionism, while attempting simultaneously to shake off the Soviet control inherited from Stalin's days. With the exception of Yugoslavia —which freed itself from Soviet control as early as 1948 to become a "nonallied country"—Rumania has gone the furthest in breaking away from the Kremlin. In 1961 Rumania began to oppose the formula of division of labor as laid down at the COMECON Conference. In 1964 it issued an announcement in opposition to the idea of "father party" and "son party." In 1965 it refused to take part in a meeting of communist parties called by Moscow. Next in line come Hungary and Poland. The communist leaders of these two countries were once purged by Stalin and spent time in jail; they served as a bridge between the government and the people during the anti-communist revolution and campaign. It is easy to figure out how they feel about Moscow. Then there are Czechoslovakia, which is industrially more highly developed than most East European countries, and Bulgaria, which is economically backward; both countries have made consistent efforts to extricate themselves from Soviet control. East Germany comes last. Its party leader, Walter Ulbricht, is a Stalinist dogmatist. Faced with the external threat of German unification and the internal anticommunist pressure, however, he has found it necessary to seek the military protection of Soviet revisionists. The prospect of freedom from Soviet control confronts Soviet Zone German Communists with a problem of contradiction.

Judging from the foregoing, it can be concluded that the seven countries of Eastern Europe will follow the line of polycentrism proposed by Palmiro Togliatti. Moscow will probably seize whatever advantage it can from this situation to establish necessary links when the Warsaw Pact is revised. This development is only a reaction to the overcentralized control during the days of the Third International. It would be an exaggeration to call it the emergence of a democratic force. The Communists in these countries still stand for internationalism. They are striving not for national independence but for equality for their parties within an internationalized system.

The mistake the free world is most likely to make is to concentrate on tendencies within the various communist parties of Eastern Europe while neglecting to study the hopes and aspirations of the peoples of these countries. Westerners seem to have the impression that the communist parties in these countries are really controlled by and representative of the peoples under their rule. If this were true, the Communists would not have built the ignominious wall in East Berlin.

If the countries of the free world believe that by intensifying their economic, cultural, and political relations with the communist regimes of Eastern Europe, they can exercise great influence in that part of the world, they are greatly mistaken. For the peoples under communist rule may very well regard such moves as attempts to support their murderers. It should be noted that peoples who have lived under communist domination and experienced communist tyranny are far more firmly opposed to communism than people in the free world. They do not need to be influenced. As for the Communists in power, they cannot be influenced to step down from their thrones of their own accord. The question may be asked: Since the Communists are unable to control their peoples, why has there been no revolution? But do we not remember the Hungarian anticommunist revolution of 1956? When the free world watched with impassioned calm while Soviet troops marched into Hungary to slaughter the freedom fighters and restore the fallen communist regime, the last words from the Budapest radio station were: "The lesson of blood has taught us that we cannot expect any help from others. It is our own strength that determines everything." These words are the epitome of endless bitterness and great wrath! History records many foolish decisions made by wise men at critical points in their careers and many tragedies that resulted from the reactions of wronged men. This is indeed a frightening thought.

NOTES TO CHAPTER FOUR

1. "An Open Letter to All CPSU Organizations and Members in the Soviet Union," issued by the Central Committee of the CPSU on July 14, 1963.

2. "The Origin and Development of Our Schism with Soviet Leadership," jointly published in Peking *People's Daily* and *Red Flag*, September 6, 1963.

3. "On Moscow March Conference," Peking *People's Daily*, March 23, 1965.

4. "From Historical Dogmatism to Experimental Dogmatism," Soviet *Red Star*, July 20, 1963.

5. "On Stalin," Peking *People's Daily*, September 13, 1963.

6. *See* note 3.

7. "A Refutation of the So-called United Action of the New Soviet Leadership," Peking *People's Daily* and *Red Flag*, November 11, 1965.

8. Liu Shao-chi's speech welcoming Albanian delegation, April 28, 1966.

9. Chou En-lai's speech welcoming Albanian delegation, April 30, 1966.

10. Khrushchev's general report at the 20th Congress of CPSU on February 14, 1956. (Engl. trans. from 84th Congress, 2d Session, House Report No. 834 [Washington: 1956], pp. XIII-XIV.)

11. Khrushchev's report on results of the conference of representatives of labor and communist parties from various countries on January 6, 1961. (Engl. trans. from 87th Congress, 1st Session, *Analysis of the Khrushchev Speech of January 6, 1961*, Senate Document No. 46, p. 63.)

12. *See* note 1.

13. Khrushchev's speech at the Russo-Hungarian friendship meeting, July 19, 1963.

14. "Long Live Leninism," Peking *Red Flag*, April 15, 1960.

15. "Promotion of the Revolutionary Spirit of Moscow Declaration and Moscow Statement," Peking *People's Daily*, November 15, 1962.

16. Liu Shao-chi's address to Korean Communists at a welcoming party at Pyongyang, September 14, 1963.

17. Khrushchev's address at the third conference of the Labor party of Rumania, June, 1960.

18. "An Outline of Split between Chinese Communist Leadership and the General Line of International Communism," Soviet *Communist*, No. 14, 1963.

19. *See* note 11.

20. "On the Soviet Struggle for Consolidation of International Communism," report to the plenary session of the Central Committee of the CPSU in 1964.

21. *See* note 13.

22. *See* note 13.

23. "The Origin of the Schism—An Answer to Maurice Thorez and Other Comrades," Peking *People's Daily*, February 27, 1963.

24. A letter written by the Soviets to the Central Committee of the Chinese Communist party, March 14, 1963.

25. "Defense of the General Line of World Communism and Opposition to Leftist Opportunism, Nationalism, and Adventurism." Soviet *Communist*, No. 14, 1963.

26. A letter written by the Central Committee of the Chinese Communist party to the Soviets, March 14, 1963.

27. "Proletarian Revolution and Khrushchev's Revisionism," Peking *People's Daily*, March 30, 1964.

28. *See* note 7.

29. "Again on the Split between Comrade Togliatti and Us," Nos. 3 and 4, Peking *Red Flag*, 1963.

30. *See* note 18.

31. "Racism in Disguise," Ukrainian *Pravda*, September 28, 1963.

32. "Again on Historical Experience of Proletarian Dictatorship," Peking *People's Daily*, December 29, 1956.

33. *See* note 14.

34. *See* note 10.

35. "Striving for Uniformity of Marxism-Leninism and Unity of Socialist Countries in Communist Movement," Moscow *Pravda*, February 10, 1963.

36. *See* note 13.

37. Khrushchev's address at Russo-German friendship meeting, June 12, 1964.

38. *See* note 10.

39. "The Great Banner of Communist Construction," Moscow *Pravda*, November 6, 1964.

40. *See* note 11.

41. Khrushchev's report at the 21st conference of extraordinary delegates of CPSU, January, 1959.

42. "The Principal Influence," Soviet *Labor*, September 13, 1963.

43. *See* note 11.

44. *See* note 42.

45. General report made by Khrushchev at the 22d Congress of CPSU in October, 1961.

46. "Our Reason Is Complete and Satisfactory Welfare in Life," Soviet *Communist*, No. 11, 1964.

47. "Improvement of Industrial Management, Streamlining of Planning, and Strengthening of Economic Incentive for Industrial Production," report by Kosygin at the plenary session of the Central Committee of the CPSU, September, 1965.

48. "Khrushchev's Pseudo-Communism and Its Historical Lessons for the World," Peking *People's Daily*, July 14, 1964.

49. New Soviet platform passed at the 22d Congress of CPSU, October, 1961.

50. *See* note 25.

51. *See* note 48.

52. *See* note 14.

53. *See* note 48.

54. *See* note 27.

55. *See* note 48.

56. *See* note 48.

57. "Unity of Thought Is the Basis for Consolidation in Communist Movement," *Pravda*, May 10, 1964.

58. "On Proletarian Dictatorship," Soviet *Izvestia*, May 17, 1964.

59. *See* note 2.

60. *See* note 48.

61. *See* note 37.

62. *See* note 20.

63. "Opposition to Dogmatism and Vulgarism in Art and Literature," Soviet *Communist*, 1964.

64. *See* note 42.

65. Brezhnev's summary report at the 23d Congress of CPSU, April, 1966.

66. *See* note 3.

67. "Striving for Solidarity in Communist Movement," Soviet *Party Life*, No. 7, 1964.

68. "Opposition to Schismatists and Striving for Solidarity in Communist Movement," *Party Life*, No. 11, 1964.

CHAPTER V

European Involvement in Asia

RICHARD L. WALKER

THE WINDS OF CHANGE

AT A PRESS CONFERENCE on July 12, 1966, Secretary
of State Dean Rusk reported on his eighth trip to the western Pacific
since he assumed office. "From Australia in the south to Japan and
Korea in the north," he observed, "new winds are blowing." The
Secretary of State was not referring to the "East Wind" of communist
victory that Chinese Communist leader Mao Tse-tung hailed in 1957
as prevailing in the world. What he had in mind were the rapidly
changing conditions in Asia and in Eastern Asia's relations with the
rest of the world. This fact of rapid change is of fundamental importance in assessing the various forces that shape international relations
around the world and their direction of movement, but a great many
Western leaders have failed to grasp it. Perhaps they are still too
much committed to the slogans and analyses of the 1950's, or possibly
they are clinging to a mythology of an unchanging East. Again, preoccupation with the central threat of Communist China may have
diverted attention from the important developments that have taken
place outside the areas of communist control. In any event, Europe
in the mid-1960's is becoming involved with a Far East that is entirely
different from that from which it withdrew during the first decade
after World War II.

It is instructive to examine the contrasts between 1956, when destalinization and revolts in Eastern Europe brought to light the first
fissures in the communist world, and 1966, when the monolithic
nature of world communism—which had been assumed by West and

85

East alike—was truly shattered. During the intervening decade many of the assumptions upon which the various powers had based their foreign policies were either called into question or proven false.

In 1956, the year after the first Afro-Asian Conference at Bandung, there was much to suggest the possibility that a presumed Afro-Asian unity constituted a major new force in the world. The leaders in the West were impressed by the rapidity of the retreat from colonialism following World War II and were sensitive to the statements of the leaders of newly independent states who found common cause in the anticolonial movement in which they had come to power. The defeat of the French in Vietnam seemed to symbolize a new power for an independent Asia. Prime Minister Nehru of India spoke glowingly and with a conviction shared by other national leaders of a multilateral neutralist third force in the world. In the West scholars and statesmen alike talked of this new force as something permanent on the world scene.

Only a decade later the situation had changed drastically, and there was need for a reappraisal of former views. The "Bandung spirit" had proved ephemeral. Antagonisms and conflicts among those who had spoken of unity and of the new spirit at Bandung in 1955 prevented the convening of a second Afro-Asian conference ten years later. Many leaders, including Nehru, had passed from the scene, and the unity they had found in deploring their former colonial status had been replaced by a preponderant concern for the problems of development and security—problems that sometimes led to disagreement rather than cooperation.

The Isolation of Imperialist China

In 1956 India and Indonesia took the lead in urging accommodation and adjustment to the new power in mainland China, accepting at face value Peking's pledges to abide by the "five principles of peaceful coexistence." During the ensuing decade, the Chinese Communist regime isolated itself from many of the Afro-Asian countries. Its border clashes with India, its complicity in the abortive coup in Indonesia, its strident assertion that "war is a great school," and its insistence that Afro-Asian unity could only be maintained on Chinese terms raised serious doubts among Peking's former supporters about Communist China's ability to contribute to constructive development and peaceful cooperation. Whereas in 1956 Peking could win accolades by an intense anti-imperialist line, ten years later the new nations of Asia were no longer as willing to cut all ties with the West. Instead of riding the forces of anti-imperialism, the Chinese Communists posed a new imperialist threat of their own. Moreover, they now seemed to have lost touch with the great changes which were taking place elsewhere in Asia.

Although Khrushchev's destruction of the Stalin myth in early 1956 had caused genuine consternation in the communist parties of Asia, a common cause still seemed to exist, as well as a general acceptance of the truth as expounded from the headquarters of world communism in the Kremlin. Even Mao Tse-tung had stated in Moscow during the celebration of the fortieth anniversary of the Bolshevik Revolution in 1957: "In the present-day world, to reject the Soviet Union is tantamount to rejecting peace." By 1966, however, it was difficult to find much substance behind the phrase "the world communist movement," at least as far as Asia was concerned. The Sino-Soviet dispute had divided and weakened the communist parties, and there was no longer a single line or strategy; unified leadership and organization had vanished. The intensity of Sino-Soviet polemics and the cynicism of great-power contention thereby revealed had undercut much of the ideological fervor within the membership of the communist parties in Asia.

Interestingly enough, the decade saw a movement toward the reestablishment of interrelations and ties between Europe—both East and West—and Asia. It would have been difficult in the mid-1950's, when the French debacle at Dienbienphu symbolized at least the apparent end of European involvement in Asia, to have visualized the extent to which both cultural and economic ties would be revived. Ironically, the awareness that events in East and West would continue to affect each other in a world grown small came with Communist China's projection of its influence into the Eastern European scene in late 1956. The subsequent Sino-Soviet dispute accelerated the growth of polycentrism in Eastern Europe. Whereas the communist leaders of that region were initially inclined to look to Peking for support of their efforts to achieve autonomy, a decade later they were exploring the possibility that Western Europe might play a more constructive role in the loosening up process. As things finally stood, the leadership in the Soviet Union seemed more tractable and more aware of the changes taking place than their Stalinist

Chinese Communist comrades, who had first set the process in motion.

But if the loosening up of what could once be accurately described as the "communist bloc" brought an awareness that events in Asia could have influence in Europe and vice versa, it was the changes outside the areas of communist control that proved their overriding importance in restoring closer relations between Asia and the West. While these developments, in both West and East, have not been as newsworthy as the Sino-Soviet rivalry and the trends toward polycentrism, they may well prove to be of longer range and more lasting significance. They reflect not only the vitality and resurgence of the countries of Western Europe, but the fact that some of the countries in Asia have begun to find their own answers to the problems of development in and adjustment to a space-age world. These Asian countries have begun to understand that the answers involve cooperation with and reestablishment of ties with the West—in many cases with former colonial rulers.

In the mid-1950's the world seemed tuned to a discussion of various ideological approaches to the problems of modernization. There was much talk of Chinese-Indian rivalry in development, and some observers even felt that the fate of Asia would depend upon whether China achieved more by totalitarian processes or India by democratic. A decade later—after the trauma of mainland China's "great leap forward" from 1958 to 1960 and the following social and economic disruption from 1960 to 1962, and after experiences with Chinese Communist fanaticism—there were few Asian leaders who would accept the thesis that the Chinese experience had much relevance for them.

The Chinese Communists have clung tenaciously to the Leninist theory of imperialism in their approach to and interpretation of the outside world, and in this they seem as far divorced from the realities of modern life as in any other facet of their behavior. The vitality and economic progress of Western Europe and Japan have proved the unreality of Lenin's theories about imperialism. The former imperial powers, freed of the colonies that proved to be more of a drain on energy, manpower, and talent than of an asset, have never been more prosperous; their people have never before had so much at their disposal in terms of social and economic conveniences.

At the same time that the myth that European power and prosperity rested upon empire was being destroyed, the leaders in Asia were themselves realizing that solutions to their problems did not necessarily lie in ideological commitment, but rather in solid and practical measures frequently unrelated to ideology. With the passing of many of those who had found common cause in their anti-colonialism at Bandung in 1955, Asian statesmen have begun to realize that they must look to the patterns of development and relations that promise long-range stability and a constructive approach to modernization. It is within this framework that we have been witnessing a renewed and intense building of interrelations between Asia and the West. It is within this framework that several Asian states have been building new patterns of relations among themselves.

Persistent Factors

But if there have been winds of change in East Asia in the past decade, many of the problems and forces of the mid-1950's have carried through into the present and served as limiting factors. Foremost among these has been the revolutionary élan and drive for regional hegemony of the Chinese Communist regime. In its continuing commitment to violence and in its buildup of military power it has for more than a decade and a half constituted a towering threat, necessitating vast expenditures of manpower and resources for security in surrounding areas. As the early illusions about the Peking regime faded over the years, concern as to how best to bring mainland China into a pattern of responsible conduct and commitment to peace has intensified.

Although Communist China and its proxies in East Asia have proved persistent in their attempts to apply Mao Tse-tung's formulas for seizure of power, this does not mean that the Soviet Union has abandoned its own efforts to create communist regimes. The Peking-Moscow rivalry may in fact have served to intensify the efforts of each communist power to create large communist party organizations that it alone can direct. Whether in the form of Soviet attempts to influence policy through aid and assistance to India or in the form of Chinese Communist efforts to extend Chinese sway in Southeast Asia, subversion, pressures, blandishments, internal interference, and propaganda have seemed to spread through the noncommunist areas of Asia in proportion to the intensity of the Sino-Soviet dispute. The extent to which communist activities have been and are likely to continue to be a source of continuing disruption in Asia was perhaps best dramatized by the attempt of the Indonesian Communist party, which was clearly under the influence of Peking, to seize power on September 30 and October 1, 1965. Had this coup succeeded, it would have been a source of major embarrassment to the Soviet Union, for the Soviets had extended more military assistance to the government of Sukarno than to that of any other country outside the communist camp, and Soviet weapons would have come under control of a communist party committed to the Chinese strategy of "people's wars." Thus the continuing communist commitment to "national liberation," which for both Moscow and Peking means the establishment of communist regimes, remains a problem in Asia—a problem in all likelihood intensified by the Moscow-Peking dispute.

Closely related to the continuing communist threat has been the problem of divided countries in East Asia—Korea, Vietnam, and China. In each case dissatisfaction with division on both sides of the continuing conflicts as well as plans and actions aimed at reunification have constituted sources of tension and violence that can escalate, as the conflict in Vietnam has illustrated only too clearly. Initiative in terms of overt action, organizational operations, pressure, and propaganda has for the most part remained in the hands of the communist parts of the divided countries.

Communist threats and violence have been in large measure responsible for a final persistent factor in the East Asian scene: the presence of the United States. From the time of its response to overt communist aggression in Korea on June 25, 1950, through the Taiwan Straits crises of 1955 and 1958, and up to its involvement in a major undeclared war against communist aggression in South Vietnam in 1965-66, the power of the United States has been the major guarantee of security for the noncommunist parts of divided countries in East Asia as well as for other countries threatened by pressures from Peking and Moscow. While Western Europe was coping with problems of economic development and cooperation behind the shield of NATO and Eastern Europe was groping toward modification of the institutions that had been imposed by Stalinism, the United States almost single-handedly provided resources for both development and security in the noncommunist parts of the Far East. This involved significant commitments of economic and military assistance, manning of bases, deployment of naval forces, treaty commitments, and the stationing of significant military forces in the area. In the divided countries military security required joint manpower commitments. In other countries, such as Japan, the major burden was carried by the United States alone.

FORCES FOR CHANGE

In addition to changes in the communist camp and the approaches of many Asian countries toward their former colonial masters in the West, new forces and trends have appeared in East Asia, pointing toward establishment of the sort of regional cooperation that has existed in Europe for more than a decade. Shielded by U.S. military protection, noncommunist countries have begun to show prospects for long-range stability and economic viability. By 1966 their leaders were already talking and planning in terms of interdependence rather than concentrating on independence. Their concepts of interdependence included long-range economic ties and exchange programs with Europe as well as with the United States.

A major emerging force in East Asia of the mid-1960's is Japan, and its miracle of economic development and progress cannot but carry overtones of politics and power. By 1966 Japan had become the world's third largest steel producer, had captured the bulk of the world's shipbuilding market, had pointed the way to meet food problems in Asia by intensifying methods of agriculture under private ownership, and had become a major trading partner for many of the countries of Europe, both East and West. Japan's foreign trade—in excess of $15 billion, four times as great as the trade of mainland China, which has seven times Japan's population—makes it a major force in world trade. The "new Japan" has been searching for its role in East Asia with imagination and finesse. It has developed plans and programs for development assistance that will make it the second most important country in this field in the Far East after the United States. Also, like some European powers, Japan has been seeking to exert a moderating influence on Peking's antagonistic world pose by developing long-term economic arrangements for industrial construction and trade. By 1966 officials in Tokyo were approaching the question of trade with Communist China with great confidence, insisting that Peking needed the trade more urgently than Tokyo. Japanese diplomacy was also moving cautiously toward the amelioration of strains with the Soviet Union.

If Japan has become once again a major force in the Far East, developments in Taiwan and South Korea have been almost as remarkable. Despite great burdens of military mobilization, these two countries now exhibit a rate of economic growth, a fiscal stability, and a degree of involvement in world trade and affairs that bespeak their increasing long-range importance both regionally and internationally. The Republic of China, the land reform and agricultural modernization of which have been acclaimed as models for what can be done in underdeveloped countries, has, for example, conducted a successful program of technical assistance in the agricultural field in a dozen countries in Africa. Both the Philippines and Thailand have similarly moved into the mainstream of world trade and into active participation in regional affairs.

Two events may serve to symbolize the new patterns of relations that have been developing in East Asia in the wake of economic and political progress in the area. The first, which took place in Manila in December, 1965, was the formal founding by twenty-two signatory countries of the Asia Development Bank with a capitalization of one billion dollars. A few facts are worth noting in connection with the Bank: Japan pledged a total of $200 million, a contribution matched only by that of the United States; two-thirds of the initial subscriptions was provided by Asian countries; six West European states joined in the venture.

The second noteworthy event was the convening of the Asian and Pacific Ministerial Conference (ASPAC) in Seoul, Korea, June 14–16, 1966. The suggestion had come from the Koreans, whose relations with Japan had been normalized earlier in the year. Foreign ministers of nine countries joined in urging "more positive and effective cooperation among the participating nations for their common good in the economic, technical, cultural, and social fields as well as the information field." The ministers agreed to continue the meetings on a regular basis and laid plans for their second conference, to be held in Thailand in 1967 with a membership that will probably be expanded through participation of other East Asian countries. The following facts are particularly significant: the initiative came from the Koreans; the United States was not involved; and, as in the case of the Asian Development Bank, Australia and

New Zealand gave clear indications that they intend to make active participation in regional affairs a major feature of their foreign policies.

Such forces for change in free Asia, coming at a time when the communist camp was in disarray, when Peking's truculence had alienated many of its former friends, and when the countries of Europe were exploring new patterns of economic and political relations around the world, may well prove of greater long-range significance than the initiatives coming from the communist capitals. In the mid-1960's many countries in Asia, though still sensitive about their sovereignty and independence, were willing to intensify their relations with the West in their plans for economic and political development to an extent that would have scarcely been considered possible a decade earlier. Though Europe hardly figured in the military and strategic picture in the Far East, the Western European nations were showing political and economic initiatives that promised to involve them increasingly in Asia's future. This growing interest was indicated, for example, by the commitment by the Federal Republic of Germany of more than DM 3.6 billion in economic assistance to Asian countries by the end of 1965, as well as by the visit of French President de Gaulle to Cambodia in the late summer of 1966.

Although stress has been placed on developments in noncommunist Asia and the opportunities offered for a revitalized Europe, it is important to note that Communist China has also been receptive to European initiatives in the economic sphere. The Sino-Soviet dispute led to a significant revolution in Peking's trading policies by the end of 1965. In the mid-1950's between 75 and 80 per cent of Communist China's trade was with countries of the communist bloc. In 1965 almost 70 per cent was with noncommunist countries, and mainland China's trade with the Soviet Union was almost matched by its trade with Japan and more than matched by its trade with Western Europe. Peking's determination never again to be as dependent upon the Soviet Union as it was in 1960, when the Kremlin withdrew all its technical experts, and its need to import grain combined to open the fabled "China market" to the West with unexpected rapidity. Perhaps of longer range significance than the changed orientation of mainland China's trade were the agreements for construction of large-scale plants that Peking concluded with Western European countries and Japan. Between 1963 and the end of 1965 the Chinese Communists concluded twenty-eight agreements involving close to $200 million. As far as Peking is concerned, because such projects last for several years and because of financing arrangements, they have implications that range beyond the field of strictly economic relations.

It is, of course, true that for the most part the trend toward renewed involvement by Europeans in the affairs of Asia has been restricted to trade, economic assistance, and economic development schemes. Yet in an increasingly sophisticated and interrelated world economic policies and trade patterns have greater political ramifications than heretofore. Although there has been no indication that Communist China's increasing dependence upon trade with noncommunist countries has exerted any significant influence on her political and military policies around the world, it is unlikely that the leadership in Peking can continue to remain isolated from the revolutionary changes in thinking that have been taking place in the noncommunist world—with which its contacts are expanding. It must be emphasized that in terms of lifting the standard of living and economic security of the masses, the real Asian revolution is taking place in the noncommunist sector—in countries such as the Republic of China, the Philippines, Malaysia, and even South Vietnam, all of which have major programs of reform and modernization. This revolution, which is bringing the Asian peoples better housing, more food and clothing, and the educational opportunity appropriate to a technical world, is based on a liberation and revitalization of free enterprise.

The stand-off between Communist China and the United States, which has caused agony in Vietnam and frequent criticism of the United States among its allies in Europe and Asia, has provided at least a framework within which the countries of Europe have been able to involve themselves once more in the future of Asia and many governments in the Far East have been able to search for and find ways to modernize, to move into the mainstream of world affairs, and to overcome some of their emotional fixations with regard to the West. In the years ahead it may recognized that it was in this period when many Asian nations began to "find themselves" that President Kennedy's proposal of July 4, 1963, for a new "Declaration of Interdependence" was accepted. The cooperation of the Europeans, who once again were acting constructively in Asia, may well prove to have been the decisive factor.

CHAPTER VI

German Reunification and the European Center Part I

WILLI BRUNDERT

Wᴏʀʟᴅ Wᴀʀ II, provoked by Hitler's policy of unrestrained force, came to an end in May, 1945, its outcome and results too familiar to require description here. Germany, which had started the war, was materially destroyed, and its people were mentally and physically exhausted. In those days Germany went through a period of want and misery such as it had never before experienced.

More far-reaching in its effects than the material distress that prevailed immediately after May 8, 1945, was the partition of the Reich, which initiated a state of affairs that still confronts Germany and Europe. The eastern provinces were placed under Soviet and Polish control, and that is still their formal status under international law. Middle Germany, consisting of the provinces and states of Mecklenburg, Brandenburg, Saxony-Anhalt, Saxony, and Thuringia, became the Soviet Occupation Zone, perpetuated under the title "German Democratic Republic." The German Federal Republic encompasses the former American, British, and French Occupation Zones. Berlin was originally divided into four sectors, but the only internal boundary that counts today is the wall separating West and East Berlin.

The continued partition imposes a burden on German politics and thus has repercussions on both European and world politics. Therefore the demand for self-determination for the people of Middle Germany is an objective necessity, not only for all Germans, but also for Europe and the rest of the world if the tensions that wrack a divided nation are to be eliminated. The tensions within Germany can at any time become aggravated and constitute the tinder for a European crisis. What this means for the world as a whole requires no elaboration.

This somewhat pessimistic evaluation of the consequences of partition leads directly to the questions: How can reunification be achieved? and What importance does the demand for reunification have within a new European policy? It must be admitted that during the 1950's the reunification problem figured more actively in world politics, and in the foreign policies of non-German states, than it does today. The decline in interest is to be regretted from a German point of view. But disappointment can be a spur to new activity, and the year 1966 has seen a number of proposals. New initiatives have been launched and new possibilities opened to debate, especially within the Federal Republic. All efforts to date have, however, been stalemated by the obstructive tactics of Walter Ulbricht, who on this subject must be considered a spokesman of Soviet policy.

The frequently repeated assertion that reunification is a matter for Germans alone is a propaganda slogan with no relation to the actual condition of the world. Of course, the Germans have a primary responsibility to do whatever they can. It should not be forgotten, however, that the great powers that assumed responsibility for Germany on May 8, 1945, still remain charged with the obligation to bring about reunification. The question we must ask in the present context is: To what extent can and must the German Federal Republic's efforts to develop a new European policy be coordinated with efforts to achieve reunification?

The thesis advanced some time ago that the West European problem should be solved first, thus permitting greater power to be brought to bear on the reunification issue, has been frequently misunderstood and requires clarification. If this thesis is to be interpreted to mean that the Federal Republic and Western Europe are to constitute an enlarged power-bloc to be employed in a policy of force toward the East, especially toward the Soviet Union, then a European policy based on such a thesis has no justification. Such a policy might even be interpreted as an incitement to armed struggle against the East, and this interpretation is therefore to be emphatically rejected. Reunification can only be accomplished on the diplomatic level and with political means. The maintenance of peace is more important than reunification—a statement this writer makes in full understanding of its significance and notwithstanding his own desire to see his home in Middle Germany reunited with the western provinces.

The efforts of the German Federal Republic to coordinate its policies of reunification and European unity from a European perspective must, under present circumstances, be limited to the psychological and moral sectors. Insofar as we succeed in making clear to our neighbors in Western Europe that reunification is a concern of Europe as a whole, and that the German Federal Republic requires the moral support of the West to strengthen democracy in the center of Europe, Germany will be reunited that much sooner.

Over and above periodic declarations and demonstrations of the will to secure reunification, the following must be our tasks:

1. To make clear to the states of Europe that so long as power politics generates tension in Germany, no permanent European peace is possible.

2. To convince the entire world that Germany, after its tragic recent history, has dedicated itself to the pursuit of peace and the securing of democracy, for which reasons it needs support from abroad for its demand that the right to self-determination be recognized.

3. To convince the countries of the Western world in particular that the best way to induce the East to solve the German problem through matter-of-fact diplomatic procedures is to impress upon those who control the Soviet Occupation Zone the fact that the Federal Republic enjoys the political and moral support of Europe and the West in its efforts to strengthen and secure democracy and peace through the realization of the policy of self-determination.

This last objective can best be achieved through the cooperation of Western Europe and the Federal Republic in dealing with this question. Understood in these terms, the unification of Europe and the efforts of Germans to reunify their country appear as parts of an integrated policy.

CHAPTER VII

German Reunification
And the European Center
Part II

KARL THEODOR BARON VON GUTTENBERG

W HAT PROFESSOR BRUNDERT has written about the innate connection between German and European reunification applies with special emphasis to the European center. There can be no German reunification without the restoration of a center of Europe that is once more European, and no revival of the European character of the central region of our continent is thinkable without German reunification.

There is an indissoluble *causal* relation between these facts. Putting it another way, we may say that Germany has lost its central region because no European center exists at present. We Germans do not say this for "programmatic" reasons. We do not speak of the common identity of the German and European situations because we expect immediate gain from this assertion. We speak of this connection because it constitutes historical reality and because any other perception would be arbitrary, tendentious, or the product of wishful thinking.

Such historical reality has a certain inevitability. One can run away from it for a while, one can close one's eyes to it for a limited time, but it is necessary to realize that, in the long run, the force of reality is always stronger than all the acts and speeches of those—whether they be doctrinaires, bigots, dreamers, or merely cowards—who conjure up their own reality. Germans can, for this reason, be assured that the compulsion of European reality will ever again provide them with helpers and allies. These allies will not be motivated by transitory feelings of sympathy or antipathy; they will be guided by what de Gaulle has called *la raison des faits*—the logic inherent in facts. It is neither theory, nor wishful thinking, nor escapism, but down to earth reality that impels our French neighbor to say: "Le problème allemand, c'est le problème européen par excellence."

But what kind of problem is this German and European problem— of what nature is the division of our country and continent? *Among other things* it is the result of the traditional, historical, national power goals and aspirations of the state currently the most powerful in Europe, the Soviet Union, and naturally of the misdeeds and megalomania of Hitler's Reich as well. But these are not, as many would suggest, the only causes, and above all they are not the determinative causes of the persisting division of Europe. If they were, and if the splitting of Europe in two parts were nothing more than the final result of a collision between German nationalism and victorious Russian nationalism, then we would today have new *geographical* boundaries in Europe, drawn by force, and not the clearly *political* boundary that separates our continent into two regions—one guided by the imperative "Grow according to your own nature," and the other subject to the command "Grow to be as we are."

An analogous meaning is found in the statement that the *geographical* center of Europe continues to exist as it did before, but that Europe is currently deprived of a *political* center. Europe today exists divided into two parts; its traditional order and structure have been torn apart, its center, its traditional heartland, suddenly transformed in 1945 into a double border zone.

Too many people in the West are inclined to belittle this situation nowadays. Their enemies are not so much the Communists as the "incurable anticommunists," whom they accuse of "mourning the passing of the Cold War." They deplore as a symptom of "ideological vertigo" any reference to the simple fact that a chasm continues to divide Europe into separate intellectual worlds between which no bridges exist. When one asks these super-experts what arcane knowledge justifies their speaking of a softening communism and even of its approaching demise, they refer knowingly to the "rising standard of living," "technical progress," "increases in production," and "changed methods of rule" in the countries beyond the line that severs the two parts of Europe. They fail to see how much they have been taken in by communist propaganda or to what degree they have begun to think in Marxist patterns.

The "anti-anticommunists" behave as though communism were nothing more than another "social system," a different "economic order," a variant "method of production"—in other words, as though its distinguishing characteristics were purely technical! It remains a constant source of mystery where these misapprehensions of the phenomenon of communism have their origin. How is one to explain that a noted German historian recently said to the writer in all sincerity that the Berlin Wall could be removed as soon as the standard of living in the Soviet Zone more closely matches that in the Federal Republic? How could a prominent representative of German intellectual life—no Communist by any means—ascribe the stream of refugees blocked by Ulbricht's wall to purely material motives?

When people talk in this way, we must ask ourselves about their knowledge, not of communism, but of freedom; for the two worlds with no bridges between them are definitely *not* those of a so-called socialist society and a so-called capitalist order. Who can deny that mixed forms combining these social and economic systems can and do exist? No, one world is that of the ideologues and totalitarians, and the other, our world, is that in which freedom is possible if we exert ourselves.

It is not enough to be anticommunist: the times demand a positive commitment to freedom, for—as we have experienced—one can very well be opposed to communism and an enemy of freedom at the same time. It is impossible to proclaim oneself an advocate of freedom and then to excuse communism the crimes for which we condemn fascism. Europe is rent asunder, not into communist and capitalist sectors, but into a free and an unfree part. There are compromises, bridges, and forms of transition between socialist and capitalist structures, but not between freedom and slavery.

This is the only sensible answer to the hopeful polyphony of voices that hail the economic advances, the higher standard of living, and the "more humane" methods of rule beyond the line separating the two parts of Europe as portents of an early end of communism. There is, no doubt, a historical process that involves the dampening of revolutionary élan, the withering of ideology, and thus the progressive betterment of the lot of the oppressed. The limitation of terror, the "humanization" of the regime, the economic and technical progress in communist countries are to be welcomed and encouraged, and they may even be signs of this historical process. But they do not constitute a recovery of or return to freedom. There are grades and levels of oppression; there is a wide gamut of totalitarian methods. There are brutal tyrants and moderate dictators—but there is no mixed form combining freedom and slavery.

The essential difference between freedom and slavery must be understood clearly by all those who address themselves to the reunification of Germany. For what is reunification other than the restoration of human freedom and political self-determination throughout Germany? Is not the German demand for reunification simply another way of expressing our insistence that the lack of freedom in the Soviet Zone give way to freedom? Is it not obvious that this demand is morally self-evident and requires no further justification, and that it may not be corrected, modified, or rendered worthless by the elapse of time or the presence of the most stubborn obstacles to its realization?

There are some, however, in Germany and other countries of the Western alliance who urge such a correction and modification of the demand for reunification. Since the enemy remains silent, such people hasten to proclaim the "collapse" of German aspirations. What a triumph it would be for this shrewd and implacable enemy—and what testimony to Western smallness and hypocrisy—were their advice to be taken!

What is the real objective of those who urge a new and "realistic" policy concerning German reunification? Whether or not they state their ends clearly and in so many words, all of them aspire in the long run to the same purpose. They advise us to abandon our policy of not recognizing the "German Democratic Republic" and especially the so-called Hallstein Doctrine. Instead, they say that we should recognize the "reality of the GDR" and enter into dialogue with the communist regime in the Zone—in other words, begin reunification talks with Ulbricht.

This "modification" of the reunification policy would amount to a total reversal of our policy as it has been conducted so far: the reunification of Germany would be placed in the hands of the "two German states." The German problem would thereby have become a problem for Germans only; it would have ceased—for one brief, fatal historical moment—to be a European and international problem. What the Soviet Union and the East Berlin Communists have been dreaming of for years would fall into their laps.

In considering this possibility, two points must be kept in mind. To begin with, German reunification, left to the Germans themselves, is only possible under two conditions. First, both parts of Germany must be able to decide freely; and, second, both parts must be able and willing to sacrifice their positions, at least in part, in order to reach a compromise. Neither of these conditions exists. The "GDR" is unfree and controlled by Moscow. And any compromise between a free state based on the rule of law and a totalitarian regime is, as already mentioned, a contradiction in itself.

The second point to be kept in mind is that to remand German reunification to the "two German states" is not only a measure unsuited to its objective, it is also something more, something different —the first step on a road that must almost automatically separate the Federal Republic from its allies. No one should succumb to the error that the Germans will consent indefinitely to the dismemberment of their country, that, having recognized the "GDR," they will simply coexist with it. While it is true that interest in reunification fluctuates, the problem remains vital, and its permanent and primary place is in German consciousness. While latent at the moment, it can become virulent at any time.

Should the decisive step desired by the East be finally taken and the "second German state" recognized as an equal partner and active participant in reunification, there would be only one road toward that objective: that of confederation with Moscow's satellite. The concept of reunification as a common Western undertaking would be dead and buried. In its place would arise the demand for an accommodation between free Germany and the Kremlin's satraps in East Berlin. The German Communists would have secured a foot in the door of the German question. They would have gained the right to present their conditions for German unity. And their first demand would be for German "neutrality."

The party to whom the German demand for reunification should be addressed is and remains Moscow. The East Berlin ploy can fool only those who fail to observe that the "German Democratic Republic" totally lacks both internal and external sovereignty—that it has never been released from Soviet tutelage. Those who enter into "negotiations with East Berlin" will soon find that their actual partner is the Soviet Union, and that reunification can be had only with Soviet consent.

What will induce the Soviet Union to agree to German reunification? Hundreds of proposals to this end have been suggested in recent years. Those coming from the East have always been in the same vein: confederation, neutrality, and adoption of the "social achievements" of the "GDR" by the Federal Republic. But the Western proposals have also been nothing more than variations on the same theme: Moscow should be offered economic and military concessions as the price of reunification.

These Western offers have ranged from payments of billions of German marks, through a gamut of demilitarized or partly demilitarized zones, to a proposal to permit the Soviet Union to retain its troops in Germany—even to a proposal for absolute German neutrality. Moscow's reply has always been a stereotyped "nyet." Insofar as the Western proposals were intended to demonstrate to the world that not Western but Eastern obduracy was preventing German reunification, they have fulfilled their purpose admirably. Is there any point, however, in continuing this competition of goodwill gestures that, if escalated too far, may lead ultimately to a sellout of Western positions?

To put matters briefly: there never has been and there is not now a price for which the Soviet Union would be prepared to let its Zone depart in freedom. It has believed and believes now that its interests are better served by preventing reunification than they would be by reunification itself. This understanding points the way to our political objective: we must bend every effort to produce a change in the economy of interests confronting Soviet policy.

This is the point of departure for what has been called the "Europeanization of the German question." It is necessary to understand that the Soviet policy of maintaining a firm grip on the "GDR" is an integral part of Moscow's European policy. Release of the Zone from the Kremlin's control is therefore dependent upon a change in Soviet European policy as a whole. As long as Eastern Europe continues to be a Soviet colonial empire, the "GDR" will continue to be the Central European crossbar holding this empire together. In other words, a Soviet Union that feels itself in unchallenged possession of its East European war booty has no incentive to relinquish its control over the "GDR." On the contrary, it has every reason to employ the "GDR" to protect its other possessions. Only a Soviet Union for which Eastern Europe has become an intolerable burden will be willing to talk seriously about releasing the "GDR."

These are obviously perspectives of a long-range character. It

would be self-deception, on the other hand, to try to build a reunification policy on short-range calculations, expecting them to material-
ize according to a timetable. One additional factor merits emphasis
at this point. Unpredictable and sudden changes are a specific characteristic of communist regimes. The frequently expressed opinion that
German unification is in any case and beyond all doubt an event lying in the remote future is therefore unduly pessimistic. It is, in fact,
an imitation of the ostensibly "scientific" clairvoyance of the Communists.

The relationship between developments in Eastern Europe and
the German question confronts German policy makers with a two-
fold dilemma. The perception that a general relaxation in the satellite area may some day open opportunities for reunification is
counterbalanced by the more immediate fear that Moscow will answer every German attempt to promote such relaxation by tightening its grasp on the Soviet Zone. Secondly, our nonrecognition policy
compels us to remain, to a certain extent, diplomatically distant from
the states that support Moscow's two-Germanies policy. In the case of
Poland, there is also the problem of the Oder-Neisse territories, and
their unilateral predetermination in favor of Poland is now—as
earlier—the prime objective of Warsaw's German policy.

There are, nevertheless, a number of opportunities for action open
to German policy makers in Eastern Europe. Experience to date indicates the desirability of a continuous expansion—notwithstanding
the lack of full diplomatic relations—of cultural exchange, personal
contact, and such economic activity as is politically wise to the extent
possible without arousing unnecessary suspicions in Moscow. It must,
however, be realized that the internal ferments and independence
movements observed in Eastern Europe are almost entirely the products of conditions in the communist system or of a nationalist nature,
and only in slight degree attributable to Western influences. For the
present, and as far as we can see ahead, the power and influence of
Gomulka, Novotný, Kádár, and Maurer in their own countries are a
thousand times more effective than any influence the West can exercise. And most particularly no one should believe that these gentle-
men are ready to carry cooperation with a Western state to a point
that would endanger their own authority.

In view of these limitations, there are two categorical imperatives
facing Bonn. The first of these is a continuation of the policy of unifying the Six (members of the Common Market). The most effective

Eastern policy remains that of creating a powerful and united Western Europe. Only an attractive and flourishing Western Europe can stimulate that change in Eastern Europe without which German reunification is impossible. The attractive force of this achievement already extends beyond the line of demarcation; it will not be long before the first ambassadors of East European states assume their posts in Brussels.

The second imperative is to grasp the hand of partnership extended by France. Wherever Germans and French appear together in Eastern Europe, the cry of "Bonn fascists" will be silenced or will remain unheard.

It cannot, of course, be pretended that Germany and France agree on all things. The questions of German boundaries and of common alliances remain points of contention. But there is fundamental common ground joining German and French aspirations on which the exercise of mutual goodwill permits the establishment of a common Eastern policy—a policy based on the will to work actively to end the partition of Germany and to solve the German question, the "European problem par excellence." Many have doubted the seriousness of France's offer to become the advocate of the German cause. De Gaulle's visit to Moscow has taught them differently—even though the General himself returned home slightly sobered by his new experiences.

An active East European policy is therefore not to be confused with that kind of "coexistence" that is today hailed in the East, and in many parts of the West as well, as the *remedium omnium laborum*. For the East this coexistence is merely a slogan intended to deceive; its true meaning is at best a temporary, limited, and tactically conceived coexistence alongside an "ideological enemy" against which no other weapons are currently available. Where coexistence is mentioned in the West, however, people think mild and kindly thoughts about a kind of "neighborly" relation, which may range from respectful distance to mutual toleration and cooperation, as Rudolf Liess has demonstrated in his book, *Is Eastern Thought Still European?*[1]

The Westerner must learn to understand that permanent coexistence with communism is impossible, and, more particularly, that no peaceful order can be founded upon such coexistence. While this statement may seem repetitive, it deserves renewed emphasis, since European coexistence hopes have led to calls for the withdrawal of troops on the ground that the peaceful intentions of the Soviet Union can be trusted. Americans of this persuasion point to their preoccupation with Vietnam (where Soviet peacefulness is not in evidence), while the British plead the precarious situation of the pound sterling. Proposals for unilateral disengagement in Europe are not, however, limited to costly conventional forces, but include projects for a "denuclearization" of Western Europe.

There is, however, a German saying that things are never eaten as hot as they are cooked. Europeans would be extremely busy if they sounded the alarm every time a proposal of this kind appeared in the newspapers. Naturally the Germans should therefore support America's efforts, burdens, and sacrifices undertaken to ward off communist expansion in Asia. Such support must be carried to the point of accepting transfers of troops that are temporarily necessary. But there is no plausible reason whatever for planning a gradual denuclearization of Europe or of European troops. On the contrary, any such intention must be interpreted here as a concession to the Soviet Union at the cost of European security.

We Germans appreciate that our American partner is not currently, and perhaps will not be for a considerable time, in a position to conduct an offensive policy designed to overcome the partition of Europe. But we continue to repose undiminished trust in this partner as a solid and reliable defensive power, which joins us in guaranteeing European security and thus the Atlantic peace. But since we Europeans—and we Germans in particular—cannot reconcile ourselves to the status quo of a Europe rent asunder, and since mere coexistence would be both inadequate and dangerous, we therefore look for outlets for our own independent activity. The thoughts developed here reflect the belief that reunification of Germany, the restoration of European freedom, and the recovery of the European center are offensive tasks that must be primarily accomplished by Europeans themselves—particularly when their transatlantic partner is more and more occupied in other parts of the world.

NOTES TO CHAPTER SEVEN

1. Rudolf Liess, *Denkt man im Osten noch europäisch?* Vol. 13, Politikum-Reihe (Stuttgart: J. Fink-Verlag, 1965).

CHAPTER VIII

Germany and Russia's European Policy

WENZEL JAKSCH

ALTHOUGH THE ISSUES raised by the Soviet Union's European policy are part of a total situation in which the Vietnam war currently looms in the foreground, they are nevertheless conditioned by the specific structural problems of Europe. It is important for the peoples of the West to become familiar with and to work toward the solution of these problems.

Since the rapid development of Russia as a world power during the nineteenth century, the western neighbors of that empire have lived under the threat of Russian imperialism, the modern form of which is pan-Slav world-revolutionary messianism. The rulers of Russia have presided over three partitions of Poland. As early as 1849, their armies of intervention entered Europe to suppress the first Hungarian revolution. Marx and Engels then predicted that Moscow would extend its western borders as far as a line drawn from Stettin to Trieste. Bismarck's foreign policy was one uninterrupted attempt either to distract the expansive force of Russia from the West or to confront it with a consolidation of the European Center. These were the motivations for the Dual Alliance and the Triple Alliance. After World War I it was fear of the communist world revolution that brought Hitler and Mussolini large numbers of supporters. Hitler, with his insane war, brought the Red Army into the heartlands of Europe, and the blindness of Western statesmen after the war allowed the additional territories of Bohemia, West Saxony, Thuringia, and Mecklenburg to slip into Stalin's hands. But Stalin's insatiability made inevitable the formation of a countercoalition in the West, in which the German Federal Republic—formed of the Western occupation zones in 1949—plays an important role.

Russian diplomacy is, of course, well versed in the art of maneuvering so as to split opposing coalitions. In the Crimean War, for instance, it was able to take advantage of the German fear of Russia since Prussia covered the Czarist empire's European rear. Around the turn of the century Russia gambled on French distrust of a growing Germany. Result: the Entente Cordiale against the European Center. At the present time the Eastern bloc is raking over all the bitter memories of the Hitler era so as to provoke distrust of the Federal Republic within the NATO coalition and to spread fear of a reunified Germany. The Federal Republic is particularly disliked in the Kremlin, for two reasons: (1) because as the nucleus of German statehood it represents Germany as a whole, and (2) because the existence of an economically successful German democracy provides constant encouragement to oppositional forces in Middle Germany and throughout Eastern Europe.

Here, we encounter once more the structural problems of Europe. The problem of German unity involves the structure of the European Center, and here is interwoven the thread of intercontinental world politics. If the United States is to free itself from Soviet Russian blackmail of its Asian policy, then it must view the German question in terms of the future of the European Center. In France and Great Britain short-sighted nationalist interests will never abandon their attempts to conduct bilateral policy with the Russians at the expense of the European Center. This is why West European integration is only a makeshift solution. The future of Europe will be decided on the Elbe, the Moldau, and the Danube. *Within this zone, there is a vacuum in self-determination, independence, and security that must be filled if the United States is to be relieved of its burdens in Europe.*

Seen in this perspective, the Federal Republic is not a political fragment but a nucleus of statehood, a magnet, and a crystallization point of European self-determination. Moral support of Middle Germany against the Ulbricht regime is therefore not a question of altruism for our Western allies, but a question of serving their own direct interests.

A sketch of European structural problems must naturally include so-called Eastern Europe, that is to say, Europe behind the Iron Curtain. Only by associating itself with Central Europe can Eastern Europe recover a relative degree of independence. This insight is gaining ground. Uneasiness about the war in Vietnam is greater in Eastern Europe than in Western Europe. We know that assistance rendered the Viet Cong aggravates the latent economic difficulties of the East European countries. The Soviet Union has, for the same reasons, been forced to modify its Five-Year Plan. The behavior of Soviet diplomats is, however, the same as though they held all the trumps. Actually, the Russians are speculating on the probability that the United States will progressively raise its offer of concessions in exchange for Russian inactivity in Vietnam; that it will perhaps even be willing to pay the price of recognizing the partition of Germany and Europe. In this tragic situation we should avoid pressing an excess of advice upon our American friends. It is our duty, however, to warn against a weakening of the American engagement in Europe.

American and European Consolidation

The best initial approach to the situation in Europe is to consider some of the results that would ensue from an American withdrawal from Europe, even if it were to proceed in gradual stages.

First, the Federal Republic would find itself forced into a relation of dependency on Gaullism in foreign policy. The term Gaullism is emphasized, since there is more reason for confidence in the European convictions of the French voters than for trust in General de Gaulle's European policy.

Second, American, British, and French pressure upon the Federal Republic to extend its contacts with East European countries will probably have results that are the reverse of those intended. A West that seeks contacts at any price must seem weaker and more insecure to the Eastern bloc.

Third, the American experts on Eastern Europe—of whom Professors Zbigniew Brzezinski and George F. Kennan are typical—are wrong in anticipating an *automatic development of polycentrism* within the satellite area. Every unilateral concession by the West to the rulers of these countries tends to act as an obstacle to liberalization, which was introduced in response to pressure from below but is already retrograde in Poland and Hungary.

Fourth, it is futile to expect any gratitude on the part of communist governments. Poland and Yugoslavia have accepted millions of dollars in gifts from the United States without letting this in the slightest influence their anti-Western policy. As one of the incidental effects of the Vietnam war, Moscow's political influence has again increased in Eastern Europe, even though the sympathies of the people there are by no means on the side of China or the Viet Cong.

Fifth, should the Federal Republic be forced into more intensified contacts with East European countries regardless of the hardening of Eastern bloc policy, then Moscow would in the long run become a stronger magnet for our Eastern policy than either Warsaw or Prague. A self-interested German foreign policy would naturally be inclined to address its economic offers directly to the Soviet Union, so as to overcome objections to reunification by the political control center of the Eastern bloc.

The *sixth* and final point is that every success attained by the Soviet Union in the European arena will cause a hardening of its policy in Asia.

Turning to the situation in Germany and Central Europe, we must begin with the conservative assumption that the Vietnam war will continue to be a factor of disturbance in international politics for a long time to come. We should not, however, fail to notice the forces of consolidation in Western Europe, as well as the growing need of the peoples for a normalization of relations between Western and Eastern Europe. One of our great postwar hopes has not disappointed us, namely, our belief in the evolutionary power of the European idea. Our only disappointment in this area has been the delay in the association of Great Britain and the entire Free Trade Zone with the Common Market. This is not, however, the fault of Professor Hallstein. Apart from this one setback, the Brussels Commission has fulfilled the objectives of the Treaty of Rome with clocklike precision. By advancing the customs union to 1968, it has overfulfilled its norm in a way the entire Eastern bloc cannot match.

The numerous agreements reached in Brussels in recent years are a tribute to the tremendous human accomplishment of men like Professor Hallstein, Herr Mansholt, and M. Marjolin, who should be accorded the recognition they reserve. Brussels, with its work of integration, has become the European counterforce to Moscow. Failure to appreciate the accomplishments of Brussels is, by the way, one of the main roots of Western inferiority complexes vis-à-vis the Eastern bloc. It should therefore be recalled constantly that in the daily confrontations between the works of the Common Market and those of the Council for Mutual Economic Aid (COMECON), unbloody battles in the East-West conflict are being decided.

Through the agricultural agreement reached at Brussels, the prerequisites for worldwide tariff reductions in the course of the Kennedy Round have been achieved. If the wisdom of the negotiators in Geneva does not fall behind the energy of the Brussels Commission, then the road will be open to closer economic cooperation on a world scale. The Eastern bloc has no such bonus values to throw into the balance. Moscow is compelled to watch impotently while the leadership of the world economy passes into the hands of the free nations of the West, where it promises to remain for some time. Why should we hang our heads at precisely this moment? Why should we exhaust ourselves in mutual criticism, or undermine the Western alliance?

Our American friends are well aware that an integrated Western Europe is more than an American bridgehead. It is at the same time the only conceivable point of departure for a Western political and economic offensive against the Eastern bloc. The European unification movement thus appears as the natural ally of American patriotism.

This brings us to a question that deserves the sober consideration of our American friends: How far would West European integration have proceeded without the energetic support of the Federal Republic? To ask this question is not to belittle the contributions of France, Italy, and the Benelux countries. German democracy should not, however, be denied recognition of its contemporary accomplishments. Discussion of the German question in the West unfortunately tends to take a retrospective view rather than to see Germany in total perspective. Hitler, Himmler, and Eichmann have, so to speak, become the household gods of political literature since the war. Occasional mention should be made of the names of those Germans who have rendered Europe signal service during the last two decades. The list of those who have labored fruitfully in the vineyard includes not only governmental leaders such as Konrad Adenauer, Professor Heuss, and Heinrich von Brentano, but also Kurt Schumacher, trade union leader Hans Böckler, and Mayor Ernst Reuter of Berlin, all of whom drew a clear line of separation between social democracy and on the one hand free trade unionism and on the other Soviet communism. By doing so, they blocked Stalin's further political advance into the West. For years Professor Hallstein—with an avoidance of publicity that is hardly typical of the times—has been performing a giant task on behalf of dynamic European democracy. The same can also be said of the SPD triumvirate, Brandt, Erler, and Wehner. What would happen to West German stability without them?

It would be false modesty to fail to mention the contribution of the expellee organizations to West German stability in this connection. Every fourth German encountered in the streets of German cities comes from the other side of the Iron Curtain. This means that after five and one-half years of war he had to endure expulsion from Eastern Germany or flight from Middle Germany. These fourteen million Germans are also allies of the free world. Their fate is a part of German reality.

In Germany as well as elsewhere there are superficial observers of this drama whose argument runs something like this: "The expellees and refugees are now integrated; they have jobs and dwellings—it is time they left us in peace." But man does not live by bread alone! Negroes who are citizens of the United States are likewise integrated in the economic sense, but their feeling of discrimination leads to the burning of entire city districts. The "Provos" in Amsterdam are neither hungry nor freezing, yet they too march against the established order.* Compare their situations with that of a half-million expropriated farmers from the German eastern territories and the Sudetenland, who were absorbed into West Germany as unskilled laborers or who must spend their old age in an attic room with a subsistence-level old age pension. Would their bitterness not be the ideal tinder for political explosions?

Who could seriously doubt that ten million deportees from the East and a further four million refugees from Middle Germany constitute an ideal recruiting ground for a new nationalism? The term *new* nationalism is in order because it is arrant nonsense to brand every assertion of legitimate German interests without further ado as "neonaziism." As the author of the first pamphlet attacking national socialism, which appeared immediately after Hitler's "beer hall putsch" in Munich in 1923,[1] this writer feels justified in stating, on

---

* The "Provos" are a variety of Beatnik, whose philosophy is that of general protest against the established order. They have won several seats on the Amsterdam city council.—*Eds.*

the basis of long experience, that *the chances of a successful neo-naziism in Germany are exactly zero.* From time to time there may be a surge of protest votes for splinter parties—even that could be prevented by wise policies—but after its experiences with Hitler's brown dictatorship and Ulbricht's red dictatorship, the German people is the least inclined in Europe to submit to the blandishments of new dictators. There is, however, a strong probability that a strengthened German national consciousness will emerge in the field of maneuver between Gaullism and Soviet patriotism.

THE GERMAN PROBLEM AS A FOCUS OF EUROPEAN POLICY

The July, 1966, conference of the Warsaw Pact states, held in Bucharest, made public the Eastern bloc's price for a peace treaty with the Federal Republic: recognition of the status quo of a partitioned Germany and a divided Europe. This demand is supplemented by the proposal for a so-called European Security Conference, the manifest purpose of which would be the exclusion of the United States and the creation of a military vacuum in Central Europe between the Soviet and the French atomic forces. These proposals must be understood as facets of an offensive Soviet European strategy. The year before Moscow had already pulled the reins tighter in its European satellite region. This policy found its expression in new trade agreements with Pankow, Warsaw, Prague, Budapest, and Sofia—every one of them expiring in 1970, but all serving a single purpose: to confine approximately 70 per cent of the satellites' foreign trade within the Soviet sphere of hegemony. The Five-Year plans of the Soviet Union and its European satellites were likewise timed to end in 1970. Rumania retained a somewhat greater economic mobility, but despite the brave declarations of its ministers it was compelled to submit once more to Russian political leadership within the Warsaw Pact.

Three solid facts emerge, therefore, from the fog of wishful thinking about East-West relations in Europe:

1. The consolidation of the Eastern bloc since the intensified American engagement in Asia.
2. The stabilization of Russian policy on the German question along the lines of the status quo.

3. The intensified compulsory economic integration of the Eastern bloc countries in the structure of the Soviet Union.

How do the people in the German Federal Republic react to this situation? So far as superficial public opinion is concerned, confusion about the German question is greater in West Germany than anywhere else. It is no secret that a considerable part of the public opinion ventilated by news media in the Federal Republic tends in the direction of the Soviet status-quo proposals. The formula of "two German states" already appears in the declarations of West German politicians. The self-accusation of stand-pat-ism is going the rounds. Leading daily papers draw a totally negative balance for German policy to date. Other periodicals whose views are taken seriously explain that we must look to the East "quite differently than heretofore." A "rethinking of our relations with Middle Germany" is also recommended. Circulars delivered from door to door containing the same arguments urge recognition of a national-communist government in Middle Germany and economic aid for Ulbricht.

This is in any case a significant German echo of the Bucharest resolution. It is necessary to reread the section of the resolution on Germany in this connection. It declares "the question of unifying the two German states" to be dependent on a relaxation of tensions. The road to this goal leads

> via the gradual rapprochement of the two sovereign German states and via agreements between them; via disarmament treaties in Germany and in Europe, based on the principle that the future united Germany will be a truly peace-loving democratic state, which will never threaten its neighbors or the European peace.

Back of these words stands the challenge to the Germans: First affix your signatures to the ukase partitioning your country, and then wait and see what comes of the "gradual rapprochement of the two sovereign German states." A more insignificant *quid pro quo* for the renunciation of self-determination can hardly be imagined. The Soviet peace offer from Bucharest, however, contains one feature that seems very tempting. *It offers West Germany* (West Berlin being no longer mentioned) *an imaginary military security within a Russian and French security system in Europe*—an alternative to the pressures and frictions associated with NATO membership.

Now that the cards of the Eastern bloc have been laid on the table, the Federal Republic is no longer dealing with nuances in the fields of foreign and all-German policy. The decision facing us is that between the recognition of the status quo of Yalta and a new round of resistance against the partition of Germany.

WHAT KIND OF GERMANY?

Our American friends should consider very carefully the direction in which they intend to influence German decision with their advice. Many of our Western advisers make the mistake of desiring three or four different Germanies at the same time, for instance:

an economically strong Germany that carries the main financial burden of West European defense, participates in every action to support the pound sterling, and conducts active development aid programs in many parts of the world;

a politically weak Germany that renounces its self-determination, that writes off its eastern territories, and that accepts the expulsion of fifteen million Germans as "just and final" in the terms proclaimed by Herr Ulbricht;

a Germany that submits to military discrimination, that does not even demand a share in deciding questions of atomic defense, but that supplies a sufficient number of patriotic young men to assume the main burden of conventional defense in Western Europe; and finally

a Germany that is a loyal ally of the United States, but at the same time a pleasant partner of Kremlin diplomacy.

Friends of freedom should never be misled into desiring an unpatriotic Germany. *A Germany without patriotism would fall victim to the Kremlin without a struggle.* This must be stated with clarity, because much of our own and the Western discussion of the German problem is already infected with arguments of the Eastern bloc. What is the meaning of "recognition" of the Ulbricht regime? According to democratic principles, a regime can only be recognized by the population it represents. The only conceivable recognition of the Ulbricht regime would be that accorded through free elections in Middle Germany. And who continues to demand them? What is the meaning of stand-pat-ism in German foreign policy? This question was well answered by Senator Lecanuet, the democratic candidate who opposed de Gaulle, in his lecture in Bonn. He reminded his German listeners of the most profound cause of stand-pat-ism in European politics: the Soviet Union's adherence to the position of Yalta. Even Stalin's concessions at Potsdam were violated by his successors, who would otherwise have to permit all-German administrators for particular functions and keep the question of German eastern boundaries open until settled by a peace treaty.

One of the most objectionable frauds perpetrated upon Western peoples is the propaganda myth of *Russian fear of Germany.* Every cadet at any Western military academy knows that in the age of atomic weapons a medium-size, thickly populated country such as Germany —divided or united—can be wiped out with a half dozen hydrogen bombs. Eight hundred Russian medium-range missiles stand ready to deliver this blow at any hour desired. The same Soviet leadership that demonstrates its immense military potential every first of May operates in its propaganda with the distorted picture of a belligerent West Germany, which is only waiting for the right moment to launch a third world war. And the satellite governments, although armed to the teeth, make sure that all Western visitors are told the canard about the fear their peoples have of Germany.

THE GERMAN PROBLEM AND EAST-WEST CONTACTS

There is a tendency in the West, present also in the Federal Republic, to place exaggerated hopes in dialogue with governments, peoples, and individuals in Eastern Europe. To achieve any concrete results, a common West European conception of integration is needed as a basis for discussion with the evolutionary forces of these countries. Without a Western outline visualizing the possibilities for economic and cultural cooperation, such dialogues must remain sterile. The same is true of the contacts made by French diplomacy in East European capitals.

Instead of chasing after pipe-dreams, however, a pragmatic Western policy concerned with Eastern Europe must first answer the concrete question: *How much room for maneuver* do the individual East European governments actually enjoy?

The case of Yugoslavia has shown that worldwide diplomatic activity does not alleviate the internal problems of a communist-governed country. It has also made clear that generous Western credits cannot help even a relatively liberal economic collectivism to overcome its structural problems.

Rumania has recently recognized that the increased Western trade to which it aspires depends on the quantity of goods it can export itself.

Poland is tied far more closely to Moscow than the expert opinions prevailing in the United States were willing to admit for some years. The prohibition of Cardinal Wyszynski's trip to the United States, the demonstration before the American embassy in Warsaw, and Gomulka's deliveries of war material to the Viet Cong have been a bitter lesson for the West against counting on the gratitude of communist governments.

Events this year in Poland, however, have shown that the autonomous will of the East European peoples is still alive. The great religious demonstrations celebrating the thousandth anniversary of Christianization were the pledge of an enslaved people to its own history, to the West, and to Europe.

As reports by visitors to Eastern European countries indicate, it is most important to differentiate clearly between governmental points of view and public opinion in Eastern Europe. For the peoples of that region union with Europe is their only remaining hope for the future. It is surprising how strongly the concept of Central Europe again figures in conversations with Poles. The same is true in the case of Slovaks and Czechs, Hungarians, Slovenes, and Croats. It is striking how, under the weight of communist foreign rule, ancient feelings of regional association revive among these people. It was more than incidental that when the Turks stormed Central Europe, Hungary, Bohemia, and the Austrian alpine lands joined in a Central European community to meet their common destiny. A Polish relief army under King John Sobieski played an honorable role in lifting the second seige of Vienna in 1683. Traditional sympathies for Vienna and Austria thus constitute a silent acknowledgment of the European Center throughout Eastern Europe.

At the same time European tourism from East to West and the attraction of the German labor market for guest workers from southeast Europe help objectify the image of Germany. The people who come to us from Eastern Europe find no disguised SS state, no armed camps of *revanchistes,* but a free, modern, friendly country. Conversely, the flow of German tourists to Eastern Europe helps spread the message of our democratic reconstruction, our economic accomplishments, and the high level of mass culture in the Federal Republic. When the noncommunist majorities in East European countries figure things out on the basis of information from independent sources, they easily come to the conclusion that without the support of the German will to reunification, all Eastern Europe would remain a domain of Moscow for an indefinite time to come. *The German will to unity is therefore a natural ally of the self-determination rights of Eastern European peoples.* Every iota of Polish or Czech independence that may exist in the future requires the backing of German democracy and a free Germany.

Political science is capable of giving direction and meaning to the treadmill of day-to-day politics by making both the intellectual elite and the broader public of the voters in the countries concerned aware of the perspectives of great historical choice. Fundamentally, the confrontation of ideas concerning the unity of Germany and of Europe involves a struggle between two conceptions.

During the great democratic movement of 1848, men of different conceptions, such as the Czech historian Palacký and the German revolutionary Karl Marx, joined in preaching the need for the *solidarity of non-Russian Europe* against Russian imperialism. The imperative of this solidarity exists to this very day. De Gaulle's formula of one Europe to the Urals is a retread of the later concept of Franco-Russian community of interests against the European Center. The first concept, that of European solidarity, is most closely related to the idea of united Europe. It also corresponds to the interests of the Anglo-Saxon peoples, who—precisely because of the tremendous tasks facing them in Asia—need the backing of a consolidated European continent.

The times call for the creation of a Europe of full stature between the giants of East and West. If we refuse to let ourselves be bluffed by Soviet status-quo propaganda, the Soviet Union will sooner or later find it necessary to seek a peaceful compromise with the economic potential of Western Europe and the freedom potential of Eastern Europe. Our task is to hold the door to Europe open for the East European peoples.

NOTES TO CHAPTER EIGHT

1. *Marxismus oder Hakenkreuz: Wer sind des deutschen Volkes Verderber?* [Marxism or Swastika: Which Will Ruin the German People?] (Teplitz-Schönau: 1924). The title of this pamphlet indicates the unfortunate extent to which the Social Democratic struggle against national socialism was carried on from the false platform of Marxist ideology. In those days, however, we considered it necessary to conduct our simultaneous struggle against the Communists on the basis of Karl Kautsky's democratic and humanist interpretation of Marx.

Part Two
Christian Churches and Totalitarian Rule

CHAPTER IX

Christian Faith and Totalitarian Rule

WILL HERBERG

THE TWENTIETH CENTURY is the age of totalitarianism. Not only does a great portion of the human race live under pervasive totalitarian rule, but totalitarianism emerges as a crucial problem at every level of twentieth century life and is largely the source of the great conflicts, economic, political, and spiritual, that are tearing apart the contemporary world.

What has Christianity to say about this massive historical reality that gives our century its characteristic aspect? Few of the utterances and interventions of influential Christian spokesmen in recent decades can be regarded as contributing to the clarity and responsibility so desperately needed in this time of crisis. The confusion in the churches is itself a major factor exacerbating the crisis and facilitating the advance of totalitarianism on many fronts. The effort to achieve a Christian understanding of totalitarian movements, therefore, involves a drastic criticism of many things that have been said and done by the churches, and in the name of the churches, in their fateful confrontation with totalitarianism.

I

Our Western political institutions, especially our Western political conceptions, derive in large part from the experience of the ancient Greek city-state and from the political philosophy developed around it. For Aristotle, it will be remembered, the *polis,* the State, was "by nature." Man, according to Aristotle, was "by nature a political animal," that is, a being with a nature that demanded organized community for its proper life and was always straining to establish it. Indeed, for Aristotle, as for Plato before him and for the intelligent, educated Athenians of their time, the *polis* was, in fact, the *human-making* institution, in which man's human potentialities could be actualized and perfected. The full perfection of humanness could be achieved only within and through the *polis.* When the Greek city-states began to lose their autonomy and vitality, political philosophers began to talk of a "universal *polis,*" a *polis* of the *cosmos,* a *cosmopolis*—sometimes identified as the Roman Empire, sometimes conceived as a "heavenly city" of the wise and the virtuous. But Greek political philosophy still remained essentially *polis*-oriented.

Greek experience and Greek philosophy founded on this experience did not, and apparently could not, distinguish between society and State. Man's sense of community, which makes society "natural" to him, was held to include the coercive organization of society as well. In Greek political thought, therefore, there was a strong totalitarian element. The pervasiveness of society in bringing forth, educating, and molding the individual into a civilized human being was easily understood as the total jurisdiction of the State as a mind- and character-forming power. Even Aristotle, a careful, moderate, and realistic thinker, complained that

> in most states, these matters [education, occupations, domestic affairs, etc.] have been neglected [by the authorities]; each man lives as he likes, ruling over wife and children in the fashion of the Cyclops. The conclusion to which we come is that the best course is to have a system of public and proper provision for these matters. (*Nicomachean Ethics,* 14; 1180a14.)

In other words, in any well-conceived community such matters as marriage, vocation, and domestic life would properly fall under the jurisdiction and control of the State. The fact is that, *in principle,* though fortunately not always in practice, Greek political rationalism, as Hajo Holborn points out,

> had no organ for the free individual. The idea of the right of the individual to possess a sphere of his own was alien to the

Greeks. The government was in total control of the community, and whatever freedom the individual might acquire, he could gain only through participation in government. The Greek soul did not demand a field all to itself beyond the social order.[1]

The distinction between society and the State was well understood by the Jews of the time as a result of their own experience and of Old Testament traditions about the kingship, and the early Church fully shared their way of thinking. Community, conceived in terms of ever widening circles of covenant, was part of God's creation and therefore (using the Greek vocabulary) "natural" to man. But the State, as the *coercive* organization of society, most emphatically was *not*. The State with its vast, complex machinery was the outcome, not of human nature, but of human *sin*. And yet, it was ordained of God, indirectly but no less truly. Here is how Paul, in that celebrated thirteenth chapter of Romans, conceives it:

> Let every one be subject to the governing authorities, for there is no authority but from God, and the powers that be are ordained of God. Therefore he who resists the authorities resists what God has ordained, and those who resist will incur judgment. For rulers are not a terror to good-doing, but to evil-doing. Would you have no fear of the magistrate who is in authority? Then do what is good, and you will have his approval, for he is God's minister for your good. But if you do evil, be afraid, for he does not bear the sword in vain; he is the minister of God to execute his wrath on the evil-doer. Therefore, one must be subject [to the authorities] not only to avoid God's wrath, but also for the sake of conscience. For the same reason you also pay taxes, for the authorities are the ministers of God . . . (Romans 13:1–6.)

What one may call the theopolitical logic here is clear enough. Were it not for man's sinfulness, were it not for man's propensity to do evil, there would be no necessity for the coercive State, for the magistrate with his sword. But since man is sinful and prone to evildoing, God, in His infinite mercy, has instituted the political order as an *order of preservation,* to save mankind from itself, to save it from destroying itself through its sinful self-aggrandizement. Hence, the State authority, from emperor down to local magistrate, is carrying out a divine vocation. The ruler is, in Paul's forceful language, a "minister of God," though he may not himself know or acknowledge it—remember that the "public authorities" Paul is talking about are the pagan Emperor Nero and his pagan officials throughout the Roman Empire! The magistrate with the sword is necessary and must be obeyed by the Christian out of his Christian conscience; but he is made necessary by the dreadful consequences of human sinfulness, and he is to be obeyed, not on his own claim, but in obedience to God.

Paul's sweeping injunction "Obey the governing authorities!" finds its own limitations elsewhere in the New Testament. There is, first, Peter's declaration, "We must obey God rather than man" (Acts 5:29); this, however, was strictly limited in scope, meaning that a Christian could not obey the magistrate when the magistrate called to idolatry or forbade the proclamation of the Gospel. Much more fundamental was the teaching that emerges from Revelation 13. Romans 13 defines the *legitimate* government, ordained by God as a divine order of preservation. And in Revelation 13 we have the definition of the *illegitimate* government, which is an agency, not of God, but of the devil. Here is the operative section of Revelation 13:

> Then, out of the sea, I saw a Beast rising . . . The Dragon conferred upon it its power and rule . . . The whole world went after the Beast in wondering admiration. Men worshiped the Dragon who had conferred his authority upon the Beast; they worshiped the Beast also, and chanted: 'Who is like unto the Beast? Who can stand against him? (Rev. 13:1–5)

This celebrated passage has a reference that is directly political. The Dragon, of course, is Satan. The Beast is the Roman Empire, or the Emperor. Here, the "public authority," which Paul had seen as the minister of God, is denounced as a servant of the devil. And how is its diabolical character discerned? By its self-exaltation against God! Instead of confining itself to its God-ordained function of preserving society against sinful evil-doing, it now demands to be worshiped and exalted. (The chant "Who is like unto the Beast? Who can stand against him?" is, of course, a devilish parody of the Song of Moses, Exodus 15:1–8: "Who is like unto Thee, O Lord . . . ?") Because it claims for itself what is owing only to God, the State is no longer to be obeyed as an order of preservation; it is to be opposed as an agency of Satan in rebellion against God. This is the *illegitimate* State, in fact, the anti-State.

The Pauline conception of the State as an institution, not of the created or "natural" order, but of the sinful world, designed to protect mankind against itself, came to govern the thinking of the Western Fathers and most thoroughly the thinking of the great Augustine. For Augustine, the political order, embodied in the coercive State, is emphatically not "by nature," as an order of creation. On the contrary, it is *propter peccatum,* because of sin. In the order of creation there is no rule of man over man; that emerges, as Paul had shown, out of the necessity of curbing man's evil-doing, his sinful self-aggrandizement that, uncurbed, would destroy the entire human race. The State is, therefore, not only *propter peccatum*; it is also *remedia peccati,* a remedy for, a protection against, sin. One must, therefore, obey the public authorities except when they order something *contra legem Dei,* which, to Augustine as to the other Fathers and the New Testament writers, meant a call to idolatry, a prohibition to preach the Gospel, or both. Under such circumstances the Christian would have to obey God rather than man, but his disobedience to earthly authorities would always remain passive, leading to martyrdom. Of the distinction between the legitimate and the illegitimate State, there is only the most shadowy suggestion; it seemed so little relevant to the new age of the Christian Emperors.

We cannot sufficiently admire the profundity and realism of this biblical-patristic view of the State. To the Christian it should be self-evident that political power, to be in any sense legitimate, must ultimately come from God, the true Sovereign Lord. From where else is the legitimacy of an arrangement that gives some men power over others to come? From the mere will and power of the ruler— whether monarch or people? That would be the sheerest idolatry. If I am to recognize the legitimate authority of the rulers, be they kings or parliaments, I must see these rulers, whether or not they themselves acknowledge their role, as ministers of God and their authority as authority coming from God, conferred upon them for preservative purposes. This view carries with it, let us never forget, implicit limitations on the scope of the authority of the State. The limits passed or violated, the State loses its legitimacy and becomes a diabolical agency for the oppression and subversion of mankind.

But our admiration of the profundity and truth embodied in the

Pauline-Augustinian doctrine cannot blind us to one glaring defect: if the State is justified by the necessity of curbing the evil-doing that comes out of the sinful self-aggrandizement of men, how is it that the ruler—whether prince or parliament—is overlooked? Is not the ruler a man, a sinful man, driven on, as are other men, by sinful self-aggrandizement, by the *libido dominandi*, the "lust for dominating" that Augustine saw as the paramount "law" of the Earthly City? Does not the ruler, therefore, need curbing on his part as well? This germinal idea of a constitutional order setting restraints on the power of rulers, however legitimate, seems to have been completely overlooked until the Middle Ages—or, perhaps, not entirely overlooked since there was some notion of the Church's acting as a check on the inordinacies of the State. In any case, the groundwork of the Christian understanding of the State, its nature and its limits, was firmly laid.

II

This conception, however, did not fully satisfy Thomas Aquinas in the thirteenth century. He was engaged in a massive enterprise of reconciling, by proper distinction and redefinition, the philosophical and the Christian traditions: Aristotle with Augustine, Augustine with Aristotle. And so he revived the Greek doctrine of the State "by nature," while retaining the Pauline-patristic teaching of the State as an order of preservation made necessary by sin. Thomas effected this reconciliation by an acute distinction. There are two kinds of subjection of man to man, he said. The first is *subjectio civilis,* civil subjection, the kind made necessary by the very nature of civil society, in which the various positions and tasks would require some sort of public authority for their allocation, even if every citizen were a saint: this kind of subjection is "by nature" and is presumably the kind Aristotle had in mind in his book on politics. On the other hand, men are obviously and emphatically not all saints, they are sinners who act out of sinful self-aggrandizement and have to be curbed in their evil-doing. Here the subjection is *subjectio servilis,* servile subjection, the kind Augustine had in mind. Hence, therefore, the State is both by nature and by sin.

The tenability of this appealing synthesis has been much argued. For our purposes, however, no conclusion on this question is necessary. What is necessary—most emphatically necessary—is to note that, for all his desire for reconciliation, Thomas brought out even more clearly the fundamental points of difference between the Greek and biblical views. Although Aristotle did not, and could not, distinguish between society and State, Thomas could and did: he expanded Aristotle's characterization of man as *zoön phusei politkon* ("by nature a political animal") into *animal naturaliter sociale et politicum* ("by nature an animal social and political"), thus making the vital and far-reaching distinction between society and State. But of even more importance, of really fundamental importance as Jacques Maritain has pointed out, is Thomas' emphasis on the transcendence of the human person beyond all social collectivities and institutions, beyond society itself. Consider these two texts:

Every individual person is related to the entire community as part to whole. (*Summa Theologica*, II-II, qu. 64, art. 2.)

Man is not ordained to the body politic according to all that he is and has. (*S. Th.*, I-II, qu. 21, art. 4, ed. 3.)

Here we have the first clear and explicit challenge to totalitarianism. Although by nature part of civil society, the individual person is not to be swallowed up whole in society or the State. On the contrary, by virtue of certain aspects of his being—what Kierkegaard was later to call his "God-relationship"—man as such is elevated above political society and the social order. It is man's ordination to the divine that thus raises him above everything social and political that would totally engulf him. Who denies this denies both God and man.

Not only does St. Thomas make explicit the Christian rejection of totalitarianism, which is radical and uncompromising, he also makes quite plain the meaning of legitimate and illegitimate government. Government is instituted by God, but the divine ordination may operate through a variety of ways and institutions, all the way from dynastic succession to popular elections. The ruler must remember that he is there to keep order, dispense justice, and maintain the law, which it is his to make only to a very limited degree. The ruler must be careful that his actions are neither *contra legem Dei*, against the law of God, nor *ultra vires*, beyond his proper powers as these are defined by natural and public law, by custom, tradition, charter, coronation oath, and the like. If he avoids violating the divine law and keeps within what may now be properly called the constitutional limits of his power as publicly defined, he is a legitimate ruler, entitled to honor and obedience without qualification. But, if he deliberately, systematically, and incorrigibly insists on violating the divine law and running beyond his constitutional powers, he becomes an illegitimate ruler, a tyrant. And against tyrants in the last resort St. Thomas, as is well known, allows rebellion (on the part of the magnates of the community) and even tyrannicide. With St. Thomas, the Christian doctrine of legitimate government against tyranny is well established. The Reformers did not go beyond him. Both Luther and Calvin called for unqualified obedience to constituted authority, so long as it remained legitimate in the biblical-Augustinian sense. Both permitted resistance when the ruler went *contra legem Dei*; both required that this resistance be passive, leading to martyrdom, though both allowed a loophole, subsequently enlarged (by the Calvinists) along Thomist lines to permit armed rebellion and tyrannicide. One more point, though: Calvin's keen sense of the involutions of sin as *libido dominandi* led him to make an explicit argument in favor of republicanism or government by committee against government by the will of a single ruler:

> The vice or imperfection of man, therefore, renders it safer and more tolerable for the government to be in the hands of many, that they may afford each other mutual assistance and admonition, and that, if anyone arrogate to himself more than is right, the others may act as censors and masters to restrain his ambitions. (*Institutes*, IV, xx, viii.)

III

Direct and conscious confrontation with totalitarianism did not arise for the mass of Christians in Western Europe and America, and for the Church as such, until the appearance of naziism as a massive power on the continent of Europe. In both Soviet Russia and fascist Italy totalitarianism had emerged earlier, but it emerged slowly, and concern over it was pushed to the background by excitement over other aspects of the new regimes (such as the atheism of Soviet communism and Mussolini's imperialist adventures in Africa). Indeed, in Germany itself it was not until 1935 that even Karl Barth came to realize that the nazi State was not a State in the sense of

Romans 13, legitimate, to be prayed for even if unfortunately harassing the Church and acting with painful injustice in many ways. In fairness, however, it must be noted that it was largely the writings of Karl Barth in the years that followed that revealed the inner nature of totalitarianism and its demonic character from the Christian standpoint—though Barth's strange reversal at the end of the war, when it became a matter of communism rather than naziism, has no doubt been a major factor making for confusion and demoralization in Christian ranks throughout the world.

What is it that characterizes totalitarianism as a special kind of State, a State radically different from the State designated as legitimate in the tradition of Paul, Augustine, and Thomas?

1. The totalitarian State by its very nature recognizes no majesty beyond itself; it exalts itself as its own highest majesty, its own god, and demands to be "worshiped" as such. In short, it demands for itself what is owing only to God: worship and absolute devotion.

2. The totalitarian State, in line with its own self-absolutization, claims jurisdiction over all life, public and private, and over every aspect of life. "Everything in the State, and through the State; nothing outside the State." In principle, the State swallows up society, State and society swallow up the individual person; in practice, every device of modern mass control is employed to implement the totalitarian claim. Nothing outside the State, nothing voluntary or private can be tolerated.

3. The totalitarian State refuses to recognize in man any dimension of his being or doing that carries him beyond the totalitarianized social order. To claim such a dimension of being is regarded, and quite logically in its own terms, as the most radical challenge, not merely to the regime, but also to the totalitarian idea and system as such.

Such is totalitarianism in its essence. It is not merely an oppressive regime. Indeed, in principle it does not have to be particularly oppressive at all—at least not to large sections of the population. What is involved is something much more fundamental. The old-fashioned despot demanded obedience, taxes, and manpower for his armies. The totalitarian regime wants much more: "It's your souls they want," as someone once put it, referring to the Nazis. It is total possession of the whole man totalitarians want. And they will brook no rivals in engaging man's loyalties, hopes, and affections. Totalitarian rulers will sometimes tolerate less than they demand in principle, but this "moderation" is only temporary, awaiting more favorable conditions. A real abatement of their total claims is not to be expected.

It needs no extended argument to show that the totalitarian State, thus described in its essence, is the contemporary embodiment of the *illegitimate* State pictured in Revelation 13 and further defined by Augustine and Thomas. It deifies and exalts itself; it demands a quasi-religious commitment on the part of its subjects; it runs constantly *contra legem Dei,* and it operates systematically *ultra vires,* beyond the inherent constitutional limits of States; and, finally, it refuses to recognize, and strives incessantly to destroy, man's personal being and his God-relationship.

But we cannot leave it at that. Every established order, every society, and every political system has its inner totalitarian strivings. Sören Kierkegaard, himself a thoroughgoing political conservative, was among the first to see this. Over a century and a quarter ago, he pronounced these impassioned words:

> The deification of the established order is the secularization of everything . . . In the end, one secularizes also the God-relationship . . . [This God-relationship] must be, for individual man, the absolute; and it is precisely this God-relationship of the individual that puts every established order into question. The established order refuses to entertain the notion that it might consist of . . . so loose an aggregation of individuals, each of whom severally has his own God-relationship. The established order desires to be totalitarian, recognizing nothing above it, but having every individual under it, and judging every individual who is integrated in it . . .[2]

"Every established order desires to be totalitarian," exalting itself and demanding everything. But there is a difference: the legitimate state, especially the modern constitutional state, possesses built-in institutions and traditions of resistance to these totalitarian "desires" and strivings; the totalitarian State is the very political embodiment of these totalitarian potentials and lives only to promote and realize them.

IV

On the basis of this analysis, what should be the Christian attitude to totalitarianism, the totalitarian State, and the actual totalitarian regimes in operation today? Certain points deserve particular emphasis.

1. Since the totalitarian State is so obviously the diabolical State of Revelations 13, the illegitimate State of Christian tradition, the Christian as a Christian owes it no allegiance, support, or obedience whatever; on the contrary, the Christian as a Christian stands in radical opposition to the totalitarian State and all its works, for the totalitarian State is, in fact, an instrument of the devil against mankind. It is war without possibility of compromise.

Many Christians find it hard to understand or go along with this notion. Some Christian leaders have even allowed themselves to become so bemused with the idea of "socialism" as a kind of wave of the future and with the "liberal" delusion that the "enemy is always on the Right" that they cannot see the flagrantly totalitarian character of the Soviet, Soviet Zone German, Chinese, and other communist regimes and tend to adopt attitudes running from friendly "neutralism" and "critical cooperation" to outright support. Without further elaboration, it can be predicted that this betrayal of the Church will not, in the end, pass away entirely unrequited.

But for large numbers of Christians these considerations are not the ones that make them so embarrassed when it is pointed out that intransigent opposition to totalitarianism is the truly Christian attitude. The fact is that many Christians, especially on the Continent, have been so habituated to the Pauline doctrine of Romans 13 that opposition to government, let alone such intransigent opposition, is entirely out of their field of vision. They cannot conceive that something like it might become their Christian duty. They cannot see that totalitarian government is a very different kind of thing, a diabolical thing, a device of the devil. We are paying for the superficial, unreal, even plainly misleading political education of the Church in recent decades and centuries.

2. This radical opposition to totalitarianism as the work of the devil does not itself entail public disobedience or outright rebellion at every point. It does entail a total inner withdrawal of allegiance and obedience. But let us not forget that, along with this inner posture of radical opposition, there are considerations of prudence and worldly responsibility that cannot be ignored. Revolution against the totalitarian State in principle is always justified in the Christian conscience. But the actual translation from principle to action must depend on a careful and realistic assessment of the situation. It is impractical to lay down rules. Sometimes a demonstrative action without much hope of success may be in place. But sometimes, too,

prudence may have to be carried to a far point indeed. All this must necessarily be left to the conscience and good sense of those who live and suffer under totalitarianism.

3. There is still another consideration of far-ranging importance. The primary function of the State, it will be recalled, is to curb evil-doers and assure the community's security and justice. The totalitarian State is prone to pervert even this elementary function, politicalizing its justice and converting the security it affords into a weapon of State control. But in totalitarian countries, as in all others, the elementary preservative services must be carried out or else the society itself would go under. Fires must be put out, traffic must be regulated, theft, burglary, and nonpolitical crimes of violence must be suppressed, and so on. It seems obvious that responsible inhabitants of a totalitarian country, no matter how uncompromising their opposition to the State, would have to give some support to the activities of the State in these elementary preservative areas.

Augustine somewhere speaks of a man held captive for ransom by a robber band and therefore obliged to live in the robber community for months, perhaps for years. Clearly he will feel it necessary and proper to support the efforts of the bandit leaders to maintain order in the bandit community, preventing violence, fighting fires, dispensing its very limited and partial kind of justice ("Even a robber band has its justice," as Plato pointed out). The captive will do this without in the least recognizing the legitimacy of the bandit government, or abdicating his right to escape if possible or to help destroy the entire bandit enterprise should circumstances prove favorable. This kind of "cooperation," if "cooperation" it can be called, is very different from the cooperation offered by many radical Christians to totalitarian regimes. The cooperation they offer in Soviet Zone Germany, for instance, is to help build "socialism," the name given to the State-controlled economies of such countries. In the one case, the totalitarian program is being supported and promoted; in the other, it is only those activities of the State without which it would be impossible to live that come into consideration.

These conclusions are not particularly sensational, nor are they intended to be. They are simply some of the more obvious conclusions to be drawn from the fundamental Christian understanding of the State, the legitimate State of Romans 13, and the illegitimate, self-deifying State of Revelation 13. The principle may be summarized in this way:

The legitimate State of Romans 13 (whether democratic or not) the Christian acknowledges as a divine order and is bound in conscience to obey unless it commands what is *contra legem Dei,* against the law of God. On the other hand, the illegitimate State depicted in Revelation 13—in our time, the totalitarian State—must be denied the allegiance and support of the Christian, and there is no obligation in conscience to obey it, though in its elementary preservative functions the Christian can support it without commitment.

It need hardly be pointed out that we must not fall into the egregious error of identifying the legitimate State with the democratic State. The legitimate State is not identifiable with any particular system and can find expression in any one of a variety of regimes, provided it meets the requirements described. The absolute monarchy of the eighteenth century was certainly not democratic, but it was quite legitimate in the proper sense: (1) it recognized a higher majesty beyond itself; (2) it did not claim total jurisdiction over all of life, many areas being left, in theory and in practice, to institutions and agencies outside the State and to the individual himself; (3) it never questioned the reality of the God-relationship that raises the individual human being above every social order, including the absolute monarch's own political order; and (4) it acknowledged the preservative function of the State and fulfilled it with not inconsiderable success. There are self-styled democracies that have not met, and do not meet, these requirements. So let us therefore keep clearly in mind what we really mean when we speak of legitimate and illegitimate States.

In the last analysis, the struggle against totalitarianism and the totalitarian State is, for the Christian, a religious struggle, a struggle for men's souls, for the totalitarian State is not simply a political institution. It is, as Karl Barth saw so clearly when naziism was in the foreground, an "anti-Christian counter-church," making an "inward claim," and "demanding the adoption of a particular philosophy of life" utterly opposed to Christianity. With this kind of State no Christian who is serious about his faith can make his peace.

NOTES TO CHAPTER NINE

1. Hajo Holborn, "Greek and Modern Concepts of History," *Journal of the History of Ideas,* Vol. X, No. 1 (January, 1940).

2. Sören Kierkegaard, *Training in Christianity* (Princeton: 1951), p. 92.

CHAPTER X

The Church Under Totalitarian Rule

BISHOP PAOLO HNILICA, S. J.

THE HISTORY of religious institutions under communist rule is too broad and too differentiated to be treated adequately in a single chapter. This presentation is therefore limited to Czechoslovakia, the country in which this writer acquired his own experience with totalitarianism. What has happened to the Roman Catholic Church in Czechoslovakia since 1945 is, however, in many ways typical of its treatment under communist regimes in other countries.

To understand the present situation of the Church in Czechoslovakia it is necessary to take note of developments over the entire period between 1945 and 1966. It is possible to distinguish a succession of phases during this period, both in Church-state relations, and in the life of the faithful. The limited scope of this presentation does not permit detailed analysis of these phases, which will be found in specialized literature on the subject. We limit ourselves here to comparing the situation of the Church in Czechoslovakia while it was still free with the present state of affairs and to analyzing the more important laws and administrative measures under which the Church has to operate.

Even a brief description of the measures taken by communist regimes in the field of religion, however, indicates clearly their objective of slowly but systematically stamping out both the institutions and the life of the Church. The guidance given by Lenin on this score is as follows: "We must fight against religion. The battle against religion is the A B C of all materialism and hence of Marxism as well. Marxism is not, however, a materialism that stops at A B C; it goes further and calls for knowledge of the way to fight religion. To acquire such knowledge, it is necessary to interpret materialistically the roots of belief and religion in the masses." Lenin writes elsewhere: "To accomplish the radical destruction of religion it is necessary to attack it from within, by provoking disunity and schisms among the faithful, and by sowing confusion, doubt, and uncertainty among them, so that they finally lose their faith." To achieve this end, Lenin writes in still another passage, it is necessary to organize "a methodical, persistent, purposive and patient propaganda and agitation campaign—within the institutions of society and in those organizations, even the most reactionary, where proletarian or semiproletarian masses are always to be found."

The present situation of the Church in Czechoslovakia is the result of a comprehensive plan that has been executed with rigorous logic. But while the entire program has been based upon deep hostility toward the Church and every religion, the tactics employed in Bohemia and Moravia were quite different from those utilized in Slovakia.

The present situation of the Church in the CSSR (Czechoslovak Socialist Republic) is the consequence of an unsuccessful attempt by the government to exploit and destroy the Church for purely political purposes. The Catholic Church, however, which was more influential and better organized than other religious bodies, refused to yield to subjugation by the worldly power. As the price of resistance the Church had to suffer hostility, oppression, and finally persecution by the state.

Several phases of this development can be distinguished. These, each with its particular characteristics and each masquerading under the nomenclature of "Church-state relations," are all steps in an inexorable campaign to wipe out the Church and its influence on the lives and consciences of the peoples of Czechoslovakia.

THE FIRST PHASE: RELATIVE FREEDOM (1945–1948)

The situation of the Church under the National Front government prior to the "February Revolution" may be briefly described as follows:

Covering an area of 127,860 square kilometers and divided into three administrative districts—Bohemia, Moravia and Silesia, and Slovakia (the latter with its own autonomous statute)—and embracing a population of 12,164,000 (1948), the Catholic Church, with its 9,300,000 members, constituted an important and respected power. Although it had undergone severe trials during the war, particularly in Bohemia and Moravia, its organization remained highly effective. Developments in Bohemia and Moravia were, however, different from those in Slovakia.

The entire CSSR contains 13 dioceses and three Apostolic administrations with 18 bishops, of whom nine work in Slovakia. As of 1948 the Catholic Church had 10,475 churches and chapels in 4,568 parishes and 5,845 diocesan priests. The seminaries contained 887 theological students, of whom 148 were ordained as priests in 1948. There were 248 monasteries housing 2,193 male members of religious orders, including 1,197 priests and 450 theology students. The 10,451 sisters of the various orders lived in 720 convents and administered 595 charitable institutions.

The work of the Church was carried forward very actively in Catholic schools. Of the 2,500 elementary schools and 340,000 pupils in Slovakia, for instance, 1,800 schools and 250,000 pupils were Catholic. These schools were operated by 4,000 Catholic teachers, primarily laymen. Of the 110 intermediate schools 25 belonged to the Church, so that of the approximately 460,000 students and pupils in Slovakia 275,000 or almost 60 per cent attended Catholic schools. Another flourishing area of Church activity was the Catholic press, including not only newspapers and magazines but also various publishing houses. In Slovakia alone there were one daily and four weekly Catholic papers, and 30 monthly magazines with an annual circulation of 20,500,000 copies.

Such a scale of activity could not fail to impress a party that understood the power of organization. After the seizure of power the government adopted an ambiguous position toward the Church. On the one hand, it declared publicly that it had no intention of intervening in Church affairs; on the other, it proceeded without delay to adopt measures demonstrating clearly its hostility toward the Church as well as its firm intention of destroying religion. The latter objective could not, of course, be realized with one blow. The initial policy of the government was therefore directed at subjugating the Church so that it could be used to buttress the regime. Atheism remained, however, the final objective.

The Church refused to make propaganda for the communist regime. The other churches—that is, the Protestants, the Orthodox Church, and the "Czechoslovak" Church, with a combined membership of 1,800,000—submitted to the state and hailed the communist regime as the standard-bearer of progress and prosperity.

ANTI-CHURCH MEASURES AFTER THE COMMUNIST SEIZURE OF POWER

After seizing power on February 25, 1948, the Communists at first attempted to secure the support of the Catholic Church for the new government. The Church was promised freedom of organization in ecclesiastical affairs on the basis of religious freedom. But the very first measures of the new government violated its promise: all the more influential Catholic newspapers and magazines, for instance, were suppressed on February 26, 1948—after the Communists had been in power exactly one day!

Most properties were taken over by the state under Law No. 46/1948. Law No. 218/1948 placed the entire property of the Church under the direct control of the state. Under Decree No. 260/20-3-5/ 5-1949-VB/52 contributions and collections were made subject to state control. All private support of priests was made impossible. They were made entirely dependent upon the state.

All Catholic printing plants were seized by the state and the printing of magazines was forbidden. A single exception was made for the weekly magazine *Katolicke noviny* (*Catholic News*) in the Slovak and Czech languages, but the edition was arbitrarily reduced by 80 per cent. Both editorial offices were "purged" and placed under the supervision of editors-in-chief appointed by the state. This state of affairs has now lasted for 18 years. Only three books could be printed during this period: the Old and New Testaments, a prayer book, and the catechism—all in very small editions.

In Slovakia all Catholic schools were taken over by the state and their property confiscated as early as 1944, the pertinent legislation being Laws 5/1944 and 34/1945. The same took place in Bohemia and Moravia in 1948 under Law No. 95/1948. Religious instruction was not eliminated immediately from the elementary schools, but it was forbidden in intermediate and higher schools by Law No. 31/1952. In the seven grades of the elementary school where such instruction remains, it can only be given after regular school hours.

Both parents must sign a request that their child attend the religious classes. All kinds of measures of intimidation and deceit are used by the administration to prevent attendance at the classes, with the result that the majority of children stay away from the religious instruction. Only persons authorized by the state may give religious instruction, and then only in the presence of a teacher who frequently interrupts with contradictions. In 1958, 58.5 per cent of the children were still registered for religious instruction, but this percentage had dropped to 35 in 1962. These children are to be found almost entirely in rural districts; religious instruction has all but disappeared in the cities.

In December, 1948, the national office of Catholic Action was closed and its directors imprisoned. By a decree of the Ministry of Interior dated February 1, 1949, all youth meetings whatever off church premises were forbidden. A further ministerial decree dated May 9, 1949, prohibited any meeting whatever without previous permission by the state authority. Contacts with young people, who are entirely caught up in the net of communist propaganda, have become difficult if not impossible. The local cells of the party are required to conduct cultural events for youth at exactly the same hours that religious services take place. Young people who attend church are persecuted and excluded from higher educational institutions.

An intensive program of communist reeducation for university students was also launched after the 1948 coup. All ideas that conflicted with atheist and materialist doctrines and that were potential obstacles to their acceptance were rigorously banished from the curriculum: ideas in the fields of faith, tradition, culture, and even science. Each individual had to be reborn as atheist Man to fulfill Lenin's demand for new people with whom to build a new society. To form these new people the best pedagogues were enlisted—many from Russia. At no time in history has a system devoted such energy and effort to the creation of a new society as has the communist system.

HOW THE COMMUNIST REGIME ENSLAVES THE CHURCH

The Communists make decisions in Church affairs without first negotiating with the Church. They do not desire the separation of state and Church, since that might involve freedom for the latter.

On the contrary, they employ a variety of administrative measures to make the Church totally dependent upon the state. Through a number of devices, they distort the organic structure of the Church for the purpose of destroying it.

One of these devices was the State Bureau for Ecclesiastical Affairs which was headed by a minister and established by Law No. 271 of October 14, 1949. A subsequent decree provided it with regional and district offices which were directed "to regulate religious life in accordance with the principles of people's democracy." Their true purpose, however, was always to destroy the structures of the Church.

The entire life of the Church is regulated by state Law No. 218/ 1949 and by decrees issued thereunder (219-223/1949). The clergy, including the bishops, must obtain state permission for any exercise of pastoral functions. Transfers of priests are for practical purposes controlled by the state office, to which the churches must account for their movable property. Priests who support the government are offered much better pay than they received in the past.

In order to destroy the unity of clergy and faithful with the hierarchy—since the latter had refused to submit to the communist regime—the "ecclesiastical offices" summoned to Prague 17 priests whom they considered favorably disposed toward the regime and 800 laymen chosen by the Communist party. This was done with the excuse that negotiations with the state had broken down through the fault of the hierarchy. In this assembly a so-called Catholic Action manifesto was read on June 10, 1949, in which these "representatives" of the Church declared—in opposition to the bishops—that they were "assuming charge of the peaceful development of relations between the Catholic Church and the state." This manifesto of the schismatic Catholic Action was then presented for signature to Catholics in organized meetings in factories and other locations. The intention was clear: the establishment of a procommunist and therefore schismatic church. On June 15, 1949, the bishops joined in conference and issued a pastoral letter that put a rapid end to this attempt. There followed a period of bloody persecution. But the attack against the Church had failed; the unity between the faithful and the hierarchy was not destroyed.

Parallel attacks were made against the Holy See, with which diplomatic relations were broken off. In March, 1950, the last chargé d'affaires of the Papal Nunciature was expelled and the Nunciature closed. The bishops, the vicars-general, and all other employees of the Curia who had not submitted were either imprisoned or interned *in situ*. In total violation of law, so-called patriotic priests and lay commissars—the latter almost exclusively atheists—were appointed and took full control of Church affairs. Propaganda trials on charges of "espionage connections with the Nunciature in Prague" were set in motion against a number of selected priests, against the heads of religious orders, and against a number of bishops. The trials took place in April and November, 1950, and in January, 1951.

All male members of religious orders were removed from their monasteries during the night following April 13, 1950, and all religious sisters forced to leave their convents in August of that year. They were transported to "concentration cloisters," where they were guarded by armed police. After a while the youngest members were released, but others were sentenced to varying terms of hard labor in a series of trials.

The writer remembers vividly his own experience on the night of April 13, 1950, at which time he was living in a monastery having nearly completed his studies for the priesthood. He and his two roommates were awakened at midnight by heavy blows on the door. Three policemen entered the room and gave the order for immediate departure. In the buses that were waiting outside each seminarian was accompanied by his own "guardian angel," armed with a machine gun.

In the concentration camp, where the writer remained for many months, the life was one of hunger, hard work, inhuman treatment, and—worst of all—intense cold. It was often impossible to sleep for lack of blankets. But the worst material privations were easier to endure than the spiritual martyrdom to which the 700 inmates who belonged to religious orders—priests and seminarians—were daily subjected. They were required to listen in silence to ridicule and insults heaped upon their most sacred values: God, Christ, the creed, the Church, religious superiors, and many more. Those who had dedicated themselves to love and truth were forced to live in an atmosphere of hate and falsehood, against which any protest was forbidden. They had been torn from the masses of the faithful and from the apostolic work which alone gave meaning to their lives.

It is hard to describe the reactions of human beings forced to endure such an unnatural life. In such a situation of pain and futility the individual must find rational meaning in his experience if he is to survive as a personality. The meaning discovered by the imprisoned clergy of Czechoslovakia was that their religious mission for the time being was not to preach or work miracles, but to suffer and die for humanity, to bear witness in a godless age by joining the suffering Christ on the cross. As St. Paul once said, "I must complete by my suffering whatever is lacking in the suffering of Christ." The smuggled writings of priests and monks sentenced to hard labor indicate that most have achieved a new serenity while some have found a new field of missionary activity in the camps and factories, even among the guards and overseers.

Along with the arrests of priests and monks, over 10,000 Czech and Slovak nuns were torn from their duties in schools and hospitals and quartered in factory buildings that serve as concentration camps. "Our sisters are collapsing physically," a typical letter states. "The causes are irregular meals and disturbed sleep. One group leaves for work in the morning and returns at three in the afternoon. Another group works from one to ten A.M., while the third begins at ten P.M. and returns at six in the morning. We live in a factory hall with forty-four beds, but it is impossible to sleep with sisters coming and going the entire night." Working conditions, especially in the textile mills, have led to a high morbidity, and even the communist press has admitted that one-half the nuns have contracted tuberculosis. As in the case of the priests, however, the nuns have achieved new religious experience in self-denial and sacrifice.

The Eastern Rite Catholic Church was liquidated on April 28, 1950, at a "Congress of Greek Catholics" at Presov, Slovakia. At this assembly a number of delegates sent by the Communist party declared for "return to the Mother Orthodox Church." After a great deal of unpleasant argument approximately 30 priests subscribed to the Declaration of Presov. Two bishops were arrested, and about 80 priests were either imprisoned or taken away and put to forced labor.

All but two of the Roman Catholic seminaries, with a total of 1,275 theology students, were closed. Even the two permitted to continue in operation, at Prague and Bratislava, were taken over by the state (Decree No. 112/1950 of July 14). The seminarians were advised to apply to Bratislava and Prague seminaries, but only a few were admitted. Under the pretext of military service the others were forced to perform various tasks for periods of seven to ten years. It was later discovered that the instruction in the seminaries is truly Catholic, even though rather mediocre in quality. The state controls the instruction and admissions, and determines the number of theologians under a *numerus clausus*.

Statistically, the results of this phase of the antireligious struggle were as follows: of the bishops, eight were imprisoned, six prevented from exercising their office, and five remained in office but were subject to detailed scrutiny and control. Of the 7,042 diocesan and regular priests, 2,000 were imprisoned. A total of 10,451 religious sisters were imprisoned or sentenced to forced labor, with a few serving as nurses for infectious diseases or abnormal children.

THE PRESENT SITUATION: RELAXATION OF PERSECUTION

The period of open and brutal persecution of the Church has been followed by a gradual relaxation, which became noticeable in 1960 and 1961. It is not possible to state categorically the causes of this phenomenon, but there are a number of probable reasons for this shift in Church policy behind the Iron Curtain: the Second Vatican Council, the popularity of Pope John XXIII throughout the world, and the end of Stalinism. Amid the reaction against the so-called personality cult and in the climate of dialogue that became prevalent after 1953, it was difficult to continue the use of methods identified as Stalinist. This was true with respect to all oppositional ideologies, including that of the Church.

There is also an economic factor. The opening of borders to tourists and the increasing travel of East European citizens abroad made possible economic comparisons between the two worlds and forced the communist rulers to pay more attention to economic questions. Ideological problems were relegated to second place. In Czechoslovakia, moreover, the communist rulers believe that they have accomplished their intention; they believe they have brought the Catholic Church so thoroughly under state control that it no longer presents any serious danger to the state ideology. One communist leader recently declared that the day of the Church's death could be calculated.

The laws concerning the Church and its activity are so well thought out that they eliminate every Church influence over the people—or so it seems. Although certain general laws have been amended and many of the communist leaders condemned during the epoch of the "personality cult" rehabilitated, nothing has been done for the bishops, priests, and Catholic laymen convicted under the same laws during the same period. The laws pertaining to the Catholic Church have not been amended. Although there has been much talk of abuse of administrative powers, no public measures have been taken to change the situation. The same paragraphs are still in force; the same methods are still employed.

While attendance at services remains satisfactory, the Church is prevented from conducting direct and free missionary work. Masses may be celebrated only by priests recognized by the state, and only in state-recognized churches. Outside the elementary school religious instruction may not be imparted outside the churches, and inside them it may not be given in the form of the catechism for children. Catholic organizations no longer exist. The Church has no access to the radio, to television, or to motion pictures.

There are no Catholic publishing houses. The only books published are the three mentioned earlier and occasional publications licensed following advance censorship. Religious newspapers and magazines account for only 0.32 per cent of the total press in the CSSR. Of a total annual production of 5,200,000 copies of "religious" periodicals, approximately 2,000,000 actually reach the hands of Catholics. This means that among the 10,200,000 Catholics in the CSSR the average individual can buy a Catholic magazine only once every four years. Even then, he obtains a periodical of only four pages, which are written by persons loyal to the regime and consist mostly of "peace" propaganda.

The individual Catholic is able to purchase a book with a religious content only once every thirty years, since the government holds the editions down to that level. The shortage of religious books is such that Catholics have taken to digging up graves to retrieve missals and prayer books from the hands of the dead. One Christmas a typical pastor received a shipment of six books for a parish of five thousand. For this reason Catholics behind the Iron Curtain are particularly dependent on Western broadcasting stations such as Radio Vatican, to which they have addressed repeated appeals.

BISHOPS AND PRIESTS

There are only four bishops left to serve the thirteen dioceses and three Apostolic administrations. The prelates are subject to slightly more moderate supervision than formerly and are permitted to travel to Rome. Their official acts, however, must be confirmed by the Ministry of Education, which has replaced the Office for Ecclesiastical

Affairs. Priests are transferred by the same office; all the bishop does is sign the decree. In many dioceses capitular vicars have been appointed under the direct or indirect influence of the communist regime, a practice injurious to the Church.

There are far too few priests for the parishes, and their number continually grows smaller. On average 70 priests die each year; there are only 20 to 30 new priests to replace them. The average age of priests is now approximately 58 years. Old priests are required to retire on pension, and those remaining have insufficient energy to manage two or more parishes at once. More than 50 pastoral positions thus become vacant each year.

Priests belonging to religious orders have been denied permission to engage in pastoral work (including the celebration of Mass in a public church)—the orders themselves having been dissolved in 1950. These priests are denied the protection of the law and are employed for manual labor only. Approximately 900 have been forced to work in mines, as have been 400 to 500 diocesan priests who were imprisoned earlier and have not yet been rehabilitated.

The zeal of parish priests is assessed by state officials according to the number of baptisms, funerals, church weddings, and liturgical ceremonies, the number attending church, the acolytes, the children receiving religious instruction, the number taking communion (with rationed wafers), and so forth. Should these statistics show a priest to be too zealous and therefore dangerous, he is shunted from place to place until he becomes tired or lands in a place where he can accomplish nothing.

As a substitute for the ill-starred "patriotic priests" movement the government started a "clerical peace movement," which attempts to intervene in Church administration. Some of the priests who belong to the "peace movement" serve the government to varying degrees, and the government utilizes these priests in its fights against the bishops. It is safe to say that 50 per cent of the priests remain true to the Church. Another 25 per cent are good in some respects but permit themselves to be influenced by the state on many subjects. Approximately 15 per cent obey the state willingly, but only a very few work exclusively for the government.

Approximately 120 theological students are presently studying at the two remaining seminaries. There has been strong pressure not to exceed the *numerus clausus* in recent years. Admission is in practice dependent on the recommendations of the communist authorities.

Truly gifted candidates, especially when they come from good Catholic families, are as a rule denied admission.

Contact with youth becomes less and less possible. Religious instruction—in practice restricted to rural villages—is limited to the schools, and even there it is subject to state control and official discouragement. No catechism classes for children are permitted in the church. A priest who entered a camping place with acolytes was deprived of his license for pastoral work for two years and compelled to work as a mason.

ANTIRELIGIOUS PROPAGANDA

Militant atheism does not confine itself to fighting the Church, but conducts a comprehensive program of antireligious propaganda. This propaganda is especially directed toward young people in the schools, but it is also conducted in factories, through books—approximately 1,000 antireligious books and pamphlets appear each year with editions running into the millions—and through courses and conferences for all levels of society.

THE UNDERGROUND CHURCH

The ideological corruption of the official Church and the continued persecution of clergy and laymen who oppose a procommunist orientation of religion have created the environment in which an underground Church—a new Church of the catacombs—has emerged and is expanding its secret apostolate. After the writer's release from concentration camp, he found a bishop who agreed to ordain him secretly to the priesthood. The place of ordination was a hospital, and the writer was forced to extract from between the inner and outer soles of his shoe the document testifying to his theological studies. After the ordination he telegraphed to other seminarians: "Operation successful, patient can receive visitors." This was a signal that they, too, could be ordained.

Three months later, the writer was consecrated secretly as a bishop. The simple service, without the usual ornateness and ceremony, took place in the cellar by the light of two candles. The consecrating bishop, who like the writer was dressed in civilian clothes, spoke a word of warning: "What we are doing today is not a matter of fame and honor. Instead, consecration as a bishop means consecration to martyrdom." Needless to say, the writer felt totally inadequate for his task and was sustained only by the conviction that God had decided to work through him.

The most moving and significant activity of an underground bishop is the consecration of new priests. This ceremony is conducted without the superficial pomp usual in the West, in the utmost simplicity and secrecy in a forest or hospital. The candidates are all employed as workers and have prepared themselves for the priesthood in their free time. Their enthusiasm and their determination to fulfill their vocations, even at the cost of martyrdom, have often lifted the writer from his own feelings of depression. The underground priests must continue their labors in the factories and mines and must fulfill their mission in what for a Westerner is a totally unaccustomed frame of reference.

CONCLUSION

The effects of the antireligious campaign can be read from the official statistics concerning the religious beliefs of the population. Thirty-five per cent classify themselves as devout believers, 45 per cent as indifferent believers, and 20 per cent as atheists.

The official press speaks of a revival of religious life, particularly in those strata of the population that were directly persecuted or were victims of religious discrimination. The communist leaders, however, see the situation as follows:

1. Communism anticipates no further difficulty from the Church as an institution. The measures to destroy it have achieved their goal.

2. Atheist ideology has not proved capable of winning the people. On the contrary, methods that were often brutal and seldom convincing have contributed to deepening the religious faith of the people and making it more resistant to the pressure of atheism.

3. Atheist propaganda has produced a vacuum in the souls of young people. A considerable number of young people who have gone through the complete curriculum of communist education eventually turn away from atheism.

4. Discrimination and favoritism have increased the number of "Communists without ideals." These have acquired bourgeois atti-

tudes to such a degree that they are incapable of winning Christians and young people for atheism.

For these reasons the communist ideologues are demanding new methods of persecution:

1. The Church is to be made to die of suffocation, which will be accomplished by denying it all means of sustenance, such as books, a press, communication through live media, and so forth.

2. Church members must be convinced that the Church has lost all meaning in life, that it lacks vital force, and that it is not capable of providing answers to modern problems. Priests write, in this connection, that the preparation in the seminaries is so sketchy that new priests are not qualified to give answers to the questions of young people, particularly those of students.

3. All media—including the radio, television, motion pictures, the press, and organizations—must be employed as instruments of atheist propaganda.

4. All strata of the population must be made the targets of personal and individual atheist agitation.

Part Three

Colloquium on Change in Eastern Europe

CHAPTER XI

Recent Developments
In East-Central Europe

A.   POSSIBILITIES AND LIMITATIONS OF EVOLUTION
—JERZY HAUPTMANN

SINCE THE FIRST SIGNS of change in the Soviet bloc appeared following Stalin's death in early 1953, many Westerners have been fascinated by the evolution supposedly taking place in that part of the world. Regarding change in Eastern Europe as automatic and inevitable, the "evolutionists" have watched passively. Sometimes helping "good" Communists, they have avoided too active a Western policy, which, it is feared, might slow developments. The critics of "evolutionism" claim that the policy of "being kind to the Gomulkas," which suffered its first setbacks in 1956, tends to strengthen communist rule and to discourage the anticommunist opposition. The attempt to "soften" the communist regimes in Eastern Europe, these critics contend, has turned out to be a means of stabilizing them.

In this symposium five specialists on specific countries have reported, in condensed form, the most significant political, economic, and social developments of recent years. The information has been selected for the purpose of enabling the critical reader to form his own judgment as to the correctness of the "evolutionist" and the contrary interpretations of recent events.

It cannot be denied that a large number of specific changes have taken place in the states behind the Iron Curtain. In determining whether these constitute evolution in the sense of interrelated changes leading to a structural mutation, the reader will want to evaluate the data in terms of a number of critical questions bearing on the economic, political, sociological, and cultural aspects of change.

In the economic field, note can be taken of reforms such as greater autonomy for individual enterprises and attempts to mobilize the price mechanism and consumer demand. New economic models have, however, remained within the framework of planned economy, even though the planning has been loosened somewhat. These new models excite great wonder among Western "evolutionists," who see in them the incipient liberalization of other aspects of political and social life—incidentally, itself a Marxist reaction, since it ascribes fundamental importance to economic phenomena. It must be asked, however, whether these new models will really work. Are there enough people in Eastern Europe interested in such reforms? To what extent will they be hampered by bureaucratic inertia and the power of the ruling party? And even if these reforms are successful in the economic field, what assurance do they hold that changes in other areas will follow?

A certain "liberalization" is discerned in politics, including a greater role for public opinion and even limited choice in elections. But are these "political rights" permanent? Are they indicative of a real intention to give the citizen a share in governmental decisions? Or are they only a safety valve for oppositional feelings? The new liberties have their limits: despite the additional candidates, those at the top of the list always win; certain subjects are never criticized in public; a censorship still controls criticism. Whether this development can lead to greater freedom remains very doubtful.

And how about the possibility of expressing *political ideas that present alternatives to communism?* The existence of additional parties in some East European states, such as the Polish Peasants' party or the Czech People's party, is often cited to show that the Communists desire no monopoly of power. Little can, however, be expected from these groups, which are franchised, tolerated, and exploited by the Communists and have little or no influence on political decisions. Anyone who suggests a genuine opposition, even in the evolutionists' darling, Yugoslavia, is quickly suppressed, as the cases of Djilas and Mihajlov have shown.

And to what extent have there been fundamental changes in *ideology?* Names such as Schaff and Kolakowski and their Czech and Hungarian colleagues are cited to show that the old, rigid Marxist communism is beginning to change and give way to a new, more humane Marxism. Such optimism forgets that communism still remains an expansionist ideology, which demands the whole world as well as the whole human being. This totalitarianism is nowadays camouflaged with pleasant words about ideals, alienation, and freedom for the oppressed. Although certain ideological changes have actually occurred, people forget in evaluating them that they hardly touch the core of Soviet Marxism. As Professor Bochenski has pointed out, such changes remain on the periphery of ideology—but the optimists still insist on discovering fundamental changes.

There must, it is urged, be changes taking place in the *communist parties* themselves. The succession of generations must bring more open-minded young people to power, and the circulation of elites, although not democratic, already shows signs of greater fluidity. The Novotnys, Kádárs, and Gomulkas, it is claimed, will have to give way to progressive Communists. But must developments continue in precisely this direction—have not our experiences with Khrushchev and Gomulka taught us just the opposite? If the Communists intend to stay in power, and there is every evidence that they do, they cannot simply watch the circulation of elites; they must control and limit it.

Optimists are fond of pointing to the field of culture, where new tendencies have indeed made themselves felt: in music, literature, art, and theater. Looking back over the period since 1945, however, it can be seen that similar cultural "thaws" have occurred in the past only to be terminated whenever the exigencies of party politics so required. Can this happen again? There are also limits to the degree of freedom a communist regime will permit, as Hungarian, Slovak, and other writers who have felt these limits can testify. Creative activity is still supervised, and those who overstep the limits must reckon with disciplinary action.

And how about the situation of religion? Until recently "progressive" Western circles hailed the exemplary coexistence of Church and state in Eastern Europe. We were told that the Communists had discontinued the oppression of the Church, and that relaxation was now the order of the day. Then came the Polish religious struggle—certainly not an isolated phenomenon. It is a matter of common knowledge that religious activity in Eastern Europe is strictly limited, that communism remains atheist, and that its fundamental dynamic compels it to remain hostile to all religion.

But have there been changes in foreign policy? In the field of foreign *economic* policy Rumania is always cited as a shining example. The Rumanians are said to have achieved greater mobility and to be pursuing their own road, at least in foreign trade. But have they really achieved such a change of course—do not the Eastern bloc and the Soviet Union still account for the bulk of their trade? Perhaps the so-called mobility is only an effort to improve Rumania's *relative* position with the Soviet bloc, with Western trade being used as a threat. Ties within the bloc are still strong; COMECON is still a reality, despite some modifications in integration policy.

In the field of foreign policy in general Mao's China, Tito's Yugoslavia, Gomulka's Poland and lately Ceausescu's Rumania are cited as examples of polycentrism and independence. It is difficult, however, to see what their "independent" policies actually are. If they do exist, are they not perhaps typical zigzag phenomena of communist policy? Here again there is a limit, described at the last conference in Chicago as the accordion theory of politics.

In the field of military policy various states are said to be attempting to loosen the Warsaw Pact system, following, perhaps, the example of General de Gaulle's NATO policy. It tends to be forgotten, however, that military policy is only one sector of foreign policy, that both the Warsaw Pact and NATO could be loosened without changing the basic relationships among the states concerned. The Soviet Union is in a position to enforce the military status quo, since it is an atomic power and its army divisions in the Soviet Occupation Zone of Germany are available for use as pincers against any satellite the military policy of which becomes too independent.

B.   CZECHOSLOVAKIA—HEINRICH KUHN

The question whether the communist system in Czechoslovakia has undergone changes in recent years calls for an examination of the immediate past. Until a few years ago the Prague regime was regarded as a "model pupil" of the Kremlin, prepared to conform abjectly with every shift in Moscow politics and tactics. But is this still true today?

Foreign Policy

The "main principle" of Czechoslovak foreign policy, the alliance with the Soviet Union and the socialist camp, has not changed since 1948, despite certain very recent nuances suggesting greater autonomy within the alliance. One of these nuances has been the opening of the state boundaries for unrestricted and state-promoted tourism and travel from West to East. This receptivity is a sign that Czechoslovakia is interested in the "normalization" of political as well as commercial relations with its Western neighbors.

Czechoslovak foreign policy between 1960 and 1964 concentrated on the establishment of contacts with the developing countries. Success in this undertaking promised to bring the Prague regime new prestige and importance within the socialist camp. Since 1964, however, such contacts have assumed secondary priority behind those with certain states of the Atlantic Alliance.

This shift of emphasis has led to the Czechoslovak government's concentrating on developing its contacts with Great Britain, Canada, France, Italy, and the Scandinavian states. The visits to Czechoslovakia of the then British Foreign Minister Michael Stewart and of his French colleague Couve de Murville made apparent a primary goal of Czechoslovak diplomacy: to isolate the German Federal Republic within its alliances and, by means of the threat of such isolation, to soften it for negotiations in which Prague can dictate its foreign policy demands. These demands are, in the order of priority:

First, recognition of the "GDR" as a second German state. The party leadership in Prague rates the potential dangers of German reunification as more serious than those of the "threat of revenge" against their own state. An example of this feeling is registered in an editorial published in *Rudé právo* on August 27, 1966, asserting that there would be no "peace boundary" following German reunification, but only a threatening "monster" endangering Poland as well as the CSSR.

Second, annulment of the Munich Agreement, if possible *ex tunc*—as though it had never existed. Such a step, Prague believes, would liquidate "West German irridentism" by eliminating its legal foundations.

These demands—simultaneously axioms—of Czechoslovak foreign policy are also the most important foreign policy goals of the "German Democratic Republic," the Polish People's Republic, and—at least for the time being—the Soviet Union. They amount to a recognition of the present status quo in the heart of Europe.

The Prague government also pursues two additional foreign policy goals of secondary importance:

Nullification of the "Berlin Clause"—an objective designed to maintain community of foreign policy with the Ulbricht regime in East Berlin.

Creation of an atom-free zone in a Central Europe that includes the "two German states," Czechoslovakia, and Poland.

This priority of diplomatic objectives indicates clearly that Czechoslovakia cannot possibly be interested in a loosening of its relations with the socialist camp at the present time.

The Propaganda Role of the "German Question"

For the masses in Czechoslovakia, every event on the international scene—from the Vietnam war to the visits of African heads of state in Bonn—is interpreted in its (existent or nonexistent) relation to the "German question." The news media present every diplomatic act or omission of the German Federal Republic as a machination of "the militarists and irridentists in Bonn." This association has actually convinced the population that the "German problem" is a vital threat to the security of their state. Fear of "West German irridentism" has thus become not only a propaganda weapon but also an impelling motive of Czechoslovak foreign policy, while reliance on the "protecting hand" of the Soviet Union is the single pillar of a diplomacy largely deprived of its powers of perception.

It cannot be denied that wide strata of the population have fallen victim to this artificially cultivated psychosis against a "new Munich" and "bloodthirsty revenge" by the Germans. This receptivity to induced fear of "irridentism" is psychologically explicable as the result of collective guilt feelings arising from the cruel expulsion of the Sudeten Germans reinforced by feelings of individual guilt evoked by the public acts of brutality that swept Czechoslovakia in 1945 and 1946. While confrontation with increasing numbers of tourists from the German Federal Republic demonstrates the irrationality of this fear propaganda in many cases, the psychological guilt roots are so deep that the Czech sense of reality remains for the most part obscured.

Relations with the Communist Bloc

When the ideological struggle broke out between Moscow and Peking, the Prague regime at first assumed a noncommittal attitude which was reflected in the neutral tone of Czechoslovak press reports. Very recently, however, it has become apparent that Czechoslovakia supports the Kremlin but plays down the ideological conflict for reasons of domestic policy.

After a long period of tension relations with Yugoslavia have improved recently. The atmosphere was doubtless warmed when Czechoslovakia recalled its ambassador, Antonín Kroužil, known for his ideological hostility to Tito. Relations with other states of the socialist camp—aside from Albania, with which diplomatic relations have been reduced to the chargé d'affaires level—may be described as normal. Enthusiasm for Cuba, the recipient of large quantities of Czechoslovak development aid, has ebbed markedly.

Until three years ago any unfavorable reporting on the Soviet Union would have been taboo in Czechoslovakia. Since then, however, personal differences between the Czechoslovak President and party leader Novotný and Khrushchev's successors have opened the way for an unprecented anti-Russian campaign in the Czechoslovak press. Themes such as alleged unfairness to Czech tourists in Moscow have served as outlets for the pent-up resentment of the population. Among the indications of less than cordial relations were Novotný's refusal to receive the Soviet Foreign Minister while he was visiting Prague and the unprecedented brevity of the *Rudé právo* story on Brezhnev's recent appearance in that city. These symptoms of friction should not, however, be permitted to obscure the fact that the Czechoslovak Socialist Republic remains tied to the Soviet Union through thick and thin. At no time during the "domestic quarrel" did Czechoslovak news media interrupt their harping upon the theme that the USSR alone is able to guarantee the boundaries and forestall a "second Munich." The brief "estrangement" could not in the nature of things last long and—as of this writing—already belongs to the past.

As a member of the Warsaw Pact organization, the CSSR plays an integral role in Soviet military strategy. In marked contrast to Rumania, Czechoslovakia considers its alliance with the USSR a *sine qua non* for the defense of its borders. The strategic role assigned to Czechoslovakia within the Eastern bloc became quite apparent during the recent maneuvers conducted under the code name "Operation Vltava"—the most elaborate to be held in Bohemia and Moravia since 1945. The maneuver was based on the assumption that the potential enemies would be the West German *Bundeswehr* and United States troops stationed in Germany, which would attack Czechoslovak territory via neutral Austria(!). Elements of the Czechoslovak and Soviet armies were joined by detachments from Soviet Zone Germany and Hungary in this maneuver. While previous integrated maneuvers on Czechoslovak territory had served mainly to test logistic arrangements and had been concentrated in the eastern part of the country, the recent exercises included a number of practice crossings of the Vltava (Moldau)—an operation suggesting not only defensive conceptions but a testing of offensive planning.

Czechoslovakia's strategic position, including its natural geographic defenses, plays an important role in Moscow's military planning. The atomic rockets probably stationed in the republic command the flanks for a possible attack launched from Bohemia and Moravia, as well as providing tactical security for an invasion of West Germany via the Soviet Zone.

The Czechoslovak People's Army is reputedly well equipped and trained; it poses no danger to the party leadership, since all Western influences within the officers' corps have been systematically eliminated since 1948. For the Kremlin the Czechoslovak army with its Soviet-trained officers represents an additional pledge of loyalty to the alliance and an assurance of permanent communism in Czechoslovakia.

Ideology and Domestic Policy

As recently as 1962, Novotný stated that Czechoslovakia was approaching the consummation of socialism, and that the transition to communism would be possible in the near future. The Party Congress of June, 1966, however, made it quite clear that the Prague leadership regards this stage as still a long way off. This admission was dictated by the economic situation, which is such that any decisive steps to achieve communism would have catastrophic results. Ideologically, therefore, Marxism-Leninism has to a certain extent become stagnant in Czechoslovakia.

Between the "Slanský trials" in the early 1950's and the Central Committee meetings of April, 1963, at which those convicted between 1951 and 1954 were rehabilitated, Czechoslovakia experienced no major political shocks—other than perhaps the overthrow of Interior Minister Barák. With the accession of Antonín Novotný in 1953, the party acquired a strong leader who, furthermore, stood in favor with the successive rulers in Moscow. Through skillful use of a personnel policy, Novotný secured firm control over the *apparat*—a situation that remained static until the April Plenum in 1963.

Intra-party opposition crystallized around the "bourgeois nationalists" of Slovakia, whose leaders, once rehabilitated, took the offensive and managed to overthrow various pillars of the Novotný power machine, including Premier Viliam Široký and party secretaries Karol Bacilek and Bruno Köhler. For a time Novotný's position and his Kremlin support seemed in jeopardy. But his reelection as President of the Republic and, at the 1966 Congress, as First Secretary of the Central Committee indicates that he still holds the levers of power.

It would, however, be wrong to underrate the strength of the oppositional forces, the principal backing of which is to be found in Slovakia. Taking advantage of the rivalry between Prague and Bratislava, they have provided the intra-party motive force for a more liberal cultural and economic policy, the effects of which can already be observed.

Economic Policy

The economic crisis, which led to the introduction of a "new system of management," has a number of structural causes. One cause is the fact that, since Czechoslovakia emerged from World War II with a then advanced and only slightly damaged industry, it succumbed to the temptation to postpone necessary modernization and replacement. Another is the neglect of agriculture, which had already been seriously impaired by the expulsion of the Sudeten Germans. A third cause of economic distress was the practice of awarding executive positions to party hacks rather than to capable managers. Finally, subordination to Russian economic demands within COMECON led to unbalanced development of the Czechoslovak economy.

The economic reform that was initiated in 1965 and has by no means been completed is intended to overcome gradually this lack of proportion, thus restoring a more healthy economic basis. Such a goal can, however, only be achieved by setting out on the "Yugoslav road" and adapting it to local conditions. Certain steps in this direction have already been taken, among them measures to permit a greater spread of wages and to strengthen the responsibility and autonomy of concerns and factories at the expense of centrally administered planning. The main problem facing the economic reformers, however, is that of agriculture. A fundamental reform in that field is not in prospect, since the principle of collectivization is to be retained. The technological basis for a successful economic reform likewise seems to be lacking.

National Committees (municipal councils) are to finance investments in local enterprises through locally collected taxes and bank credits. Concerns and factories are also to be permitted to borrow at interest. This relapse into capitalist financial practices is presented to the public as an "improved form of socialist economic management." All these reforms naturally meet with resistance from bureaucrats whose interests are affected adversely—all the more so since business accomplishment is henceforth to be better rewarded than services to the party. It therefore remains to be seen whether the reforms will achieve even a partial degree of success.

Whatever the reforms accomplish, they will be in vain if Czechoslovakia does not succeed in expanding its trade with capitalist states. Its political commitments to the members of COMECON and its dependence on the Soviet Union for raw materials are such, however, that an expansion of Western trade sufficient to carry the economic reform is hardly possible without Kremlin approval.

Cultural Policy

The shift to a relatively liberal cultural policy—at least in comparison with those of Poland and Soviet Zone Germany—took place over the course of a decade concurrently with the internal stabilization of the communist system. The initial liberalization launched by the Union of Czechoslovak Writers in 1956 was braked and suppressed by the party, but the trend could not be halted. Cultural life today is free insofar as literary and artistic criticism does not challenge the existence of the communist system itself. The recently replaced Minister of Education and Culture, Dr. Cestmir Cisař, despite his background as a party secretary, did much to promote a degree of liberalization and restore the traditional autonomy of the university. The new minister, Professor Jiři Hájek, has not yet made his mark, but there are signs of a return to "reactionary" cultural policy.

Cultural exchange is conducted actively, but it is largely one-sided, serving as cultural propaganda and as an entering wedge for Czechoslovak foreign policy. By presenting performances of unquestioned artistic merit, the government hopes to achieve an atmosphere of cordiality and sympathy for Czechoslovakia—an endeavor that has largely succeeded, even in the supposedly "irridentist" German Federal Republic.

In contrast to the relatively successful "liberalization" of cultural policy, the political education of youth has been an abject failure. Despite all its efforts and threats, the regime has not been able to implant communist ideology in the minds of the younger generation. For the vast majority of young people "Marxism-Leninism" is simply a required exercise that must be gotten over with in the school or youth organization. The regime's own economic reforms appeal increasingly to personal material interests and thus intensify rather than dampen the trend "away from politics."

Communist antireligious policy has changed its methods but not its objectives during the sixteen years since 1948. Catholic priests are still arrested, interned, or prevented from fulfilling their pastoral duties, and the atheist campaign continues unabated. At the same time, however, the regime has sought an agreement with the Vatican, in order to "prove" to the outside world that "constitutionally guaranteed" freedom of religion actually exists in Czechoslovakia. A compromise under which Cardinal Beran was released from internment but exiled to Rome seemed expedient to the regime, since the population still regards the priests who have capitulated and joined the National Committee of Catholic Clergy as an "assembly of apostates."

During the last two years the regime seems to have adopted a "softer" policy toward the Catholic Church—which does not alter the fact that the Church is still a thorn in its flesh. This is particularly true in Slovakia, where most of the population, including minor party functionaries, continue to attend services regularly. In Bohemia, on the other hand, the prevailing attitude is one of religious resignation: few outside the older generation attend church, while at least the antireligious aspect of communist youth education seems to have taken effect. What is probably a more immediate cause of the religious indifference of youth, however, is the craving for worldly goods that is an unintended product of dialectical materialism. This "personal materialism," which is intensified by contacts with Western tourists and their standard of living, leads Czechoslovak youth away from both the Church and communism.

Concluding Evaluation

The communist regime in the Czechoslovak Socialist Republic feels itself to be saturated and consolidated. An internal opposition such as might endanger the system does not exist. The only danger to the state from within lies in the latent antagonism between the Czech and Slovak nations, which has risen increasingly to the surface in recent years. The Kremlin holds the key to further development: it can support agitation for an "independent communist Slovakia," or it can assist Prague to suppress the unquestionably genuine Slovak demand for self-government. In either case Moscow has the CSSR firmly in its grasp, and the scope for autonomous Czechoslovak foreign policy is correspondingly limited. The Prague regime, however, has learned how to exploit the little freedom that it enjoys.

In the domestic field the Kremlin accords Czechoslovakia a wide degree of freedom within the limits of the communist system, these limits being contiguous with the economic interests of the USSR. It is therefore improbable that Moscow would remain a passive spectator at a total reorientation of Czechoslovak foreign trade toward the West. Czechoslovak economic and cultural policy is of positive interest to Moscow only insofar as it strengthens the economic potential of the Eastern bloc and enhances the position of the Soviet Union itself. While the Czechoslovak "model satellite" has reached a certain degree of maturity, it remains—for the obvious structural reasons pointed out here—ideologically and materially dependent on the Soviet Union.

C.   HUNGARY—HELMUT KLOCKE

The revolution of 1956 was the single expression of several different forces. It was, to begin with, a blow struck in desperation against a Stalinist system exaggerated to the nth degree. Revolt first broke out in a sector of the party against the terror and inhumanity of an imported system. Historical tradition also played a role: in the region between Germany and the Soviet Union, Hungary—along with Poland—had always manifested the most intense patriotism and nationalism. The excessive massing of population in the capital, with an unbelievably intense concentration of abstract-urban intelligentsia and industrial workers, also provided favorable structural conditions for the ripening of a revolutionary situation, for the outbreak of revolution, and even for its victory. Instant liberation of agriculture, the forced collectivization of which had been intensified only in recent years, became the spontaneous battle cry in peasant areas. More than half the so-called agricultural production cooperatives dissolved themselves.

Although the revolution was overthrown by Soviet military intervention, it was impossible to return to office those responsible for Rákósi's prerevolutionary reign of terror. In installing Kádár, Moscow chose a man who had himself suffered under the Rákósi dictatorship, and the entire affair led to changes that were broader and deeper still. Thus a portion of the workers' self-administration established during the revolution in imitation of Yugoslavia was permitted to continue for the time being. Recollectivization of the dissolved agricultural production cooperatives was also undertaken with the utmost caution and at a deliberate tempo.

Political Developments

Even though genuine workers' self-administration was tolerated only for a short time, while farm collectivization—as in all other East European countries except Poland—was completed by 1961, the Kádár regime nevertheless allowed considerable leeway for intellectual confrontation and discussion. The situation that developed after 1961 was regarded as tolerable by much of the population, especially when compared with the state of affairs before 1956. Kádár's well-known epigram of October, 1961, "Who is not against us is for us," was a departure from the spirit of neighboring systems. It helped considerably to spread a feeling, particularly among intellectuals, of the need to make some positive contribution to the system so as to render it more human, more elastic, and more rational in the long run.

Individual opinion could, of course, be expressed only in a limited manner. Literature took recourse to symbolism, expressing many ideas in seemingly historical comparisons or in generalized human images and stories that were often cryptic to the uninitiated. It remains an open question whether this conscious intellectual reaction was motivated by unconscious forces; the remarkably sharp drop in births and the corresponding increase in abortions would suggest that it was not, even though complex causes were doubtless involved.

After the Kádár regime had, with Soviet support, restored the institutions of domestic power, it turned its attention to the aftermath of the revolution of 1956. A partial amnesty was proclaimed in April, 1960, and political offenses committed since 1945 were declared free of punishment in 1963, even though a few hundred people remained in prison. The authority and influence of the secret police were clearly restricted. Four bishops were released from house arrest in May, 1963, but were not permitted to resume their ecclesiastical functions. Limited concessions were made in connection with the elections of February, 1963, when the regime accepted the defeat of an appreciable number of popular-front candidates for the position of national deputy. The domestic policy as a whole brought the regime a diplomatic success: after U Thant's visit in 1963 the Hungarian question was removed from the agenda of the United Nations.

An agreement with the Vatican was reached in September, 1964, providing among other things that only bishops agreeable to both sides would be appointed. Five new suffragan bishops were consecrated, so that each diocese once more had a bishop. Hungarian priests were again permitted to study in Rome.

Ideology and Culture

While these developments were taking place, the ideological line of the party remained unambiguous and actually became stricter with the passage of time. Its goal remained the total elimination of religious influence. The weak position of the Hungarian episcopate was, on the other hand, made evident by a statement published in the Catholic journal *Uj Ember* on November 13, 1965, to the effect that "an intensification of the ideological struggle does not correspond to the tasks of the Church." It is significant in this connection that the Hungarian bishops were not invited by the Polish Church to its millennial celebration, and that they criticized the basic position of their Polish colleagues.

The pressure exercised by all levels of the party and the state on the population is indicated by a reduction in the percentage of primary school pupils taking religious instruction from 30 per cent in 1956–57 to 15 in 1965. Participation must be requested by the parents. Party and state ecclesiastical policy is not, of course, the only cause of the insufficiency of young priests to fill vacant pastorates. As early as the summer of 1965 priests were again being tried and sentenced to long prison terms. Stricter entry rules for foreign clergy were announced during the summer of 1966, neither tourist nor transit visas were granted for private visits. This anti-Church policy does not inhibit the Hungarian regime from employing "peace priests" to expand its influence within the Church. Developments in general indicate that the regime's struggle against religion and the Catholic Church has again been intensified since 1965, and that the position of those bishops currently in office is extremely tenuous. Relations between the government and the Church are further complicated by the fact that Cardinal Mindszenty is unwilling to leave Hungary and insists on being restored to his former authority.

Literature has played a consistently important role in Hungarian political and national development during the nineteenth and twentieth centuries. As it was under the absolutist regimes of the past, literature in the period since World War II has again become a forum for various forces that have no other channel of expression. This aspect lends particular interest to the congress of the Hungarian Writers Association held in late 1965. The Association had been dissolved in 1956 and reestablished at a congress in 1959; 100 of its 350 members belong to the Communist party. Leaders of the regime hold office in its presidium and secretariat; its president Jozsef Darvas was Minister of Education from 1950 to 1957. At the 1965 congress Darvas inveighed against the "disintegrating" West and in favor of a "nationally engaged" literature: a tendency followed today by hardly any of the creative poets and writers, from Tibor Déry to Gyula Illyés. So far as the state is concerned, anything not openly antagonistic to the regime may be published. Official cultural policy thus remains ideologically constrained, but it is largely ignored by the poets and writers who were on the revolutionary side on 1956 and, having served their prison sentences, are again writing.

Economic Policy

The essence of the Hungarian economic reform is a reform of prices. Csikos-Nagy, chief of the Price Office, has formulated the objective as follows: "Prices must become an effective mechanism of the economic system, their function being to stimulate the growth of production." The full significance of a price reform under present conditions in Hungary is evident from the fact that only about 10 per cent of existing prices correspond to the cost of production and

90 per cent are either higher or lower—the prices for 85 per cent of commodities are administratively fixed. The purpose of the price reform is to achieve a stable economic basis for prices, limiting price controls to 22 per cent of commodities. Whether the Hungarian practice of concrete prices will correspond entirely with these principles after January 1, 1968, remains to be seen.

The Central Committee's resolution of late May, 1965, and the commentary to the Five-Year Plan issued in late June indicate clearly that the political leadership reserves the right to use a variety of direct interventionary measures. Such intervention is demanded by the dogmatic advocates of a centrally administered economy. The latter will doubtless try to modify the final text of the economic reform laws in line with their centralist precepts. It is quite probable that they will nullify many of the measures intended to establish a market mechanism. It may be observed, however, that Hungary has for some time now employed methods of price formation that deviate considerably from the former rigid practice.

A significant phase of the reform already realized is a charge of 5 per cent for the use of productive facilities. The principle of interest has thus become operative, since state funds for industrial financing are no longer granted free of charge. The demand that enterprises show a positive balance has at least been declared. Such economy is necessary because of a shortage of production factors, including manpower, which imposes a limit on global economic growth.

The entire economic reform situation in Hungary is characterized by an understanding of the objective need for the measures described, an understanding that the leading theoreticians and economists in the political leadership have assimilated. These measures, however, encounter a variety of difficulties, for example, the political reaction to the new prices and the problem of explaining to the nonagrarian population that it has been living beyond its means for years. Influences from abroad, such as the unwillingness of the Soviet Union to countenance more than the most cautious and halting steps toward reform and events in Yugoslavia that may be exploited as arguments for extreme hesitancy, also impinge upon the program. The political leadership has to face a further perennial question: whether it can continue to wield its accustomed centralized political power if it limits its planning to establishment of a framework, according substantial free play to the market and thus to decentralized economic decision making. The schedule established by the Central Committee indicates that, even if the reform proceeds without interruption, its practical effects will hardly become apparent before 1970.

The Western world is certain to raise the question of expanding commercial relationships and economic cooperation with Hungary. Basically, some two-thirds of Hungary's foreign trade is committed to the Soviet bloc by the long-term trade agreement for the current planning period, which runs until 1970. The Soviet Union continues to figure as the dominant supplier of raw and basic materials. Hungary is furthermore obligated to repay Soviet credits with deliveries of goods. This relationship establishes a political limit to expansion of Hungarian trade with the industrially advanced states of the West.

The reform measures can, however, exercise a certain influence on Hungarian foreign trade with the West even before 1970 in two respects. First, as soon as the enterprises can choose their sources of supply, they will tend to prefer modern investment goods from industrially developed countries. Second, the provision permitting productive enterprises to enter into direct relationships with foreign suppliers and customers will doubtless promote an expansion and broadening of trade.

Soviet occupation—which apart from the Soviet Zone of Germany persists only in Hungary—and dependency on the Soviet Union for raw materials are facts that compel Hungary to hew to the Soviet line in foreign policy. In all questions of domestic structure, however, the discussion has already started, and the West should take advantage of it in order to loosen the rigid forms of the past.

D.   POLAND—RICHARD F. STAAR

A useful starting point for a study of postwar change in Poland is the 1952 Constitution.[1] This document provides for a unicameral parliament or *Sejm,* confirming an arrangement that had been in effect since the 1946 referendum. Of 460 deputies, 255 are members of the Polish United Workers (Communist) party, i.e., 55.5 per cent of the total.[2] Wladyslaw Gomulka has maintained this somewhat lower ratio of Communists ever since the 1957 elections, because he is able to control the two subordinate political groupings: the United Peasant party and the Democratic party.

Another innovation, patterned after the Soviet model, is the seventeen-member Council of State, the chairman of which acts as chief of state for ceremonial purposes. This collective presidency under Edward Ochab[3] approximates the Presidium of the Supreme Soviet in the USSR. The local People's Councils, similar to the soviets, are now elected for terms of four years, coinciding with the terms of the *Sejm*. The latter elects the Council of State for the same term of office.

The government, of course, merely comprises a facade, behind which the locus of power remains the Communist party or PZPR (*Polska Zjednoczona Partia Robotnicza*). This organization, which had only 4,000 members in mid-1942, now claims 1.8 million members.[4] This in itself would indicate that the overwhelming majority of members may have joined because of opportunism. More positive evidence to the same effect is found in the recent words of a high-ranking defector:

> The Party became an organization purely for opportunists, because nobody can believe now in anything the Party says. But it is necessary to be a member of the Party to get a good job, to get better conditions, and so on.[5]

The power elite that controls all important positions and comprises an interlocking party-government directorate appears, however, to consist of dedicated Communists.[6] Even this group seems to be split into factions, with the hard-liners under Interior Minister Mieczyslaw Moczar placing their own people in other ministries, the propaganda apparatus, key posts within the economy, and the armed forces—not to mention the police. Gomulka is said to be supporting Moczar against the liberals—among whom Foreign Minister Adam Rapacki and Premier Jozef Cyrankiewicz are classified—because he "fears the revival of such an organized form of protest against conditions in Poland . . ."[7]

With respect to the rank and file members, the party continues to attract proportionately more intellectuals than industrial workers. Figures on the social composition of the PZPR indicate that the percentage of intellectuals has increased from 9.6 per cent in 1945 to 42.9 in 1964, while the percentage of workers has dropped from 62.2 per cent to 40.3 over the same period.[8] A related problem is that of excessive turnover in party membership. Although it was claimed over Radio Warsaw (April 15, 1964) that only 400,000 persons had either left or been expelled from the PZPR during the period from 1956 to 1964, information pieced together from other official sources indicates that the number was 638,485 in the years 1955 through 1961 only (some 55,000 in 1955 alone).[9]

Regardless of this inherent instability the Communists have been able to transform Poland's economy to a substantial degree. Although the number of collective farms has remained stable at about 1,200, they have been supplemented by approximately 32,000 "agricultural circles" that attempt to inculcate *kolkhoz* philosophy and practice among the peasantry.[10] During 1966 the regime planned to invest a total of 16 billion zlotys (4 billion dollars at the obviously unrealistic official rate) in a program for modernizing agriculture. Only 14.6 per cent of Poland's agricultural production comes from the socialist sector of state and collective farms. Industry, on the other hand, remains 99.6 per cent nationalized.[11]

Before World War II national minorities comprised a sizable percentage of the population of Poland. With a current population approximating that in 1939 (almost 32 million), minorities today total less than one-half million persons. Of these the Ukrainians and the Belorussians together number about 350,000 inhabitants.[12] This fact supports the claim of the Roman Catholic Church to speak for the overwhelming majority of the population, a claim that encourages the communist regime to treat the religious hierarchy as its main enemy.

The most recent controversy in the struggle for control over the minds of the population was provoked by a letter sent by Cardinal Stefan Wyszyński and thirty-five Polish bishops to their counterparts in Germany, inviting them to attend the millennium celebrations in May, 1966, at Czestochowa. The communist regime reacted strongly, accusing the Church hierarchy of involving itself with foreign affairs.[13] Early in 1966 the Cardinal was prevented from traveling to the Vatican, and subsequently all foreign clergy were refused visas, including Pope Paul VI, who wanted to visit Poland. Pessimism about the future of the Church seems justified.[14]

Within the communist orbit Warsaw has joined all treaty organizations sponsored by the Soviet Union. Among these membership in the Council for Mutual Economic Assistance (COMECON) has proven most expensive to Poland, because resources required for large capital investments have been diverted to long-range economic improvement projects. This capital could have been more advantageously used for shorter-range domestic programs. The large investments promoted by COMECON include the Polish section of the Danube-Oder canal, exploitation of brown coal deposits at Turoszow, and the *Druzhba* oil pipeline between the USSR and Soviet Zone of Germany, which crosses Poland.

In an attempt to improve the Polish economy, which suffers from its membership in COMECON, the government has announced a cautious change that will decentralize planning and responsibility down to the intermediate level of industrial trusts or similar plants, but not to the individual factory.[15] Gomulka is reportedly afraid of more liberal reforms in the economy, "because he is an old Communist and that is against his ideas." The same source expresses the attitude of the population in Poland by recalling the saying that "the government is only pretending to pay the workers, so the workers are only pretending to work."[16] The Warsaw regime claims that some 8.3 million of its citizens inhabit the so-called Recovered Territories to the east of the Oder-Neisse border line, and that over one-third of the GNP comes from there.[17] The important aspect of this controversy, owing to the fact that no Western country has recognized the boundary officially, remains that it can be exploited by the communist regime against the West and in favor of the Soviet Union.

E.   RUMANIA—OTTO R. LIESS

Within the short span of three and one-half years Rumania has progressed from the status of a remote People's Democracy, a Soviet satellite with little prospect of betterment, to the spectacular role of an "individualist," a "rebel," a "broker between the Kremlin and Peking," and even "a bridge between East and West." The Rubicon leading to this unprecedented position was crossed not at a meeting of the Party International or of the Soviet bloc heads of government, but at an executive session of the COMECON where open conflict between the USSR and Rumania erupted on February 15, 1963. The Rumanian delegation took exception to the plan for "integrating" the other COMECON partners on the basis of and at the expense of an unbalanced expansion of Rumanian agriculture. This collision set a basic precedent, determining both the potentialities and limitations of its "Fronde" against Moscow: the Rumanian Communist party gained freedom of action in matters of foreign trade, commercial policy, cultural relations, and dealings with international bodies —insofar as no *fundamental* decision affecting Soviet centralism or the primacy of the CPSU was involved.

Rumanian Foreign Policy

In the field of foreign policy the development in Bucharest suggests analogies with Tito's Yugoslavia or even de Gaulle's France. Rumania indeed occupies a unique position within the magnetic field of world communism. Geographically it is encircled by the Soviet communist power area, for which reason the Kremlin was able to permit Gheorghiu-Dej and later Ceausescu greater freedom of movement than, for instance, the rulers of Hungary, Czechoslovakia, and the "German Democratic Republic," all of which have borders with West-Central Europe.

Tito's heresy against J. V. Stalin, which preceded Gheorghiu-Dej's "go-it-alone" policy by fifteen years, was made possible by Yugoslavia's Western borders combined with the either/or alternative that Belgrade faced after the collapse of its Balkan federation plans in 1948. Rumania's "Gaullism," however, is neither fundamentally nor tactically a symmetrical counterpart of de Gaulle's *Weltpolitik*. The immediate causes and the structural and functional characteristics of Rumanian "individualism" within a system of totalitarian power bear no close similarity to those of de Gaulle's quest for great-power status or of France's current influence as a "third force" between the major partners of world politics. The audacity of Rumania's go-it-alone policy and its success to date are essentially traceable to two factors:

1. A wave of nationalism among the Rumanian people, provoked by exploitation, discrimination, and indifference to Rumanian interests on the part of the Soviet leadership.

2. The Moscow-Peking dispute, which permitted the clever tactician Gheorghiu-Dej to make his first protest against the overbearing ways of Soviet tutelage.

The traditional Rumanian "see-saw" policy proved able to exploit the Moscow-Peking schism, not only within the communist camp, but also in relations with the West as well. Coordinating its actions with a case-to-case "Fronde"—administered in carefully calculated doses—the Rumanian Socialist Republic under Gheorghiu-Dej seized the initiative in foreign policy. This initiative, which became even more pronounced under Nicolae Ceausescu, developed simultaneously in three directions:

1. A degree of cooperation with communist governments in the Danubian and Balkan area, this partial federation within the Soviet bloc serving to provide better support for sovereign action.

2. No open switching of sides from Moscow to Peking, but an "honest broker" policy mediating between the two power centers of world communism.

3. A partially independent coexistence policy in relations with states beyond the communist sphere, with benefits for Bucharest including favorable trade agreements with the West, improved opportunities for training key personnel in the West, manufacturing licenses, and improved foreign-trade cooperation.

Party Policy

Until the end of the 1950's the policy manifested by the Bucharest regime toward Moscow was one of abject bootlicking. The dyed-in-the-wool "Titoist" Gheorghiu-Dej (who died March 19, 1965) pursued a policy of fulfillment toward the Kremlin until he had secured his own monopoly of power in Rumania. Within the party Gheorghiu-Dej was a master of intrigue who remained in the background but earned description as an "autocratic Stalinist" by the way he ruled over his comrades in the Rumanian Communist party. His young Moscow-trained successor Nicolae Ceausescu was borne unexpectedly to the pinnacle of power in Bucharest by a wave of national Bolshevism—at the expense of Ion Gheorghe Maurer and Alexandru Birladeanu, representatives of the older generation.

Both Gheorghiu-Dej and Ceausescu must be classified as convinced and fanatical Communists. The mistakes and failures of the Kremlin forced both to declare their opposition to Moscow's desires and expectations in order to safeguard Rumania's position as well as their own leadership in the RSR.

The leadership situation within world communism after the death of Gheorghiu-Dej made it necessary for Moscow to accord Ceausescu a free hand following the Ninth Congress of the Rumanian Communist party (July 19–22, 1965). Ceausescu, however, has diminished his agitation for coordinated anti-Soviet resistance within the bloc and bent his efforts toward securing increased freedom for Rumania in partial and marginal areas of foreign policy (military, commercial, and cultural policy and training of younger personnel).

Foreign Trade

Rumania's economic relations with communist countries continued predominant but dropped to 65 per cent of total foreign trade turnover in 1965, while the Western share rose to 35 per cent. The decisive turning point in this direction came between 1960 and 1961, when the noncommunist share of Rumanian foreign trade rose from 27.0 to 31.3 per cent. In 1965 the German Federal Republic replaced Czechoslovakia as Rumania's second largest trade partner. Trade with West Germany did not, however, amount to much more than one-fifth of Rumanian-Soviet trade.

Rumanian Trade with Major Trade Partners

1965	*Millions of Lei*
Soviet Union	5,067.5
Federal Republic of Germany	1,042.2
Czechoslovakia	989.0
"German Democratic Republic"	805.4
Italy	707.3
Poland	492.1
Great Britain	446.6
France	426.5

Commodity trade with the Chinese People's Republic expanded by almost one-third between 1964 and 1965, as did such trade with Yugoslavia. Rumania's foreign trade turnover with its COMECON partners did not expand proportionally as much as its trade with Western countries.

As a consequence of existing treaties and the Rumanian planning system, as well as of problems of machine parts, delivery quotas, and standards of quality, Rumanian dependence on the Soviet "ruble bloc" must be expected to continue for almost the entire decade to come. The new Five-Year Plan for 1966–1970 projects a total expansion of foreign trade by 55 per cent. But trade with the Soviet Union is to expand by only 30 per cent, with the "GDR" by only 44 per cent, and with Hungary by only 20 per cent. Alone among communist countries Poland is to enjoy a trade expansion of 80 per cent, according to Rumanian foreign trade planning. It follows from these figures that the increase in Rumanian trade with the West will be proportionally greater.

Current trends include decreases in imports of refinery equipment and in exports of oil, grains, and foodstuffs. The share of Rumanian machinery and tool production exported has, on the other hand, increased, as has Rumanian trade with certain countries in the Near East (including Turkey and Iran) and in Southeast Asia.

The foreign-trade picture is, of course, affected by an "autarkic" trend in Rumanian economic planning apparent since 1963. This trend is not so much a reflection of reformist agricultural decentralization as a defense mechanism against the Soviet exploitation, delivery demands, and price dictatorship prevalent up to that time. As is well known, a plan published by E. B. Valev in early 1964 contemplated the inclusion of eastern and southern Rumania in an international area composed of Soviet, Rumanian, and Bulgarian territory.[18] The notorious map of this area provoked what came close to being an open collision between Moscow and Bucharest. Specific phases of this episode included an attempted coup against Gheorghiu-Dej, mobilization of the Soviet army against Rumania, and major "maneuvers" in the latter country.

Military Policy

The Rumanian armed forces have for the time being been somewhat withdrawn from joint Warsaw Pact activities. The 1966 fall maneuvers in Czechoslovakia took place without any significant participation of Rumanian units. Former plans charging the Rumanian People's Army with coordinated offensive tasks as part of Soviet strategy against Western Europe have been changed. Soviet rocket bases aimed at the German Ruhr are, however, still stationed in Rumania, as are similar bases threatening Turkey from the Dobrudja. The operational importance of Rumania in all the military and transport planning of the Kremlin is such as to preclude its further withdrawal from the Soviet bloc.

"Bloc politics" is apparent in certain Rumanian assurances addressed to Peking. It is not inconceivable that Rumania—despite its improved political and commercial relations with the United States, France, Italy, and Germany—will dispatch "volunteers" to Vietnam as soon as Peking gives the signal and the "situation" makes such action appropriate.

Social and Cultural Policy

Rumanian policy continues in the accustomed People's Democratic pattern: a directed economy with a gradually improving standard of living, but without co-determination of co-responsibility of the workers. Rumania's collectivized agriculture continues to be neglected, and the hope of the peasants for enlarged private plots or a redistribution of farm land has proved in vain. On the contrary, Bucharest's agricultural collectivism is more stringent than Hungary's, to say nothing of Poland's. Structurally, the unsolved agrarian problem not only hampers the expansion of total production but also blocks the first steps toward building a new society in Rumania.

The succession of generations seems to raise the most serious issues: the younger generation demands luxury and leisure and rejects the fanatical self-sacrifice typical of "old Bolsheviks." The antagonism of this youth is directed at both the Soviets and the domestic *politruks*.

Developments in the field of culture and education are characterized by the beginnings of a national renaissance—a revival of national cultural traditions and of pride in Rumanian achievement. A new broad-mindedness and a more receptive attitude toward the West have become clearly apparent in Rumanian scholarship since 1963. The transitional situation and the gradual nature of internal change are, however, more evident in the cultural sector than elsewhere. The party line is more strictly enforced in certain respects than in neighboring communist-ruled countries, and the beginnings of liberalization in the education of young people have not yet proceeded as far as in Yugoslavia, Hungary, Czechoslovakia, or Poland.

Rumanian Communists are not yet ready to enter into a genuine conversation or open intellectual confrontation with democracy, in which the advantages, disadvantages, and potentialities of Western democracy and Eastern dictatorship are objectively weighed and compared. Developments have not progressed beyond the first "thaw."

Controversial Issues

Transylvania and Bessarabia, as focuses of political controversy, will for some time remain a constant source of instability in the interplay of political forces. A hostile dispute between Moscow and Bucharest over Bessarabia can hardly be avoided. Transylvania has been involved in the crossfire of intra-bloc struggle and skirmishing since the early spring of 1966. Brezhnev's unofficial visit to Bucharest during May 10–13, 1966, drew attention, not only to the struggle over Transylvania, but also to the foreign policy ramifications of this issue in Moscow, Budapest, and Belgrade.

F.   YUGOSLAVIA—JOHANN HAWLOWITSCH

Among the processes of economic and social change taking place within the communist orbit, those in Yugoslavia differ from the rest. This is true, not only because of the distinct Yugoslav concept of socialism as a principle of social and economic order, but more particularly because of Yugoslavia's kaleidoscopic national evolution, which has no parallel in either the East or the West. All economic and social life in the south Slav federation is organized under the principle of self-administration (or self-management) in a system that has arisen spontaneously over the last few years and for which no ready model was provided by ideology.[19]

The intellectual roots of the system are to be found in the teachings of Marx, Lenin, and certain syndicalists, as well as in contemporary writings advocating "liberal" and "democratic" socialism.

The process of change in Yugoslavia since the introduction of workers' self-administration has been characterized by attention to practical problems of economic and political life—problems that demanded pragmatic solutions. The result of experimentation and the search for a distinctive national road to socialism was the Constitution of 1963, which embodies a relatively complete concept of social order. Decisive changes have taken place, especially in the economic system and in government, and more radical political transformation is in the offing.

The Yugoslav economic system before 1950 was a typical centrally administered planned economy copied from the Soviet model. Two years after the break with the Soviet Union, however, workers' self-administration was introduced, and a year later detailed economic planning was abandoned. These steps were accompanied by a reorganization of the state administration, while municipal autonomy was progressively expanded in the economic field. Throughout the 1950's and early 1960's measures of decentralization and recentralization alternated regularly, both in local government and in industrial management. The oscillations represented attempts to master both specific economic situations and power plays by reformist and orthodox groups in the party leadership, whose struggles were also closely related to the nationality problem within the Yugoslav federation. And in all, Yugoslavia's structural and economic development until about 1963 leaves the impression of a struggle for a more efficient political and economic order, characterized by a succession of ad hoc measures. The Constitution of 1963 seems, however, to have marked the end of the period of experimentation and groping for new paths. The reforms put into effect since then reflect a consistent and often radical translation of relatively clear structural concepts into economic, social, and political reality—an adjustment of society to the basic ideas of the Constitution.

Productive capital in Yugoslavia is not state property; it is merely socialized, i.e., the "working organizations" (enterprises, etc.) possess certain rights in relation to the socially-owned means they manage. This specific concept of "social ownership" has its roots in the principle of self-administration and in the demand for a limitation of state power, which as the Yugoslavs see it can only be achieved by transferring property rights—especially the disposal of profit—to the immediate producers. The degree of such decentralized control over property determines the degree of economic freedom.

The individual enterprise in Yugoslavia is permitted to dispose of its assigned and earned capital almost without limitation. The rights of the state and its organs to interfere with the property of business enterprises are limited essentially to a control function.

Private ownership of business capital is limited to certain sectors of the economy:

1. Retail and service businesses, in which a private entrepreneur may not employ more than five workers. Very recently

private operators have also been licensed to open restaurants and hotels.

2. Agriculture—the area in which private property is most important, since 85 per cent of all arable land is in private ownership. Private peasant farms, which may not exceed ten hectares in area, accounted for 77 per cent of Yugoslav agricultural production and employed 96 per cent of the farm workers in 1963.

The scope of free decision left to the peasants should not be exaggerated, since the marketing of farm products is monopolized. Most agricultural products are bought at fixed prices, and the laws and regulations specifying types of crops and requiring consolidation of fields are administered by local authorities, in some cases with considerable harshness. The type of "General Agricultural Cooperative" developed in Yugoslavia does, however, represent an organizational pattern that offers the private peasant a certain incentive to cooperate.

Self-Administration and Profit Sharing

The basic pillar of the entire Yugoslav system is the concept of workers' self-administration, which is today applied in all areas of human endeavor—in factories and administrative agencies, and even to some extent in universities. Its legal basis, the Workers' Councils Law of 1950, has been repeatedly amended and expanded, most recently in connection with the reforms of July, 1965. These changes have the effect of limiting legislation to general rules, leaving concrete details—including wage scales and the distribution of profits—for determination by the bylaws of individual enterprises. The essence of the self-determination principle is thus seen to lie in a shifting of economic decision making on production and distribution to the employees of the various enterprises and to the autonomous organs they elect: the Workers' Council, the Administrative Committee, and the Director. The Workers' Council occupies the center of power, with decisive management functions entrusted to the Administrative Committee in internal affairs and to the Director in external relations of the enterprise.

The steadily increasing independence of enterprises and their individual plants poses severe demands upon the organizational structure. Although fields of competence are defined in formal legal terms, jurisdictional conflicts as well as shifts in power positions among the leadership can and do occur. To minimize this danger, recent laws have enlarged the authority of the collective management organs (especially of the Workers' Councils and the workers themselves in referendum) and reduced that of the Director. It is necessary, however, to decide from case to case how far self-administration can be accommodated to the requirements of modern management and to what extent co-determination under democratic rules can be achieved in practice.

Since 1957 and 1958 self-administration has gradually been extended to all areas of industrial management, so that the employees and their elected organs decide autonomously, not only on production methods and personnel questions, but on the distribution and utilization of profits as well—of 70 per cent of the net profit since the 1965 reform. The resulting incentive provides the motive force driving the entire system. It also explains why almost all Yugoslav workers, regardless of their political views, regard self-administration as a step forward. The immediate connection between performance and profit sharing gives the workers a feeling that they have a voice in determining their own income. Even though wages cannot always be raised at the expense of working capital, the reform in Yugoslavia is characterized by the fact that the state no longer intervenes administratively and directly in the distribution of profits. The profits remaining after paying bonuses to the employees are divided by the Workers' Council as it finds proper between investments and the social fund for employees. The only requirement is that legal minimum reserves be maintained. This expansion of self-administration in the distribution gives rise to the following problems:

1. The freedom of enterprises in the distribution of their own net earnings involves a constant risk of inflation and misallocation of resources. The recommendation by the parliament that wage increases follow increases in productivity seems to be inadequate, and there is an acute need for instruments to link the wage trend with productivity in overall terms.

2. The legitimate demand of the worker for a job and thus a share of profits comes into conflict with the drive for productive efficiency and for maximizing profits and incomes. The reform of July, 1965, gives economy a certain priority over political and social

goals: dismissals are permissible when the economic situation of the plant requires them.

3. The objective of overcoming the still substantial differences in the economic development of various regions is hardly compatible with the decentralization of investment decisions. The share of total investment undertaken by enterprises with their own funds or with bank loans has increased constantly in recent years (to about 50 per cent of all investment between 1961 and 1964), instead of coming primarily from the central Investment Fund as was formerly the case. The gradual reduction in that fund since 1964 and the reforms of July, 1965, led to decisive changes involving nationality policy. Shifts of investment funds are no longer accomplished by confiscation of profits and their redistribution to the underdeveloped republics; they are now influenced through monetary, credit, and fiscal measures.[20]

4. The development of self-administration, the progressive decentralization of investment, and the need for a rational monetary and credit policy as a tool of stabilization impelled Yugoslavia to undertake a reform of its banking system, which took effect in early 1966. All banks other than the National Bank now operate independently within the limits of credit policy and banking laws and may compete with one another without regard to regional boundaries. They are organized along cooperative lines under the self-administration principle. Municipalities and enterprises deposit their funds in the bank of their choice and participate in its administration in proportion to their deposits, subject to ceilings designed to curb the influence of financially strong enterprises and municipalities. Each bank has a credit committee staffed exclusively by professionals, which has sole responsibility for examining and approving loan applications.

The National Bank fulfills an important role in the elastic management of money and credit. As a bank of emission it is responsible only to the federal parliament and does not engage in financing investments or other bank transactions. Its main function is to manage reserve, discount, and interest policies so as to regulate the volume of credit and the circulation of currency.

Progressive decentralization has led to changes in the form and methods of planning. Until 1965 the long-range economic plans were supplemented by annual plans—the latter being limited, however, to macro-economic aggregates without dictating normative production quotas. These annual plans were discontinued in 1966. Studies of business conditions are conducted from time to time in order to assess the achievement of planned development and to permit adjustment of economic policy to changing situations. This conception of planning is an entirely new departure within the socialist orbit and has nothing in common with the planning practices of other East European states except the name.

Contemporary market relationships in Yugoslavia may be defined as those of a "competitive socialist economy." They are based on contracts concluded between enterprises, without restriction or compulsion. Enterprises compete in both the domestic and foreign markets, subject to credit and tax policies that conform with the market principles in their execution. Direct intervention by the state in economic processes is limited almost exclusively to two areas of economic policy: prices and foreign trade.

In contrast to the administratively determined prices of Eastern planned economies, prices in Yugoslavia are largely formed on the market through the interaction of supply and demand. Fixed prices are still, however, employed in limited areas, and to a large extent prices are subject to state price controls that permit reductions but make increases difficult.

Foreign trade is still subjected to a variety of restrictions. Tariffs have been reduced, however, and the preliminary draft of the new Foreign-Trade Law indicates that approximately 50 per cent of all imports will be liberalized by the end of 1967. Yugoslavia has long since abolished its state foreign trade monopoly; individual enterprises are almost completely unrestricted in their export sales and are permitted to use freely a part of the foreign exchange thus realized. A total elimination of valuta rationing is not, however, in the offing despite Yugoslavia's membership in GATT, the reason being the permanent deficit in its balance of payments. Although Yugoslavia entered an associative relationship with COMECON in 1964, its commodity trade and economic cooperation with the West continue to play the decisive role. The same is true of the large volume of Western credit and the financial support provided by the United States, both of which have contributed to Yugoslav economic development and to the achievement of an independent economic system.

Institutional Aspects of Change

The economic system in Yugoslavia has not yet attained its final form. Apart from the property relations implied by the term "socialist," it is already closer to the Western market economies than to the

Eastern planned economies, and it has outdistanced the latter by many years in terms of practical and theoretical reform. The almost complete elimination of direct intervention by state and administrative organs, the diminished role of the party in economic matters, and the upgrading of the parliament are signs of a progressive democratization of economic life in Yugoslavia. The government has, furthermore, abandoned the policy of forced industrialization at the cost of the standard of living and turned increasingly toward welfare goals in the economic plan for 1966–1970.

Experience has shown that the Yugoslav system of "socialist market economy" combined with self-administration "is unique and fraught with contradictions. For all its risks and cyclical fluctuations, it is infinitely superior to the Soviet-type global planning directed from one centre . . ." but suffers greater frictional losses and is hence less productive than a market economy along Western lines.[21]

Commitment to the idea of self-administration in the economic sector involved a reorientation of both ideology and party policy. Basic conceptions of Soviet ideology were abandoned, particularly the theses of (1) a uniform road to socialism under the leadership of the Soviet Union, (2) the necessity for a totalitarian "dictatorship of the proletariat," and—more gradually—(3) the demand that total power be vested in the state and the party. Leading Yugoslav ideologists hold that Marxism-Leninism is no eternally sanctioned doctrine but a discipline that requires further development, modernization, and adjustment to conditions and processes as they emerge in reality —to self-administration in the case of Yugoslavia.

After an institutional guarantee for self-administration had been proclaimed in the Constitution of 1963, it became increasingly urgent to open additional avenues for the expression of this principle, in the political sector as well as elsewhere. Many Yugoslav Communists have come to reject the totalitarian concepts of communism and are gravitating increasingly toward democratic forms of socialism. They seek to achieve a socialist societal and economic order with safeguards against the accretion of totalitarian power in the state and the party, as well as against bureaucratic encroachments by the executive. Ideologically, this trend is reflected in a rejection of Stalin, a critical reexamination of Lenin, and a return to Marx—particularly the young, humanitarian Marx, whose ideas the Yugoslavs would like to adapt to modern conditions.[22]

This ideological orientation implies a new role for the party. The latter is no longer an organization that determines everything, as it still is in other communist countries. Its leadership function has been particularly challenged in the economic field, and—according to Professor Antun Vratuša of the University of Ljubljana—many Yugoslavs "visualize not only the paralysis of state power but that of all other monopolistic power including that of the Party."[23] Similar views are to be read, not only in officially tolerated liberal periodicas such as *Perspektiva* (Ljubljana) and *Praxis* (Zagreb), but also in articles published by Yugoslav Communists in party organs such as *Borba* and *Politika*.

This increasingly comprehensive legal public discussion is not, however, the only sign of widening freedom and fairness in Yugoslav social and political life. Other developments in this direction include:

1. The growing importance of the federal parliament in economic and political decisions, expressed in the expansion of its jurisdiction and in the fact that government bills are often defeated or amended in vigorous debates.

2. The establishment, for the first time in Yugoslav constitutional history, of a complete system of constitutional jurisprudence in the Constitution of 1963. Constitutional courts on both federal and republic levels took up their duties in 1964. Constitutional complaints may be lodged by both private and juridical persons against the widest variety of governmental acts. The somewhat elusive doctrine of "socialist legality" has been replaced by the more rigorous principle of the legality of administration, the effective enforcement of which is evident in court decisions against organs of the state infringing certain rights of self-administration or civil liberty.[24]

3. The new constitutionally anchored election system, used for the first time in 1965.[25] Under this system, the complexity of which corresponds to that of the Yugoslav federation, candidates must believe in socialism but are not required to belong to the party. More candidates appear on the ballot than the number of seats to be filled, thus affording the voters a limited choice in the matter of ability and of "liberal" or "orthodox" orientation. The improbability that a second party will be permitted to function is demonstrated, however, by the case of the Zagreb lecturer Mihajlov, whose criticism of the one-party system was tolerated but whose efforts to found an oppositional political group were suppressed.

4. The new statute of the League of Yugoslav Communists (Communist party), adopted in 1964, which likewise contains significant changes. Among these are mandatory rotation in party office and the right to criticize party functionaries and express deviant opinions. Since these principles are given more than lip service, a kind of "constitutional opposition" has emerged recently within the party. It is also significant that the new statute no longer requires members to be atheists. The so-called Socialist Alliance—a mass organization with noncommunist as well as communist members—is achieving growing importance as a forum for airing intra-party disputes.

The Confrontation of Orthodox and Progressive Forces

The confrontation between orthodox and progressive groups has spread from the economic and political sectors to the field of literature, where it has overrun the formerly mandatory "socialist realism."[26] While cultural and journalistic creation remains under considerable surveillance by the party, consistent attempts are made to achieve a more realistic presentation of national and world events. At the same time Yugoslav foreign policy manifests the desire to achieve a bloc-free position for dealing with the East, the West, and the developing nations.

The most important cause of this development is the advent of a younger, more progressive, and more liberal generation to the highest ranks in the party. The preponderance of younger delegates with little association with international or Soviet communism was already apparent at the Seventh Party Congress of 1958; at the Eighth Congress in 1964, 85.5 per cent of the delegates were participating for the first time, and their average age was thirty-six.[27] The same emphasis on youth was apparent in the 1964 elections to the Central and Executive committees. The intellectual and political younger generation, of which Executive Committee member Mijalko Todorović is typical, has participated actively in the development of self-administration and has learned to appreciate its advantages as compared with the centrally administered societies and economies of other East European states. Many in this generation have studied or worked in Western countries, especially the United States and France. While remaining convinced Communists, they have acquired clear ideas on the functioning of a modern political system, which they hope to combine with the realization of self-administration. The advancement of such people into the leading organs is favored by the new and looser election system and the new party statute.

A further cause of the development described lies in the splitting of the party into "orthodox" and "liberal" wings, the beginnings of which could be observed as early as 1959 and 1960. The "orthodox" were unable to develop principles other than those that had already failed in practice. The contradictions between the retrograde, dogmatic, and conservative attitude of this wing of the party, which was still relatively strong during the 1950's, and the actual evolution of the Yugoslav social order became increasingly acute. This led to a crystallization of opinion on the other side: among the progressives and liberals. Intra-party conflicts thus became aggravated to the point where party unity was endangered, and events since 1960 have been shaped by the power struggle between the two groups. Economic difficulties caused by the 1962–63 recentralization—which the orthodox wing had brought about—lent weight to the arguments of the reformers, who carried the day at the 1964 Party Congress and were able to overthrow the most powerful champion of orthodoxy, Ranković, in July, 1966. The concurrent emasculation of the state Security Service may also promote liberal control of the party.

The orthodox-liberal confrontation also reflects the ethnic and regional contrasts that characterize economic, cultural, and political life in the multi-national south Slav federation. The individual republics show widely varying stages of economic development, and a resurgent nationalism has today its primary roots in economic questions. Within the party advocates of decentralization and liberal economic policy tended to come from the more advanced and financially strong republics of Croatia and Slovenia, while the dogmatists and centralists were concentrated in the poorer areas of Serbia, Montenegro, and Macedonia. Today, however, this regional differentiation of opinion has become blurred, although the economic and cultural differentials remain.

The cardinal problem facing Yugoslavia today is a growing contradiction between the self-administration principle and the political monopoly of the party. A decision taken by the Central Committee on July 1, 1966, created a commission to deal with this problem through an incisive reform of the party. Its most important objectives are: reorganization of the Central and Executive committees, the strengthening of "intra-party democracy," and the adjustment of party policy to the changing social order. Even within the party leadership there is a growing trend of opinion favoring a separation of party and state.

It remains an open question whether the process of social change in Yugoslavia can be described as consciously controlled by the party, or whether social developments have run away from party policy and ideology. Even a skeptical appraisal of recent events seems to indicate that certain ideas of freedom and justice have moved beyond the purely economic into the political sphere of social life, where they are already practiced to some extent. A lesson to be learned from happenings in Yugoslavia is that at least a degree of democratic development can be initiated within a communist one-party system, and that such development has to be won through intra-party struggle.[28]

Evolution or Pseudo-Evolution?

Critical analysis of the various changes reported in this symposium should make it evident that they do not necessarily and inevitably lead to great changes but, instead, move within definite limits dictated by the totalitarian nature of communist systems. What may be classified as "liberalization" in one East European state may not constitute liberalization in another. It should also be noted that the tendencies observed here are not limited to the formally independent communist states; they are also present in the Soviet Union, especially in its border areas (the Baltic states, Byelorussia, Ukraine, and Moldavia).

If we are really witnessing an inevitable development in communism, as the "evolutionist" politicians claim, then this means that the West can simply wait for communism to wither on the vine. The communist rulers may perhaps succeed in slowing down and in some respects obstructing this process, but they cannot, in the long run, prevent the westernization and ultimate disintegration of communism.

It is necessary, however, to face the possibility, if not the probability, that the changes we have recorded do not constitute an organic evolution, but are superficial modifications of a situation that remains basically the same. Can it be that the developments discussed in this book are largely the visible results of tactical measures? Perhaps their only purpose, both in internal and international politics, is to draw the teeth of a potentially dangerous opposition. Perhaps the true sense of freedom is to be replaced by a higher standard of living coupled with a spurious freedom in Eastern Europe. Or is it the purpose of these developments to make the West forget the danger of communism?

As this is written, the watchword in Western capitals is détente. It is hardly necessary to urge that the realism of a policy of détente depends in large part on whether the changes observed in Eastern Europe are steps in the direction of freedom or merely an optical illusion in that respect.

NOTES TO CHAPTER ELEVEN

1. Text in *Dziennik ustaw*, No. 33 (July 23, 1952).

2. Latest elections, as reported by *Trybuna ludu*, June 3, 1965.

3. Replaced the deceased Aleksander Zawadzki, according to *Polityka*, August 22, 1964; reelected the following year, as reported in *Trybuna ludu*, June 25, 1965.

4. *Trybuna ludu*, August 14, 1966.

5. "Testimony of Wladyslaw Tykociński," *Hearing* before the Committee on Un-American Activities, House of Representatives (Washington D.C.: Government Printing Office, 1966), p. 908. This man had been chief of the Polish military mission in Berlin until his defection.

6. *See* "De-Stalinization in Eastern Europe: 'The Polish Model' " in Andrew Gyorgy (ed.), *Problems in World Communism* (Princeton, N.J.: D. Van Nostrand Company, 1966), p. 70, for a listing of key personnel.

7. Tykociński, *op. cit.*, p. 907

8. *Nowe drogi*, II (May-June, 1948), p. 30; *Trybuna ludu*, May 16, 1965.

9. *Nowe drogi*, XII (December, 1958), p. 87; *Trybuna ludu*, January 16, 1960; *ibid.*, June 16, 1960; *ibid.*, March 16, 1961. During 1965 a total of 37,853 members were crossed off party lists; in the first six months of 1966 about 22,200 left the party of their own initiative, another 15,411 were crossed off, and approximately 3,000 were purged: *Trybuna ludu*, February 26 and August 14, 1966.

10. *Trybuna ludu*, June 15, 1966, and August 28, 1965.

11. N. Stolpow, "Communist Countries of Europe," *Kommunist vooruzhönnykh sil*, XLVI (February, 1966), pp. 72–75.

12. *Polityka*, October 30, 1965, p. 10.

13. *Życie Warszawy*, December 10, 1965.

14. *See* commentary by Ludwig Zimmerer, broadcast by *Bayerischer Rundfunk*, July 4, 1966.

15. Politbureau Report in *Nowe drogi*, XIX (August, 1965), pp. 3–58.

16. Tykociński, *op. cit.*, p. 907.

17. Kazimierz Secomski, "The Western Territories: 20 Years of Development," *Polish Perspectives*, VIII (September, 1965), pp. 3–13.

18. E. B. Valev, "Plan," *Vestnik Moskovskogo universiteta*, No. 2/1964.

19. The most systematic and comprehensive presentation of the Yugoslav system—especially Self-Administration—can be found in S. Pejovich, *The Market-Planned Economy of Yugoslavia* (Minneapolis: University of Minnesota Press, 1966); G. Macesich, *Yugoslavia: The Theory and Practice of Development Planning* (Charlottesville: Univer-

sity Press of Virginia, 1964); H. Schleicher, *Das System der betrieblichen Selbstverwaltung in Jugoslawien* (Berlin: 1961); D. Miljević, S. Blagojević, M. Nikolić, *Razvoj privrednog sitema FNRJ* [The Development of the Economic System of FPR Yugoslavia] (Belgrade: 1956); International Labor Office, *Die Arbeiterselbstverwaltung in den Betrieben Jugoslawiens* (Geneva: 1962); Institut druŠtvenik nauka, *Radničko samoupravljanje–razvoj i problemi* [Worker's Self-Administration—Development and Problems] (Belgrade: 1963). One of the most concise presentations of the 1965 Yugoslav economic reform is R. Bićanić, "Economics of Socialism in a Developed Country," *Foreign Affairs*, Vol. 44, No. 4 (July, 1966). For economic development in Yugoslavia, see *Yugoslavia* (Economic Surveys by the OECD: Paris).

20. *See* V. Pejovski, "Die Investitionspolitik in Jugoslawien," *Schrift enreihe Internationale Politik* (Belgrade: 1965).

21. *Financial Times,* London, January 25, 1967.

22. Westdeutscher Rundfunk, Cologne, *Der Internationale Frühschoppen*, broadcast on August 21, 1966.

23. Interview with Professor Antun Vratuša of the University of Ljubljana, *New York Times*, March 10, 1964.

24. F. Mayer, "Die Sozialistische Föderative Republik Jugoslawien—Entstehung und staatsrechtliche Entwicklung Jugoslawiens bis zur Verfassung von 1963," *Zeitschrift für Politik*, Vol. 11 (1964) pp. 360 *et seq.*

25. *See* R. V. Burks, "Verbürgerlicht Jugoslawien?" *Osteuropäische Rundschau*, Munich: No. 11 (1965), pp. 7 ff.

26. *See* D. Müller, *Jugoslawien zwischen Ost und West* (Hanover: 1964).

27. See *Practice and Theory in the Erection of Socialism in Yugoslavia,* in materials from the VIII Party Congress (Belgrade: 1965).

28. Westdeutscher Rundfunk, Cologne, *Der Internationale Frühschoppen*, broadcast on August 21, 1966.

Part Four

Cultural Aspects of the Change in Eastern Europe

CHAPTER XII

The Intellectual Shift in East-Central European Marxism-Leninism

EUGEN LEMBERG

M ENTION OF CHANGES in East-Central European Marx-ism-Leninism in contemporary conversations usually calls to mind the well-known symptoms of liberalization within the Eastern bloc: Yugoslavia's "go-it-alone" policy; the difficulties encountered in co-ordinating Eastern bloc economies through the COMECON; and the policies of national independence such as that pursued by Ru-mania. Those more interested in intellectual developments tend to emphasize the discontent of the workers, students, and intelligentsia —a discontent that boiled over in the "Polish October" and in the Hungarian uprising of 1956—and may have some inclination to read in these phenomena the indices of a rejection of communism and an approach toward Western customs and Western social and govern-mental systems.

These symptoms of a rejection of communism, which are clearly apparent in East-Central Europe, are not, however, our present con-cern. Those who know how far communism has managed to interlace itself with the nationalism of the peoples in that region will in any case be inclined toward skepticism about any rejection of commu-nism. Of greater immediate importance is the intellectual shift *within* communism.

This process of internal change may not mean the dissolution and rejection of communism that Western observers are so anxious to discern. It may, rather, be evidence of an adaptation, by means of which the communism of Eastern and East-Central Europe is emerging from the isolation imposed upon it by Stalin, is becoming socially acceptable in the intellectual world of Western science and philosophy, and is thus being preserved—albeit in modified form—as one of the forces that will continue to shape the epoch to come.

All this is reason enough to look beyond the spectacular phenomena of crises and disintegration and to take note of the intellectual shift through which Marxism-Leninism has been passing since its power spread across East-Central Europe. The extreme forms of this shift have acquired notoriety under the label of revisionism. But—as we know by analogy from the history of the Reformation—there are no rigid barriers between doctrines remaining within the range of orthodoxy and the heresies that accept the consequences of a break with the high priests of Marxism-Leninism and are therefore condemned as revisionism; rather, there are fluid transitions from one to the other.

In the study of the mental processes and disputes that culminate in revisionism, the intellectuals among the peoples of East-Central Europe must occupy the center of the stage. When Marxism-Leninism took root in this region, all historical experience in similar situations pointed to the natural expectation that, when assimilated by peoples with a thousand years of Western tradition, it would acquire a physiognomy quite different from that which it manifested in Russia, particularly in the Stalinist version that was then current. The European answer of these peoples, a certain re-europeanization of Marxism and a rediscovery of some of its original motives, could be anticipated. And as a matter of fact, this is exactly what happened when the intellectuals of East-Central Europe adopted Marxism—insofar as they adopted it at all.

An astonishing parallelism is manifested by developments in all phases of intellectual activity: in the interpretation of history, in *belles lettres* and fine arts, and in educational practice. This indicates that we have to deal, not with a tempest in a teapot among the philosophy professors, but with a trend affecting cultural life as a whole. Our first and primary concern, however, is with the dispute that has taken place in the inner sanctum of Marxist philosophy and ideology.

In order to understand the values at stake in contemporary disputes, it is first necessary to bear in mind that characteristic changes have taken place in the level and technique of ideological and scholarly argumentation in the Marxism-Leninism of Eastern and East-Central Europe—at least in certain sectors. It is no longer possible to continue the usual practice of Western intellectuals, which was simply to dismiss all expressions of overtly Marxist scholarship within this region as mere effusions of ideology and political propaganda without scholarly value. With the passing of the first wave of agitators who, with mediocre scholarly qualifications, dominated fields such as philosophy, historiography, and literary criticism, a new generation of capable thinkers and researchers has made its appearance over the last ten years. These younger scholars, who are methodologically better trained than the pioneers of Marxism-Leninism and are clearly striving for recognition by non-Marxist scholars in their respective disciplines, have already adjusted themselves to the standards of Western scholarship, both in style and in choice of argument. While adhering to the basic assumptions and categories of Marxism, they are seeking to achieve freer discussion and greater independence of thought, to attain which they are ready to advance to the border of orthodoxy—even into contradiction with it—and to take the risk of being denounced as revisionists. This development has given rise to an entire complex of problems that at least suggests that an internal metamorphosis of Marxism has taken place. What is involved will be illustrated here by analyzing the discussion of three central themes that lie at the root of Marxist self-understanding in the philosophical and ideological debates of East-Central European Marxist-Leninists.

THE CHANGING CONCEPT OF IDEOLOGY

The first theme involves the relationship between science and ideology, that is to say, a change in the concept of ideology. It appears in clearest outline in connection with Polish philosophy, for it was the younger Marxist philosophers of Poland who figured most prominently in the ideological discussion that excited all East-Central Europe shortly before 1960 and for a while thereafter.

Confronting the highly developed and internationally recognized philosophy of Poland after 1945, Marxism-Leninism did not have an easy time of it. As in other East-Central European countries during the early 1950's, in Poland Marxism-Leninism was introduced in the editorial offices of philosophical journals and in scholarly institutes, as well as in the newly founded Polish Academy of Sciences —a copy of its sister institution in Moscow—by young ideologues, scholars, and journalists with only a modicum of philosophical training. The new dispensation was not taken seriously as a philosophy. It was regarded as an ideology, which proceeded from rigid theses not subject to inquiry, on the basis of which it undertook to explain all problems of life, nature, and society and to formulate the only correct guidelines for political, economic, and social development. As a philosophy this Marxism-Leninism remained fixed in a nineteenth century stage of development long since rendered obsolete by the various divergent schools of contemporary philosophy.

A number of factors combined, however, to gain attention and respect for Marxism-Leninism. The power wielded by the party, for instance, was sufficient to install reliable spokesmen of the doctrine in professorial chairs of philosophy and to remove—at least for the time being—those who clung to contrary opinions. It would be wrong, however, to attribute the Marxist-Leninist penetration of Poland to party pressure alone, even though that pressure was more intense before 1956 than it has been since.

Whether or not Marxism-Leninism attained the level of contemporary philosophy, it did offer answers to questions that society has been asking philosophers since time immemorial but which contemporary schools had declined to tackle for reasons deriving from the theory of perception and from scientific rigor. These answers may be based on faith rather than on science: orthodox Marxist-Leninist philosophy claims that they are provable and that it has proved them.

Precisely this claim is now being challenged by the criticism of certain younger philosophers of Marxist-Leninist training. Foremost among these critics is Leszek Kolakowski, whose book, published in German under the title *Der Mensch ohne Alternativen* [The Individual Without Alternatives] (Munich: 1960), discriminates between the functions of faith and knowledge. Like Ernst Bloch and Georg Lukács, he takes a positive view of Marxism, but he accepts it as a faith, a system of values and norms such as every society needs for its survival, rather than as a science.

Kolakowski is not the only one to make the distinction between ideology and science. His Polish colleague Julian Hochfeld has also dealt with this problem. Adam Schaff, whose status as the most representative Polish Marxist philosopher has remained unchallenged, has engaged in criticism from a more orthodox point of view. The discussion of Polish revisionism has, for the time being, revolved largely around this question of the concept of ideology. That this problem is not of interest to Poles alone is indicated by the title of an essay by the Yugoslav Mihailo Marković: "Science and Ideology" (1959).

It is evident from all this that Marxism-Leninism has entered a decisive phase in the *development of its concept of ideology*. Starting with the original concept proclaimed by Marx and Engels in *German Ideology,* which defined ideology as "falsified perception" or deliberate distortion of the truth, Marxism has understood and announced itself not as an ideology, but as a science. Meanwhile, however, the fact Karl Mannheim formulated in his famous book *Ideologie und Utopie* has become self-evident: Marxism, despite its claim to be a science, because of its intention not only to explain the world but to transform it, is also an ideology. Kolakowski defines this as an "evolution of Marxism to an ideology," for, as Marković explains, "a consciousness that is not content to determine facts . . . but also has intentions . . . is not purely scientific . . . but . . . ideological." Kolakowski, however, goes beyond the teachings of even the Western sociology of knowledge concerning ideology. "The difference between ideology and science is not the difference between falsehood and truth. The two differ in their social function and not in the degree of their sincerity." According to Kolakowski, ideology serves a social group by organizing the values "that are necessary so that the group can act effectively." "Knowledge of reality in itself," he adds, "can never stimulate anyone to action."

All this represents a broadening and objectivizing of the concept of ideology—a process that is also taking place, *mutatis mutandis,* in Western thought. The Polish revisionists are mainly concerned with reducing the ideological pressure in scholarly and artistic life and with achieving a certain pluralism. Kolakowski describes this gradual relaxation of ideological pressure as follows: "In Poland, such pressure has already been eliminated in the natural sciences, and it has been greatly limited in the area of artistic creation." Artistic activity, he observes, could not exist without ideological inspiration—but inspiration is something different from direction by a political organization. Kolakowski and Hochfeld go so far as to confront "institutional Marxism," as they call the ideological apparatus perpetuated by party orthodoxy, with an "intellectual Marxism" carried forward by revisionist philosophers and intellectuals, a confrontation that opens new perspectives of credibility and scope to the Marxist movement as a whole.

This entire discussion of the concept of ideology and of the ideological character of Marxism-Leninism is of central importance to the communist movement, as is the distinction between ideology understood as doctrine of faith on the one hand and as objective science on the other. The role of this controversy in the development of communism today is analagous to that of the question whether the sun revolved around the earth or vice versa for the Church in the sixteenth century. Just as the credibility of Christian belief seemed in those days to depend upon retention of the geocentric thesis, so does belief in the superiority of communism over the religions and ideologies of the rest of the world seem to the contemporary leaders of communist parties to depend on the thesis that communism—in contrast to competing doctrines—constitutes demonstrable science.

Kolakowski was not burned alive as was Giordano Bruno. He and Hochfeld were long able to propagate their revisionism in print and over the radio. Finally, however, the party decided that orthodoxy in this question was important enough to require the silencing of Kolakowski. An ideological counteroffensive by the party became apparent in 1963, especially in Poland, where party leader Gomulka proclaimed revisionism to be the principal danger and at the same time claimed emphatically that it had been substantially defeated on various sectors of the ideological front. Other party officials boasted of the party's energetic campaign against the thesis of contradiction between ideology and science and against the differentiation between intellectual and institutional Marxism, a distinction the party considered "sterile." Official terminology continues to speak of the "scientific world view," a term reserved for Marxism-Leninism alone in contrast to all other ideologies and religions.

Perceptions of European experience such as the distinction between ideology and science, in other words between belief and knowledge, are not, however, to be anathematized out of existence and particularly not out of the minds of East-Central European intellectuals, for whom this distinction is also a token of their European thinking. Among such intellectuals, expressions such as the "scientific world view" have degenerated to the status of declamatory clichés. They are still used when they cannot be avoided, for instance, in the deliberately ambiguous language of Czeslaw Milosz as early as 1953, but they are no longer taken seriously. There has been no abandonment of or revolt against Marxism-Leninism, but it is becoming humanized and europeanized.

THE PROBLEM OF CONTRADICTIONS

Around 1963, during the same ideological counteroffensive by the party orthodox, the intellectuals of East-Central Europe were also fascinated by a second topic of discussion, which has since become another permanent feature of the disputes among Marxists in the region. This was the question whether antagonistic contradictions, blunders, disorder, and faulty development are also possible in socialist countries. Since these are all specific sins of capitalism, they should disappear automatically with the transition to socialism. The pragmatically inclined Czechs have played a more prominent role in this discussion, which formed an important part of the background for the noteworthy Kafka Conference, held in Liblitz near Prague in 1963.

Employment of certain essays by the Czech Marxist philosopher Karel Kosík—who will be mentioned again in another connection—is not meant to imply that he is the only one to express a freer point of view, one that promotes the further development of Marxism. On the contrary, this point of view is characteristic of the younger generation throughout East-Central Europe—a generation striving to free itself from dogmatism and the personality cult.

In the age of dogmatism and the personality cult, Kosík wrote in 1957, all the tensions, errors, and abortive developments experienced in socialist countries were interpreted as externally caused, as the machinations of agents from the capitalist countries—the only countries where such phenomena could occur. With this conception Marxism-Leninism retained its utopian character throughout its Stalinist-dogmatic period and even during the beginning stages of the Khrushchev era. This utopianism is now considered unworthy of true and realistic Marxism, and efforts are being made to overcome it. Socialist reality, as viewed by the Marxists of East-Central Europe today, bears no resemblance to the image once propagated from the Soviet Union as an object of belief. Socialism is now seen realistically: a system with problems and contradictions, with deficiencies and negative aspects like every other human society—something needing and meriting continuous effort to perfect it—humane in the sense of European humanism and therefore pluralist in its goals and methods.

It is important to realize what this signifies. Marxism has renounced the millennial vision with which the Communists operated while seizing power in Eastern Europe and which culminated in Khrushchev's precisely dated eschatology pinpointing the emergence of the classless society with which history would come to an end. The sober Czechs, who learned to get along without historical eschatology during their national renaissance in the nineteenth century, have brought the Hegelian, Marxist, Leninist, and now the Khushchevian doctrines of salvation down to earth by unceremoniously dumping their ideal millennium overboard and accepting the facts of life: that a socialist society differs from all other types of social organization in its system and method, but not fundamentally, sociologically, or anthropologically. This is a reorientation no less fundamental than that the early Christians were forced to undertake when they found out that the end of the world would not occur during the lifetime of the generation then living, and that it would be necessary to face long epochs of worldly imperfection and struggle. It is more than a coincidence that one of the Karel Kosík books bears the title *Dialektika Konkrétniho* [The Dialect of the Concrete] (Prague: 1963).

The realist view of socialist society advocated by Kosík and many others also means something more: Marxism's way back into international discussion. Such discussion was not possible with dogmatists, who insisted on treating socialist systems as infallible and immune from the problems of the rest of the world. Now, however, the intellectuals throughout East-Central Europe are showing a passionate concern to emerge from this intellectual isolation and to enter once more into conversation with the outside world—particularly with the intellectual world of the West, from which the peoples of East-Central Europe have never withdrawn.

Taking this realist point of view, the best minds of the younger generation in East-Central Europe view their role in socialist society as that of pioneers in the restoration of a Marxism that is open to the world and capable of development—characteristics that were lost in Stalinist dogmatism, but that they believe represent Marxism's better tradition and its destiny. Only in open-minded discussion with representatives of other, including nonsocialist, systems of thought and social organization do they see the opportunity for socialism to prove itself and have a future.

A classic example of the basic problem in which discussions of every subject merge, namely, that of the relation between a realistically viewed socialist society and the nonsocialist world, was afforded by the famous Kafka discussion at the Liblitz palace near Prague in 1963 and its continuation in related reports and publications. The conservative representatives of the "German Democratic Republic" at the conference and afterward Alfred Kurella, the well-known cultural pundit of the SED, defended the orthodox principle: that there is no longer any "alienation" in socialist society, for which reason Kafka has nothing to say to Marxists. Eduard Goldstücker, professor of German literature in Prague, launched a polemic against this opinion. He accused Kurella of conservatism and demanded an entirely new relationship with the Western, nonsocialist world. A basic weakness of the personality cult, he said, was its tendency to proclaim ideological struggle as necessary but to avoid it in practice. During the Stalinist era Marxists had paid no attention to the development that had been going on for decades in the nonsocialist world; they had contented themselves with an attitude of total rejection and withdrawn behind a Maginot Line of power, confident that the ideological struggle would one day be decided with nonideological weapons. In the discussion of Kafka and of the renewal of Marxism the French Communist Roger Garaudy declared that Kurella was wrong in defining the issue as that of supplementing Marxism. The problem was rather, in Garaudy's opinion, to bring Marxism in its full and renewed strength to bear on problems that it had hitherto passed over in silence.

This position, this striving for an opening of Marxism toward the nonsocialist world and for what might be called social acceptability in that world (despite whatever frequently unobtrusive reservations are made of Marxist concepts and categories), is today characteristic of a large part of the young intelligentsia of East-Central Europe. Despite all reversals and reprisals we are not limited to reading the new point of view between the lines of the prohibitions and anathemas of the government concerned. It is published openly in newspapers and periodicals, particularly in specialized journals. The bolder a magazine becomes, the more rapidly its circulation rises; the more incisively a book deals with these themes, the sooner it is sold out. Although theses such as those now being propounded are called revisionist or come dangerously close to revisionism, they 'actually have a *reformative* character, since they express the maxim: Away from all vulgar Marxist and dogmatist distortions of the true doctrine and back to the sources! Back to the original broadness and open-mindedness of Marxism! It is by no means so dogmatic, so backward, and so primitive as it became in Russian hands. This is how the East-Central European intellectuals justify Marxism. And what else are they to do? They must operate within its conceptual categories and atmosphere if they are to publish, that is, to exist intellectually. Not only personal conversations but magazines and books as well—read between the lines—afford many interesting and amusing proofs of this situation.

BACK TO MARX

There is today a widespread belief among East-Central European Marxist intellectuals that the opening of future prospects for Marxism requires a return to original sources and a rediscovery of Marxism's original broad-mindedness, cosmopolitanism, and humanity, as manifested so clearly by Marx himself. This idea dominates discussions of the third major theme on the cultural agenda since 1962 and is still a subject of lively controversy.

The issue is that of developing a philosophical anthropology on a Marxist base. In order to justify this process as a necessary intellectual achievement of Marxism, recourse is taken to the young Marx. Along with Western researchers on Marx, including non-Marxists, the Marxists of East-Central Europe have rediscovered the humanist motives of the young Marx. This is symptomatic of a movement that embraces broad sectors among the intellectuals: the turning of East-Central European Marxism toward humanism. The term "humanism" has indeed become one of the most frequently employed words in the intellectual literature and journalism of the region in recent years. One characteristic book of this movement, *Marxism and the Human Individual,* written by the Polish philosopher Adam Schaff, appeared recently in German translation.[1] A similar attempt had, however, already been made in 1963 by the Czech author Karel Kosík in his *Dialektika Konkrétniho* (mentioned above in another connection).

The discussion began with a controversy between the Czech academy member Arnost Kolman and Adam Schaff in 1962. Kolman, writing in the Czech magazine *Tvorba*, attacked Adam Schaff's attempt to separate philosophical anthropology, as a specific discipline, from Marxist philosophy. Kolman denied the necessity for such a step. He attributed efforts to develop a special philosophical anthropology to the feeling of certain Marxists that an alliance was needed with the existentialists (J. P. Sartre) and the left Catholics, an alliance he rejected as ideological compromise. Adam Schaff, although in no way a revisionist, defended himself against this orthodox criticism.

Karel Kosík now entered the controversy. In his *Dialektika Konkrétního* and in an earlier article in the *Literární Noviny* he justified the necessity of such an anthropology. While idealism isolates meaning from material reality and transforms it into a reality in itself, natural positivism has gone to the other extreme by depriving reality of meaning. The more thoroughly it excluded the human being and human values from its considerations, the more realistically it could approach reality. The problem was that the reality of Man, thus banned from science and philosophy, did not cease to exist. In fact, it accounted for the periodic waves of anthropologism, which called renewed attention, from time to time, to the forgotten human being and his problems.

Adam Schaff's newest book is a manifest attempt to clear Marxism of the charge that it raises the collective to an absolute value while downgrading the human individual. To achieve his end, Schaff takes up the discussion about Marx as a young man, which had been stimulated by the publication of some of his early writings in the 1930's and which had previously been given more attention in the West than in the communist area. Schaff refers to the interest that German Protestant theologians showed in the young Marx during the 1950's, citing Erich Thier's work, *Young Marx's Concept of Man*.[2] This positive acceptance of Western suggestions is itself at variance with the customs of Soviet orthodoxy and shows the extent to which an opening to the West has become possible in East-Central European Marxism, even where it remains orthodox.

Soviet Marxologists claim to observe a contradiction between the younger and the older Marx, the reason being that the political-economic teachings and the theory and strategy of the class struggle are all that is important for Soviet communism. Adam Schaff refuses to recognize this contradiction. For him, Karl Marx's life, from the humanist and indeed Christian starting point of his Hegelian youth to the political-economic theory of *Das Kapital*, constitutes an organic unity. Marx, he writes, never abandoned his original concern: the liberation of the individual and the elimination of his alienation from his own personal purposes in life. The entire turn towards economics—Schaff undertakes to prove—was only a reluctantly adopted detour to Marx's true objective: the creation of social conditions such that the personal fulfillment of the individual, hitherto "alienated" by the conditions of production, could be restored. Despite his stubborn concentration on the economic relationships and laws that needed to be studied in order to overcome them, Marx returned time and again to his individualist and humanist starting point. For Adam Schaff this is proof of the extent to which the Marxist anthropology postulated by him, with its humanist foundations, is necessary in order to correct the unbalanced collectivism and economism of the Marxist epigones and administrators.

It is noteworthy that Schaff goes so far as to ask whether the "alienation" pictured by Marx is only possible in the capitalist system, as Marx thought, or in the socialist system as well. Marx, he adds knowingly, could not have anticipated the personality cult. Schaff also asks whether private property, as Marx also believed, is really the only cause of alienation. Here again, Marx could have known no better, since he was unacquainted with Stalinism. These questions were an echo of the discussion theme, mentioned above, that played a central role at the 1963 Kafka conference and became a watershed separating the orthodox, conservative functionaries from the young, progressive, revisionistically inclined and open-minded intellectuals: the question whether alienation is also possible in socialist countries —as the younger Marxists believe—or whether the end of capitalism entailed the end of alienation and thus freed Marxists from the need for further independent thought or for studying nonsocialist conceptual systems—as the conservatives assume.

In this field, too, the internal exegesis of Marx's personality and teachings, the characteristic confrontation of two fronts, can be observed in East-Central European Marxism. There is a Marxist-Leninist orthodoxy, which no longer clings to so-called dogmatism but nevertheless regards Marxism as such a closed and comprehensive system that it need not accept suggestions from non-Marxist systems of thought, which would only distort it. This orthodoxy holds that alienation was overcome through the abolition of capitalism in the socialist countries. Opposing the orthodox front is that of the "progressive" intellectuals, who not only do not shrink from discussion and exchange of views with Western philosophies but also consider such contacts necessary, and who are in varying degrees "revisionists."

The same fronts and basic positions can be observed in connection with all three major themes of Marxist-Leninist philosophy and ideology currently being discussed by the intellectuals of Eastern Europe: (1) the controversy about the concept of ideology and the differentiation between ideology and science; (2) the argument about the realistic perception of socialist countries—a perception that makes contact with the West possible—according to which they are subject to the same kind of problems and errors and the same "alienation" as capitalist countries; and (3) the controversy concerning the necessity for and justification of a philosophical anthropology with a Marxist base—which had hitherto been missing but could now be supplied through a return to Marx's original humanism.

The Scope of Marxist Revisionism

The phenomenon that has been illustrated with brief descriptions of discussions in the field of Marxist philosophy in East-Central Europe is by no means limited to the subjects and authors mentioned. It is the manifestation of an intellectual movement or, more exactly, of a state of mind among the intellectuals of East-Central Europe, insofar as they are Marxists and—notwithstanding their revisionism—have no intention of abandoning Marxism.

It is possible to cite similar examples from Hungary and Yugoslavia, as well as from the part of Germany ruled by the SED. In the latter Wolfgang Harich and Robert Havemann proposed revisionist ideas and were made to suffer for it. In Hungary there are—in addition to Georg Lukács, who has become an institution—a large number of poets, writers, and scholars who either are revisionists or lean toward revisionism. These people—who according to an acid admonishment in the official party journal *Tarsadalmi Szemle* call themselves oppositional Communists—cite the Twenty-second Party Congress of the CPSU in support of their struggle for tolerance, pluralism, and open-mindedness. In Yugoslavia the criticism of the "new class" by Milóvan Djilas, a member of the top party leadership whose book was published throughout the world but who was himself sentenced to a long term in prison, has been followed by criticism of the Soviet Union by the university lecturer Mihajlo Mihajlov, who achieved popularity with his series of articles entitled *Moscow Summer, 1964*. Quite recently the Zagreb magazine *Praxis* has been crusading against dogmatism and for the right of free criticism with a series of articles that have attracted much attention, including orthodox replies. This periodical provides a medium for Professor Danko Grlic of the University of Zagreb, who openly denounces the "Stalinist revision of Marxism and Marxist humanism" that still dominates the older functionaries. This is a turning of the tables on the Stalinists. "Marxism," Professor Grlic declares, "that is, the true and original Marxism, has not suffered a decline. A great quantity of superstitious prejudices, simplifications, and dogmas, on the other hand, that were formerly called Marxism, are long since dead and buried, with us and throughout the socialist world. And thanks to the demise of this superstitious pseudo-Marxism, Marxism has become bolder, more authentic, and more capable of solving the problems of the world today." This is precisely the basic feeling of the younger Marxist intellectuals of East-Central Europe, as we have sensed it in the theses of Polish and Czech philosophers.

The intellectual development indicated here is not limited, however, to the area controlled by communist governments in East-Central Europe. It is also taking place among the Communists of the West European democracies, where the same arguments are addressed to the same problems. On both sides of the Iron Curtain the dispute among Communists shows a striking parallelism to a trend in the noncommunist world. These facts enjoin us from dismissing these philosophical and ideological discussions as a tempest in a teapot among Marxist ideologues.

That Palmiro Togliatti applied the word "polycentrism" to the Italian Communists is well known, as are the attempts of his successor to reach an arrangement with the Roman Church, with left Catholicism serving as a bridge. In France Roger Garaudy—whom we already encountered in the Kafka discussion—has taken a position close to the Sartre version of existentialism. The Vatican Council initiated by Pope John XXIII inspired Garaudy to an almost panegyrical appraisal of Christianity, which appeared in the *Cahiers du Communisme* in 1963. Among the basic ideas of the Council, he emphasizes the discovery of the human being, in whom the Church now reposes an entirely new confidence and whose human rights are restated in John's encyclical *Pacem in Terris*—an encyclical in which the spirit of dialogue attained victory over the spirit of crusade. To support his contentions, Garaudy is able to cite prominent ecclesiastical commentators. In this development he also sees—not without a degree of justification—the same trend toward humanism that is characteristic of contemporary Marxism. This makes him conscious of the common points of departure of Marxism and Christianity: "Marxists do not forget what they owe to Christianity . . . Marxists are proud to claim as their own the tradition of Hellenic humanism and rationalism, but are also aware that Christianity created a new dimension of mankind: that of the human person."

Garaudy's article also illustrates the satisfaction these progressive Marxists feel at seeing their ideas confirmed, when they recognize in Teilhard de Chardin a phenomenon analogous to themselves: a revisionist—in the Catholic area, of course—who, like themselves, aspires to the further development of his belief in the direction of evolutionary humanism. Thus Leszek Kolakowski, writing in 1965, calls "Teilhardism" a risk but at the same time an unprecedented opportunity for the Catholic Church, just as East-Central European revisionism means a risk but at the same time the decisive opportunity for Marxism.

It would, of course, be possible to interpret this entire development as an obbligato to certain "popular front" tendencies, which are again—as has happened regularly during power crises in the Soviet system since the 1920's—appearing on the political horizon, that is, as tactics and propaganda. But even if this were the case, the theories, conceptions of the world, self-images, and arguments thus set in motion have acquired too much momentum and specific gravity of their own and have cut too wide a swath among Marxist, revisionist, and non-Marxist intellectuals both within and beyond East-Central Europe to permit the entire trend to be stopped short by a change of course of the kind customary under Stalin. Today such changes are less frequent, and in any case they are hardly enforceable in countries outside the Soviet Union. It is therefore advisable to deal seriously and critically with this entire development within and on the fringes of the Marxist movement—if for no other reason than that we, too, are in motion, and a certain parallelism, to say nothing of a degree of convergence, of ideological processes is not to be denied.

Historical processes of this kind in the realm of ideas cannot always

be launched and guided by political authorities for tactical conveni-
ence. Some light may be thrown on their significance and autonomous laws of development if the numerous historical examples of
reception of an ideology by a particular society are brought to bear as
comparative points of reference. Such an analysis may point to the
beginnings of a theory of ideological processes. Our brief concluding
considerations will be devoted to this subject.

The facts we have observed in connection with the reception and
transformation of Marxism-Leninism in East-Central Europe, when
compared with similar processes internationally and historically, contain a wealth of material for such a structural history and functional
analysis of ideology in general. We have, to begin with, the invasion
of this region by Marxism-Leninism, an event for which many favorable conditions existed, not only political and military, but social and
intellectual as well. Among these may be mentioned the unsolved
nationality question, the chronic agrarian crisis, the economic an-
archy of the small national states, a semi-feudal society without a
stabilizing bourgeois middle class in certain countries, the rapid deterioration of East-Central European democracies—superficial imita-
tions of those in the West—into dictatorships and semi-dictatorships,
and, finally, the pragmatism of the bourgeois-national leadership of
the national states created in 1918, which disappointed the best minds
and enticed them into revolutionary movements that offered chal-
lenges, enemies, and visions. The motivations leading to a decision
for communism were not very different from those that led many to
become Catholics and impelled others toward various forms of fascism.

When Marxist ideology first came to power, it enjoyed a brief
honeymoon attributable to a number of factors: the victory over an
intolerable state of affairs, a vision of a better future, the fascinating
opportunity to participate in a rebuilding of society, and, of course,
the rush of opportunists to climb aboard the bandwagon. Soon,
however, it was forced into a defensive position. Who cares to be
identified with the errors that inevitably occur in the process of reconstruction and that are multiplied automatically in an ideological-
doctrinaire totalitarian system? It becomes fashionable to wash one's
hands of the system, at first shyly and apologetically, then cynically,
and finally with unmitigated loathing. The alternative to the system
—in this case the West—grows in fascination, and not only because of
its higher standard of living.

This is the second phase of the process described—somewhat tentatively and imprecisely—as the reception of ideology in this essay. This phase is already partly shaped by a younger generation, which has experienced in childhood the revolutionary days of pioneers and heroes or—as in East-Central Europe—a liberation with ambiguous effects, which is more matter-of-fact and accustomed to things, which is tired of revolutionary emotionalism, and which backs away from the dogmatic parvenus of the first wave.

Where, however, does this younger generation find its *raison d'être*, insofar as it does not emigrate to the West—which happens only very occasionally? For it must find some kind of adjustment, some task, and some meaning in life. It finds all of these in the further development, modernization, revision, and reformation of that same ideology under the influence of which its members live as partly or wholly convinced members of society. Just as the first wave of revolutionary pioneers found satisfaction in propagating and organizing the social system dictated by their beliefs—a task requiring an offensive, missionary approach—so the second wave, the younger generation, feels the need to develop a new program and a new goal. These must deviate in one way or another from the initial achievement, must overcome the disappointment that it necessarily aroused, and must thus give the life of this second, younger generation meaning and purpose. Since a restoration of the *ancien régime,* the system overthrown by the revolution, cannot, at least yet, be considered, this is the age of revisionism. How strongly such revisionism is dictated to the second wave by the dialectic of generations can be recognized from the fact that even true believing Marxists like Adam Schaff and Karel Kosík develop theses and arguments that resemble revisionism and, at the very best, influence the development of the prevailing ideology in the same direction.

When this entire and seemingly inevitable succession of phases—characterized here as the dialectic of generations—is viewed from a detached position, the question finally arises whether there is a law that controls the historical development of an ideology—any ideology—in the stages after it has seized power. There is much to suggest that the sequence of phenomena examined here contains elements that are typical.

If, however, there is a typical sequence of phases in the reception of an ideology, then we Western observers must feel impelled to inquire as to the future prospects for the great ideological confrontation between East and West. This is, briefly stated, the question of our rescue from an ideology that maintains its world revolutionary pretensions today as in the past. From which quarter should we expect salvation: from its refutation, emasculation, destruction through a defeat of the power that supports it, or perhaps from a conversion of its faithful? Or should we not rather look toward a softening and functionalizing of the ideology and toward its integration into the stream of world history through further development, humanization, and revision?

On the basis of all we know of the world history of ideologies, to which must now be added what we have learned from the changes in Marxism-Leninism since it extended its power over East-Central Europe, it behooves us to regard the second of these tendencies as the main chance. This is all the more so in view of the evident parallelism between the transformation of East-Central European Marxism and a trend in the rest of the world—a parallelism that shows signs of a degree of convergence of ideologies.

NOTES TO CHAPTER TWELVE

1. Adam Schaff, *Marxismus und das menschliche Individuum* (Vienna: Europa-Verlag, 1965).

2. Erich Thier, *Das Menschenbild des jungen Marx* (Göttingen: 1957).

CHAPTER XIII

The Wave of the Past

EUGENE DAVIDSON

WHEN IN THE SUMMER of 1914 the young men of Europe, swept along by their own conviction of the righteousness of their cause and their longing to rescue the fatherland from its peril, marched forth to war from under the flowers showered upon them by their exultant fellow countrymen and countrywomen, neither they nor their leaders had any idea of the kind of war it would turn out to be. Uhlans rode into battle with their lances, poilus in the bright uniforms of another century. It was the cut and thrust and headlong charge on the bloody but glorious field of battle shown in the pictures that filled the museums and history books that they envisioned—not the fields of mud, the mechanical mass slaughter of the trenches. Learned books have been written on the failure of the generals not only to foresee what would happen, but even to understand what happened after the war started; on the generals' clinging to historical habits of thought and practice while hundreds of thousands of men died of their arteriosclerosis.

Preparations for World War II were far more up-to-date—a fact doubtlessly reflecting both the criticisms made of military practice in World War I and the lessons drawn from the experimental battlefield in Spain. But even so, the Poles again sent lancers into the field, while a more advanced military theory, attempting to wrench itself free of past errors, envisaged such a wide range of possibilities that almost nothing was left out. Thus it was foreseen by some military theorists that the air arm alone would win a war, preventing mobilization of the enemy and bombing it into submission before it could begin to fight, or that a small army of highly trained specialists would replace the huge, unwieldy mass armies of World War I. It was the German army more than any other that in 1939 selected and combined from among the many choices presented by these theories the mechanized, motorized, and airborne army of specialists and foot-sloggers that produced the *Blitzkriege*. It was the then current blueprint of the national socialist revolution that made it impossible to turn these victories into anything more than armed occupations, resting on military force and a secret police, and thus made it necessary to expand further. But the ineptitudes, as in the case of World War I, were international. The French had more tanks in 1939 than the Germans, they had more troops, and they had the world's most renowned system of fortifications and alliances—alliances that represented in the early mid-thirties a massing of the forces of Europe against the German Reich so overwhelming as to represent, on paper at least, the greatest coalition of all time: Russia, Czechoslovakia, Poland, Great Britain, Belgium, Yugoslavia. It was a formidable array and it fell apart in a matter of months.

It would not be difficult to submit evidence of similar blunders by the political leadership and the general staffs of other centuries, but what makes the present examples more glaring is both their nearness to us in point of time and their contrast to the peacetime environment, smoothed, leveled, and made almost painless by the technological revolution and the millennial plans for its exploitation that far outpaced even its dynamic progress. For the general staffs and the politicians of the pre-World War I era to underestimate the military uses of the machine gun, of the gasoline engine, and then of the self-propelled armored fortress is basically the same kind of phenomenon as the foot dragging of former generations of military men in exploiting the uses of the long spear, gunpowder, and armored ships. What dramatized, as does one of Mme. Tussaud's exhibits, the failures of the men of World War I was the catastrophic loss of life that followed upon their incomprehension—a loss, it may be added, that has never been made good and can never be made good, for although the population fills up again, the generations that would have been begotten by the Alain Fourniers, the Rupert Brookes, and the young German writers whose letters have been preserved because they died on the field of battle can never exist. The current generation can never enrich its continent and its world as these young men for so brief a time enriched theirs.

Slaughter on a huge scale was by no means lacking in the wars of the past, but as the name of the Thirty Years War—an oft-cited example—shows, they were long, as well as destructive, wars; a few days on the Vimy Ridge or in the fields of Flanders or in the storming of Verdun could match their holocausts. Wrong and stupid judgments, miscalculations, and brainlessness can have more deadly consequences more quickly in the twentieth century than they had in the nineteenth or in centuries before. It is one thing to misdirect an army and lose a great battle in which a few thousand men are deployed, after which a peace treaty shifts boundaries that were changed before and will be changed again as chance or military genius determines the fortunes of states in the ebb and flow of the accepted context of a Western order; it is quite another to make a similar miscalculation in 1914 and again in 1939, and it is still another in the late 1960's. When Adolf Hitler mistook his paranoid, fanatical, and parochial view of history for a world view and imposed his rule of violence and illegality on his own people first and then on the major part of the continent of Europe, the effects were to last far beyond the twelve years of his tyranny. When Franklin Roosevelt failed to grasp the essential realities of Soviet Russia and put all his bets on postwar collaboration between the USSR and the United States and the other "peaceloving" nations of the world, the effects of such incomprehension were far longer lived than when he thought the China of Chiang Kai-shek should be one of four policemen putting down aggressors in the postwar international society of his imagination. The two men are not otherwise easily compared—what is comparable is the long-range effect of decisions made on the basis of their private worlds, the one filled with terror and concentration camps for the pariah races or for those who resisted him, the other created from humanitarianism, from cherishing the forgotten man and all those lacking the four freedoms. But the laws governing nations and human societies doubtless work as surely as those of nature, and we still bear, as we will for years to come, the burden of the violence and hatreds Hitler unleashed and of the fatuous conceptions of the nature of communism held by Mr. Roosevelt.

Hegel said that we learn nothing from history. But as it lurches from one position in time to another, it is clear that some detritus of experience is left behind and utilized, however imperfectly. After World War I had been fought in the expectation that it would resemble the wars of the nineteenth century, the German, and later the Allied, military strategists of World War II determined that they would not make the same mistakes again, that they would make every possible use of science and technology—from tanks to jets and rockets and then to the atom. And political decisions have followed a similar course: no major decision by the great powers to intervene or not to intervene in a critical area, or to form or dissolve alliances, has been made without awareness that a basic miscalculation could result in the destruction of cities and entire populations.

Other decisions and their aftermaths, too, bore the imprint of a past that was not to be repeated. The Common Market, NATO, and the French-German rapprochement marked the beginnings of a new European solidarity. For a time it seemed as though the common defense front might be deepened by additional economic and political collaboration that would further diminish the importance of national boundaries. Any idea of war between the Western partners had become truly unthinkable—a remarkable change in political preconceptions in itself, even if it owed at least as much to the threat of the Soviet Union as to the knowledge that an era was over. Other well-publicized advances in international comity such as a world organization, the product of generations of earnest if wishful thinking, had none of the vitality or the adaptability of the pan-European or pan-Western movement, the alliance of the noncommunist powers of the Continent with the United States.

Mr. Roosevelt's imagined four policemen pursuing the breakers of international law did not exist, had never existed; there is no analogy or at best a most misleading one between the criminal operating in municipal law and the criminal in international law. As one of the jurists who helped draw up the charter of the International Military Tribunal at Nuremberg pointed out when Mr. Justice Jackson was trying to impose his notion of individual responsibility for the crime of committing aggression, some day there may be such a crime, but to call it that at the present time is to go far beyond the facts of international life. No state after World War II, except perhaps West Germany, was prepared to yield an important measure of its sovereignty to an international organization. What the states were prepared to do, and what they did, was to accept a limited and prudent surrender of sovereignty for the common defense that could only be achieved in the form of an alliance and to make concessions in the fields of economics and politics and in former military notions of what made for security in peacetime. Under this international um-

brella and in this climate Western Europe has flourished as never before in its history. The United Nations has its modest uses, but not
in the form in which those who dreamed of four policemen saw it.
It can patrol the borders between Israel and the Arab countries as a
kind of international gendarme. But the moment it attempts much
more in the way of peace-keeping—as it did in the Congo—it is torn,
not only by internal dissension, but also by its built-in incapacity to
deal with rivalries and counter-purposes among the great powers.
There is no need to do more than mention its futility when a major
crisis such as that in Cuba or Vietnam occurs. That it was able to take
any action in Korea was entirely owing to the fortuitous absence of
Soviet Russia from the Security Council.

The hypocrisy of a collective security system that (as in the case of
the League of Nations) had essentially no higher motive than to preserve the status quo regardless of its injustices or its incompatibility
with the relative strengths and capacities of nations has been stripped
away in post-World War II Europe. And not only in Europe. A piece
of territory like Goa, which hundreds of years ago became part of a
great overseas empire, can actually change hands with little or no
bloodshed and without an international posse springing into action.
Under the new conditions that removed Portugal from the position
of an imperial power and that changed India from a divided conge-
ries of a hundred separate rulers to a unified nation, a territory like
Goa may change hands and come under the sway of a state like India,
the highly regarded spiritual center of nonresistance to the forces of
violence and imperialism. Change, in other words, can still take
place in our time if the major powers have no interest in preventing
it or if the minor states that continue to inflate the United Nations
cannot, or prefer not to, interpret the change as imperialism.

The more limited and realistically designed economic, military,
and political alliances of today, however, are a different phenomenon. Since the occurrence of the major tragedies of the forced migra-
tions from East Germany and Czechoslovakia, it may be said that
postwar changes in Western Europe have on the whole been benefi-
cent. Up to a short time ago it seemed that the apex of international comity had been achieved in a spirit of mutual confidence by
the Western powers. Europeans could travel from one country to
another with a minimum of red tape, and goods flowed almost as
freely. The armed forces of the nations of Western Europe were coordinated, their air forces flew unimpeded over national boundaries,

their high commands shared quarters and personnel, and the troops of late enemies and friends were under the mixed command of officers of the alliance regardless of nationality. These seemed to be the outward and visible signs of the beginnings of a movement that would before long transform the Continent even further from its sanguinary, hyper-nationalist past of separate, warring states into a cooperating, mutually dependent alliance, and then perhaps into a federation. But old, vestigial habits of thought easily reassert themselves when the clear and present danger has lost its overwhelming threat. The rules by which statesmen have lived for centuries are broken only in emergencies, by the demands of warfare or its simulacrum in peacetime, for they have stubbornly stood the tests of time and experience and, like many relics of the past, they may have an alluring patina that has no substitute in the new concepts. One does not need a French general in his seventies to reactivate these old patterns of *gloire* and security. One needs only the diminishing or the seeming diminishing of the danger that caused the new orientations temporarily to take the place of the old.

But if de Gaulle is making a mistake, the results of his miscalculations may well be far more long-lived than the General himself, for his recent policy reverts to a long tradition, however much it may be out of date. It is only a slight oversimplification to say that this policy has been mainly responsible for the tragedies that have overtaken Europe and the world in the last hundred years. For the *politique* that fitted the realities of Europe in the eighteenth and nineteenth centuries became ill-fitting in the late nineteenth and early twentieth centuries and grotesque by the time of the Weimar republic, for it was purely negative. Germany, whether in the interest of French security or French hegemony, had to be cut down to size: the wars that France lost, or won through alliances with more powerful states, served to increase her determination to accomplish this purpose at almost any cost. Thus the Germany of the Weimar republic, which was far less a threat to the peace of Europe than the succession states, was forced into the position in which it had to produce a dissembling, iron-fisted Hitler or fall victim to civil war. Not only was Germany limited to an army of 100,000 men, without an air force and without heavy artillery, not only was it bled for as long as possible through unprecedentedly large reparations that could not possibly be paid, not only was self-determination limited to France's allies and denied the Germans, but all this was perpetrated under the rubric

of legality. When the Poles seized Vilna or were awarded German
territory that had voted to join the Reich, their actions were accepted
as legal; but when the bankrupt Austrians wished to have a customs
union with the impoverished Germans, such proposals were illegal
and if necessary would be prevented by armed force. No post-World
War I statesman of any stature attempted for long to defend this
status quo in Europe up to the time when Hitler changed it; they
tended to agree that the Polish corridor and one-sided interpretations
of what was right for the victors and the vanquished held the seeds of
future wars in them, but they let matters drift. They certainly did
not know it at the time, but what they were doing was demanding a
Hitler. They were conjuring up a primitive, dark, irrational, volkish
mystique that would be expressed in the coming to power of a man
who had none of the reasonable scruples of his Weimarian predecessors and who could answer hypocrisy with counter double-talk and
the show of force with tirades and steel.

French policy and the doctrine of pseudo-legality that bolstered it
in the League of Nations were little fitted to the realities of twentieth
century Europe. A weak France as the hegemonical power of Europe
corresponded, not to the facts of international development, but to
myths that could only be maintained by sleight of hand. And for a
time following World War II the same kind of tactic was used. A divided Germany was welcomed, the more divided the better. "We
love Germany so much," said one distinguished Frenchman, "that
we want two of them." Almost every step taken toward Germany's rehabilitation after World War II was opposed by a France still aspiring to dominate the Continent. Even a central German postal
administration and the organization of German trade unions on a
national scale were opposed. The government of the Fourth Republic, which had a political Morgenthau plan of its own, retreated foot
by foot, contesting every concession its allies found it necessary to
make, including, of course, a German contribution to the defense of
Western Europe.

The change in policy was in part forced upon France by her allies
and in part by the increasing pressure of external circumstances, but
it was also helped by the efforts of some of its own leaders who saw
as clearly as anyone the need for a reappraisal of French aims, purposes, and capacities. Reacting to the Soviet threat made manifest in
the Berlin blockade, in Eastern Europe as well as in Vietnam (in
the early 1950's) and Korea, France slowly and reluctantly abandoned

her Richelieuian policies. And when it changed, France did it with grace and seeming determination. De Gaulle's journey to the Federal Republic was no ordinary occasion; it was a rite of comradeship, of reconciliation. Echoing the words of one French general uttered directly after the end of the war, "Nos ruines sont vos ruines," de Gaulle did not put aside the past; he made use of it to proclaim the insanity of mutual killing between two great neighbors. It was a masterful performance, even if it did turn out to be much the same old play but with new actors and a happy ending. France was still seeking to dominate the Continent, was still seeking—this time by other means—to attain a position to which she could only aspire by way of one-sided alliances, by way of the power of others.

It is easy to understand the desire on the part of de Gaulle and many others less intransigent than he for a third force. American policies, like those of other states, are made in part with domestic politics in mind, not to mention American security commitments far beyond the borders and immediate interests of the European states. The crises in Korea, in Cuba, in Vietnam were further away in the eyes of many Europeans than even the "remote quarrel" Mr. Chamberlain mentioned when speaking to the British people of the Reich and Czechoslovakia in 1938. American postwar policy has often seemed unduly belligerent to many foreign observers, depending on the nationality and political orientation of the critics and the circumstances that gave rise to their criticism. Thus in 1948 and later when the Russians again seemed intent on causing a showdown, many good people said that it was impossible to hold Berlin. Berlin lay in the middle of Soviet-held territory, the mistakes had been made at Potsdam and earlier in dividing the city. Now it must, in one way or another, be acknowledged a victim of its present allies and the inscrutable conqueror. The Berliners themselves violently disagreed with this view of their situation, but I have heard such defeatist notions uttered by other Germans including a professor in a well-known university who told me West Berlin should be acknowledged as lost and a new Berlin rebuilt somewhere in West Germany.

We need not go through the entire list of invitations the United States has been tendered to withdraw from its commitments or to refrain from undertaking new ones. Greece in 1947, Korea in 1950, the offshore islands of Formosa and then Formosa itself, the ultimatum on Soviet rockets in Cuba, the intervention in Santo Domingo, and the defense of South Vietnam: all these acts taken to

resolve crises far removed from Germany or Europe have been denounced in succession as war-breeding or immoral or both. Not only
traditional diplomacy but long experience have taught statesmen to
ask: "What's in it for us? What can we gain and what do we stand to
lose by being drawn into the folly of war of utter destruction through
the whims of a foreign power intent on its own concerns?"

The answers to such questions must depend in large measure on
our view of the nature of the enemy or, if that seems too strong a
word, of the opposing side. First let it be pointed out that in none
of these cases has the attack come from the West or from the United
States. First came the attack on the Greek government by communist
forces inside the country using infiltrated aid from the then pro-So-
viet government of Yugoslavia; next the attack on West Berlin by
means of blockade and the attack against South Korea mounted by
the North; then followed the attack by the Red Chinese on the offshore islands of Formosa, the preparations for a direct Soviet attack
on the United States by installation of missile sites in Cuba, the attempt to extend by civil and guerrilla warfare the Castro branch of
Soviet imperialism to Santo Domingo and other Latin American
countries, and finally the attack by the North Vietnamese on the
South. What were we to do about these? Retreat from each one
separately as so many Americans and Europeans have urged as each
crisis arose? Retreat from some of the areas and stay in others, depending on their strategic importance to the continental United
States or to its allies? The latter would be called a flexible strategy—
which is what all strategy should be. But how far do we retreat?

Let us begin, as we might have, with Quemoy and Matsu, the offshore islands. Even Mr. Kennedy as a presidential candidate suggested that these islands might well be the subject of negotiations.
Had we persuaded the government of Chiang Kai-shek to surrender
the islands, what then? Would this have appeased Red China, caused
it to accept a noncommunist Formosa and to withdraw its claim to
that island? Might it not have whetted the appetite of the Peking government, which, like all other communist governments, establishes
its boundaries as deep in other people's territories as its power or its
threats can move them? And had Greece, or West Berlin, or Formosa
been surrendered, would that have appeased the dynamic forces of
world communism? Would Soviet Russia then have settled down to
negotiate the reunion of East Germany and the Federal Republic?
Would Red China have renounced its further claims to the leader-

ship of a world revolution and the territory of its neighbors and of the imperialist enemy? Was it not the refusal to surrender, despite all demonstrations that withdrawal was prudent and moral, that has kept the peace, that has in fact produced the détente that enables General de Gaulle to journey to Moscow and indulge himself in the illusion that he is aiding the forces of security and of French prestige in leaving his place in the alliance that has sheltered the recovery of France, of Europe, and of its extension, Japan?

So far as the United States is concerned, Mr. Roosevelt's policies, based on his naïve notions about the Soviet Union, were soon to be reversed by a successor without much experience in international politics but with a considerable native sense of their realities. The latter is shared by many, one might say gratefully, by most European statesmen since World War II, for the communist threat was so immediate, so unmistakable and overwhelming that at its most virulent stage it demanded the kind of common purpose and design elicited by war itself. But the détente is a weapon, too, and perhaps a more subtle and powerful one than the bludgeoning tactics Stalin used against the war-weary peoples who stood in his path.

Soviet policy has never long proceeded in a straight line, and although there is a thaw, and although the relationships of the Moscow government to its satellites and to its own people have changed greatly, there is nothing in the structure of the Soviet Union that would prevent its tightening the reins if its leaders saw fit to do so. The Soviet writers who celebrated the appearance of a literature that dealt honestly with the horrors of the past discovered that they had done so prematurely. The one day in the life of Ivan Denisovitch did not last very long. It may be true that much that has happened to lend more personal independence and more freedom to the satellites is irreversible—let us hope that it is—and it may be true that the ideological differences with Red China have produced an unbridgeable gap in the communist camp. But the threat remains, whether communism is divided into two camps or is concentrated in one as it was until a few years ago.

Since 1917 many observers have foreseen the early demise of the Soviet state, and many more have sporadically detected a break with the principles that established it and have stubbornly remained with it throughout all vicissitudes. The changes that have occurred may be cherished. A profit motive has been reintroduced, more consumer goods provided, more freedom of action given the Eastern bloc, more criticism permitted; a bureaucracy has multiplied itself; a deposed

Prime Minister has not been killed or shipped off to some remote part of Siberia but permitted to remain unobtrusively in Moscow. Such developments in the administration of the Soviet Union are on the whole gratifying, but they do not change the character of the dictatorship or the possibility of change in another direction. As things stand, the revolution rooted in the party continues to dominate the Soviet Union and its allies; the communist ideology remains with its vision of a world order in which coexistence, too, is but a means to an end.

It is only very recently that men have decided that a war between countries that share a great and richly diversified culture would be unthinkable. Until Europe had passed through the crucible of World War II, lost provinces or the sufferings of fellow nationals under alien rule at times when the international situation became incandescent and prestige seemed at stake were sufficient to produce the flash point. The plight of the *Sudetenlaender,* of the German minority in Poland, and then of any minority in the Germany of the Third Reich or of any people who found themselves under the heel of its forces of repression: these were all real enough. The peace and unity of Europe under a totalitarian government could only be broadcast by propaganda machines; they had no reality in the lives of the people or in their feeling for justice, nor did they promise the freedom of separate national growth in a great European ecology characteristic of an earlier period of flourishing cultures on the Continent. This has all changed in a true leap forward in Western Europe during the last fifteen years or so. No one is exploited by a political system; cultural development is wholly free and its flow is almost instantaneous; Europeans travel and work and interchange ideas together, and no cause of war may be found among them. The grave problems lie outside their common borders. How long can Germany remain divided? How long can Berlin be two German cities? What will be the fate of the Oder-Neisse territories, which so many people including Germans wish to see formally surrendered before a peace treaty is made acknowledging a *fait accompli* or the continued need to make restitution for nazi crimes in Poland and Russia?

The attempts at a resolution of these problems could divide the alliance, but should they? Is not a strong and democratic Germany sharing her economic, cultural, and military capacities with the countries of a free Europe a bulwark to the alliance? The Federal Republic has earnestly attempted to fulfill its obligations to those the Third Reich so grievously injured; no one who has followed postwar German attempts at restitution can deny that millions of Germans have acknowledged their responsibility and in a spirit of humility and contrition done much to repair the part of the damage done by the National Socialists that is reparable. One has only to compare the number of cases against nazi criminals tried in the Federal Republic with the number tried in Austria to see the difference in the attitude of the two countries that has developed. Those who have found substantial evidence of a rebirth of naziism in Germany either are extrapolating from isolated events or knew what they wanted to find before they started their researches. Neonazi parties have proved transitory and unstable; their supporters write in their newspapers and periodicals for one another with the help of an occasional crackpot from foreign shores, including some from my own country.

But just as a decision in favor of a new association of European nations may be made, decisions may be made that will prevent it. Germany cannot remain forever the problem child with its head turned to the wall in expiation of the sins of another generation or on the racist assumption that some evil psychogenetic inheritance taints the German people. It cannot in the long run remain divided and deprived of equal weapons. Its alliance partners cannot long ignore its just expectations. In the present state of Germany and Europe it would be difficult to repeat the mistakes that were made in the post-Versailles era when the nationalist, particularist, and one-sided policies of the victors helped cause the overthrow of a government that was doing its utmost to cooperate with them. This is no Germany of the inflation, of unemployment and despair, open to the attack of one of the victorious powers whenever it failed to make reparations payments or whenever one of them might see a safe opportunity to make inroads on its sovereignty and territory.

Nevertheless, Germany cannot remain indefinitely and again a special case—denied the weapons that its scientists have, alas, joined the scientists of other nations in developing; permitted to take part in the European and Western alliance only with the acceptance of handicaps designed for it alone and not at all in keeping with its natural development as a great scientific and technological center. If the forces of extreme nationalism and the believers in blood and soil that have been ostracized and rendered powerless in the Federal Republic are ever given any encouragement, it will be by measures similar to those that helped Hitler come to power. If a nation is always treated as an outsider, if it is never permitted the freedom accorded other nations and the psychological and material weapons its partners possess, then the voice of the extremist will be heard in the land, and, what is more, it will be listened to.

What is needed is prudent good faith. Neither Eastern nor Western Europe has ever been composed of fixed configurations, nor are they now. Boundaries have never been eternal, and there is no reason for attributing that status to one established as a *quid pro quo* for territories acquired by the Soviet Union and expressly stated to be provisional. This does not mean advocacy of war on behalf of lost provinces. No responsible person in the Federal Republic has ever advocated the use of force for the reacquisition of the lands taken from their German owners. On the contrary, they have spoken of the need for reconciliation, of the renunciation of force, and of a just solution within a European framework of interdependent nations. It can be said that this is eyewash, that these words mask the true intent of the speakers, who are merely biding their time until a resurgent Germany will be in a position to obtain what it wants by force. But this again is a wave of the past. How could Germany, given the facts of power in the age of intercontinental missiles and their megaton warheads, impose its solutions on territories lying between it and the Soviet Union? Neither the might nor the will is there, and not even their dimmest reflections will make their appearance if the statesmen of the Western alliance continue to take account of the realities of these years, of the survival value of a common defense and purpose, and of the place of generous policies for our friends as well as for our enemies.

It would be folly to miss the opportunity that has been presented to us. There now exists an association of nations that represents a breakthrough from the past, from the wicked past of useless slaughter for ends that are now trivial for this society. We have not only a military alliance in being but also a moral alliance, and to foster it means to treat its members as equals, as partners in a defensive network, which could, at some future time, ripen into a system of security excluding no one. The rejoicing that took place when Britain was kept out of the Common Market should have been mourning. The need of the West is not to limit its system of economic and political cooperation but to expand it. No one country in the current struggle for survival of the free world may be penalized without damage to the others. When the British continued, as a result of earlier four-power agreements, to dismantle German dock installations years after the end of the last war, there might have been the same kind of self-congratulation that was to be witnessed in some quarters on the Continent when Britain was excluded from the economic community. But Britain gained little from its demolitions, made in the narrow context of another period in history. She did something far different when she gave permission for the manufacture of the Volkswagen in competition with her own cars. No one has gained from Britain's being fenced off outside the Common Market; no one, least of all France, will gain from her secession from NATO. The front of the West needs to be held and extended to all those who in good faith wish to participate in it.

The common front is not, of course, a guarantee against all dangers; before long atomic bombs will be produced by nations other than France and Red China, and our system of security must be alert to many vicissitudes. But this is clearly a stage in the political development of the West with enormous possibilities for good and evil; the time demands precisely those forces of reconciliation and mutual support the lack of which in the past has resulted in such monumental disasters. To take the scientific and technological revolution into account does not make us its prisoners. It may be, and we can pray that it prove true, that the new weapons of mass destruction will never be used, that they will remain the ultimate threat, and that the buttons will never be pressed. It may be that the rift between the two communist powers will align the Soviet Union with the West or cause Communist China to assuage her wrath—the possible permutations and combinations are many and unforeseeable. But surely in the meantime to keep the alliance as strong as possible, to foster its possibilities for peace as well as for conflict is to serve a cause that could give nourishment and hope to all mankind—including the peoples of the Soviet Union and of China. Superficially, it may seem pharasaical to say this when United States bombs are falling on North Vietnam in a bitter war the end of which is not yet in sight. But that war is part of an attack mounted against us all, and had the attack not been resisted at the strong and weak points of its varied thrusts, those who press it would have taken over much more than the southern part of a small country in Asia. Our strategy should be flexible, but our purpose should be inflexible: to resist not aggression *per se* but aggression directed against the areas vital to us. It is a common enterprise and out of it— who can tell?—may come the unification not only of Germany but of larger entities that now seem beyond our range.

Part Five
In Summary

CHAPTER XIV

Possibilities and Limitations
of Evolution in Eastern Europe

KURT GLASER

Tʜɪꜱ ʙᴏᴏᴋ, like its predecessors, is concerned with aspects of the East-West confrontation central to twentieth century world politics. Although the contributions are mainly analytical rather than operational in emphasis, the insights they contain may contribute to an intellectual foundation for rational foreign policy, both in the United States and in allied European countries.

The keynote for the Fourth International Congress on Central and East European Affairs and hence for the present book was provided by Senator Thomas J. Dodd, whose analysis emphasizes the unity of the global political struggle and the community of interests of free men on both sides of the Atlantic and—as recent events have demonstrated—the Pacific as well. Some of the more sophisticated Europeans who have been weaned on a diet of Machiavelli, Bodin, Metternich, and Bismarck, as well as American "realists" of the Morgenthau school, may be disposed to smile at the Senator's unabashed idealism, especially his assertion that American foreign policy constitutes an extension of our own Declaration of Independence into the field of foreign affairs. As the Senator himself admits, our beliefs may have at times given rise to a certain democratic dogmatism, particularly in our African policy. One of the most vigorous critics of our Congo policy several years ago was Senator Dodd himself, who after a personal inspection in the Leopoldville area and in Katanga bluntly accused the United Nations interventionary force—and by implication our own government which was providing logistic support—of taking the side of chaos against civilization.

Despite occasional lapses there is, nevertheless, a basic realism in American policy, because it is based on assumptions about man and about human nature that the experience of our total culture has shown to be true. One of these assumptions, which is stated explicitly in several of the essays and is implicit in all of them, is that the survival of the person as a moral and ultimately as a physical being depends upon his integrity. This is the concept underlying the Senator's statement that it is impossible to defend freedom in Europe while abandoning it in Asia. Another of these assumptions, brought out in Senator Dodd's discussion of the "coming collapse of communism," is that man has a fundamental will to freedom. This will to freedom reflects the instinct of moral self-preservation, the innate urge of the individual to defend the wholeness of his personality. This is why a totalitarian regime, which invades and destroys personality, is perpetually at war with the human beings it rules.

Senator Dodd also deals frankly with a number of problems that have caused transatlantic misunderstandings from time to time. One of these is the proposed atomic nonproliferation treaty, controversy about which has intensified in recent months. The purpose of a treaty of this kind is to safeguard the security of atomic and nonatomic powers alike by restricting the multiplication of national nuclear forces that might be recklessly employed to escalate minor wars—the so-called nth country problem. This basic purpose would be defeated were the treaty to be drafted or construed so as to preclude a NATO or European defensive nuclear force.

Unity within the free world has also been disturbed by charges of American unilateralism in NATO and in matters involving Franco-German and Franco-American relations. Although the United States has at times acted without due consideration of the feelings or interests of its allies—a failing which it shares with other governments—there can be no doubt of the basic commitment of the American people to transatlantic as well as European unity. A serious disturbing factor, which for the time being has temporarily obscured the common purposes of Western Europe and the United States, is the failure of many Europeans to understand the dynamics of the Vietnam war. As Senator Dodd points out, the neo-isolationists of Europe, like their American counterparts, have closed their eyes to the basic insatiability of totalitarian systems. The political metabolism of such systems, which is strongly suggested in Professor Herberg's essay, impels their dictatorial rulers to engage in foreign aggression as a means of maintaining themselves at home. The nonappeasability of totalitarian dictatorships was demonstrated by the results of the Munich Conference of 1938 and the Yalta and Potsdam conferences of 1945.

Senator Dodd undertook to assuage the quite rational fear of some Europeans that American overcommitment in too many places may impair our capacity for effective action. The Vietnam engagement, as he pointed out, has resulted in an even greater strengthening of American forces. Of the 500,000 military personnel added between January, 1965, and September, 1966, only 300,000 are in Vietnam, leaving more men available for other commitments. The increase in manpower has been accompanied by extensive renewal and modernization of equipment, including trial of various new weapons systems under battle conditions.

Contrary to the impression given by some European newspapers, American opposition to the defense of freedom in Vietnam is insignificant both in quantity and quality. As Senator Dodd points out, the professors who sign protest manifestos are, for the most part, those having no professional experience with public problems, while the student contingent is typified by the term "beatnik." American campuses are today the highest-priority target for the U.S. Communist party, and—it may be added—recent events at several European universities suggest that systematic infiltration and agitation among students has been given universal emphasis by the communist leadership.

Summarizing his observations in the form of practical conclusions, Senator Dodd urges a policy designed to open up the closed communist society, to promote its further erosion. To support this, he advocates what he calls "positive containment," holding the line against communist expansion and subversion but developing greater reciprocity in exchange programs and support for intellectuals who become victims of the communist police states. In addition to the general rehabilitation and strengthening of NATO, Senator Dodd calls for a joint NATO policy on trade with the communist bloc, which is much more dependent upon the West than vice versa. The leverage provided by trade should be used to bargain for concrete advantages, such as settlement of the Vietnam war or destruction of the Berlin Wall. This proposal for economic unity within NATO was warmly seconded by the late Dr. Jaksch, who is remembered for his initiative in formulating German policies designed to reopen Eastern Europe.

POWER POLITICS AND IDEOLOGY

The first major topic, "East Europe in the Interplay of World Forces," is introduced by Professor Meissner's analysis of Soviet politics under Brezhnev and Kosygin. The Soviet Union, he emphasizes, has never abandoned its imperialist goal in Europe. Its military policy remains frankly aggressive, dedicated to catching up with and overtaking the United States in mass destruction weapons. Local wars have been upgraded in current Soviet policy, and it is clear that the Kremlin leadership intends to provoke such wars wherever they will serve communist interests. While Brezhnev and Kosygin, perhaps as a reaction to the failure of Khrushchev's diplomacy in the COMECON, have deemphasized that organization, they have undertaken to build up the Warsaw Pact as an offensive military alliance. But while the satellites have accepted the new weapons that Moscow provides for them, they have—under Rumanian leadership—rejected Brezhnev's and Kosygin's proposals for a closer integration of the Warsaw Pact organization command structure. They have likewise objected to paying a larger share of joint military costs. Largely as the result of its own aggressive military policy, the Soviet Union faces the dilemma of rockets or butter, a situation that promises to remain acute as long as the Kremlin insists on gearing up for a first strike or preemptive attack.

The facts marshaled by Professor Meissner should suggest to the intelligent observer the ingredients of a common-sense Western trade policy. Certainly no Western country has an interest in helping the Soviets off the horns of a dilemma that is hampering the expansion of their nuclear striking force. This consideration reemphasizes the need for machinery for agreeing on and carrying out a NATO economic policy.

The foreign policy of the new Kremlin leaders, Professor Meissner points out, is distinguished from Khrushchev's by a certain difference in style, but not by willingness to make concessions that might really reduce tensions. The new leaders recognize, as several other contributors also observe, that Soviet control of Middle Germany, the Soviet

Zone, is the key to continued hegemony in East Central Europe. They therefore want no movement in the German question and are not even at present interested in bilateral talks with the United States on that particular subject.

In domestic politics the Kremlin is faced with a dilemma rooted in the fact that the needs of industrial society dictate greater personal freedom. The party apparatus fears, not without reason, that such freedom would jeopardize its monopoly of rule. Continuing this analysis and extending it to the satellite area, Professor Mosely observes that destalinization has given partial release to the forces needed for economic and social modernization. Critics of Stalinism, however, are not necessarily pro-Western, nor are they any less dedicated to world revolution. They may indeed be optimists about modernizing socialist and "Marxist-Leninist" economic systems.

Rejection of Stalinism introduces a certain empirical element into communism, while the doctrine of infallibility is abandoned. East European Communists, Professor Mosely points out, sometimes even appeal to the public with negative arguments, claiming, for instance, that their peoples are better off than the Russians or that it is better to be ruled by lukewarm local Communists than by fanatical Soviet Communists. It must be interjected here, however, that the revolts of 1953 in Middle Germany and 1956 in Hungary and Poland, to which the antistalinist campaign was a response, were not against Stalinism or bureaucratism but fundamentally against communism as a whole.

As Professor Mosely and the contributors to the symposium on individual countries make clear, the processes of change that dominate the scene in East-Central Europe are more than superficial, even though they are still to be classed as changes within the communist system. These changes, which communist leaders both need and fear, can hardly come rapidly enough to meet the demands of industrial progress, even in Yugoslavia. It is evident from several of the essays that while communist leaders attempt to control political and social evolution, they are not always able to do so. The failure of communist intellectual control, despite a monopoly of communications media, suggests that there are autonomous laws of political behavior that are above ideology and are valid in dictatorial as well as constitutional systems.

The present situation has many aspects of a détente, but there are—as Professor Mosely observes—a number of possible contingencies that might induce the Kremlin to return to a more aggressive and expansionist policy. One of these would be a shift in the balance of strategic power; another, a Moscow-Peking reconciliation; a third, a serious breakdown in the solidarity of the West, permitting the Kremlin to play the Western powers against one another. Professor Mosely's recommendations therefore are: (1) a strengthening of the strategic role of the West, perhaps through a European deterrent; (2) greater emphasis on German reunification; and (3) differential treatment of East European governments, reflecting their differing degrees of independence and liberalization. The puppet Ulbricht regime would be at the bottom of the scale—treated as a pariah and dealt with only indirectly through the Federal Republic.

In the discussion of world power relationships affecting East-Central Europe, Professor Possony seconded the warnings of Professors Meissner and Mosely about aggressive Soviet military intentions, pointing out that if the Soviet Union continues to expand its missile force at the current rate, while the United States adheres to the policy of replacements only, parity will be achieved between 1970 and 1972. Secretary McNamara, he indicated, has admitted as much to a Congressional committee and has said that a Soviet first strike would cost an estimated 135 million American casualties. A full-scale anti-ballistic-missile system, analogous to that now being deployed by the Soviets, has been repeatedly deferred as too expensive, although it would cost only about 5 billion dollars per year—less than half the cost of the Vietnam war at present—and it would afford a considerable reduction in casualties. In connection with Soviet-satellite relations Dr. Uschakow observed that a shift in the juridical basis of the newer bilateral pacts has indicated a limiting of the *casus foederis* and hence *theoretically* a greater independence of policy for smaller East European states. Dr. Bradebond, in the same discussion, observed that Gomulka had his own reasons, in addition to any Moscow may have had, for not wanting the Pope invited to Poland.

No consideration of East-West relations in Europe would be complete without reference to the Moscow-Peking dispute, which looms on the horizon as a factor that might, in the future, upset existing power relationships. Analyzing the ideological aspect of this conflict, Dr. Wu Chen-tsai, Director of the Institute of International Affairs in Taipei, points out that the Soviets believe that the era of imperialism has ended, that the nature of the times has changed, but that the Chinese think the age of imperialism still continues. The Russian

Communists recognize that large-scale wars are disastrous for both sides. They believe such wars can be avoided. Therefore they stress peaceful coexistence as a form of struggle short of total war, while clearly rejecting any ideological compromise with capitalism. The Chinese, however, believe that the balance of power is already on the side of socialism and the "revolutionary peoples," that is, the peoples of colonies and former colonies, whom they count on their side—whether they actually are or not. Indeed, the Chinese talk as though they were ready for a showdown with the United States and its allies, which, in any realistic sense, they obviously are not.

In the field of economics the Chinese charge that Soviet reforms decentralizing planning decisions and introducing the principles of profit and incentive pave the way for the revival of capitalism. In discussing the effects of the Russian-Chinese schism on Eastern Europe, Dr. Wu Chen-tsai warns against expecting to exercise much influence through economic, cultural, and political relations with communist regimes. He urges more careful distinction between rulers and peoples in the formulation of policy.

A fundamental insight is contributed by Professor Walker, who shows that the real revolution in Asia—in terms of fundamental improvement in human welfare—is taking place outside the communist area of control. Free governments in Taiwan, Japan, Korea, and elsewhere are pioneering in novel programs of economic development— to which the "revolutionary development" program of the South Vietnam government is a recent addition—and transforming the entire region. Thus the Republic of China, having succeeded with its own land reform, is carrying on agricultural-technical assistance in a number of African countries. International cooperation is expanding through the Asia Development Bank as well as through the Asian and Pacific Ministerial Conference (ASPAC), to which the United States does not belong and which was organized at the initiative of Korea. International relations in the Asian sector have changed markedly since 1956. The Bandung spirit proved ephemeral. An attempt to hold a second Afro-Asian conference at Algiers aborted when neither Russia nor China was able to exert the necessary leadership. The Chinese have continued their drive for hegemony, but their policy blunders have isolated them from other Asian nations. The overthrow of communist influence in Indonesia, which made possible the settlement of the Indonesia-Malaysia conflict, is a case in point. Wherever progress is achieved in Asia, however, it takes place under the umbrella of United States power, and this is one reason why the importance of the American holding action in Vietnam goes far beyond Vietnam itself.

In the discussion on Far Eastern affairs, Dr. Jürgen Domes observed that the army and the Red guard were, at least for the time being, eclipsing the regular party machinery in Communist China, while the power struggle among Mao's would-be successors was continuing. In the past any economic betterment has been followed by a new radicalization, and this sequence might well be repeated. Messrs. Carrington and Broekmeijer pointed out the importance of an infrastructure for economic development, which is something lacking in mainland China. Professor Mosely's observation that the more primitive and less sophisticated elements were coming to the fore was seconded by several contributors who emphasized the irrational and fantastic elements in Chinese policy. The ultimate answer to the Chinese economic problem, as Professor Mosely somewhat cynically but not unrealistically suggested, might very likely be a Malthusian solution—not the first in history—that is, a reduction in the number of consumers.

Three contributors to this book—Mayor Dr. Brundert of Frankmurt, the late Dr. Jaksch, and Baron von Guttenberg—deal with problems involving the reunification of Germany and its implications for Eastern Europe. The commitment to German unity, they point out, has been a major factor in stabilizing German democracy, the latter being a problem that the Allies of World War I neglected in the days of the Weimar republic. Although the reunification issue seems to have dropped into the background at present, it can and should be reactivated as part of a comprehensive peace policy. It might be commented here that since the Soviets are currently following a stand-pat policy, the West enjoys an excellent opportunity to develop and advertise its own conceptions.

Despite the partition of Germany and Europe, Germany continues to fulfill its role as a cultural link between the East and the West, the use of German as *lingua franca* and the expansion of east-bound tourism being cases in point. There is, of course, a certain danger that the East may come to visualize Western values too much in terms of minks and Mercedes. A United States withdrawal from Europe, such as that conceived by some believers in the automatic liberalization of communism, would create a power vacuum that could only be filled by Soviet Russia. Above all, the West should not be taken in by the myth of Russian fear of Germany, which acts as a stumbling-block to more positive policies. Dr. Jaksch and Baron von Guttenberg both made clear that, although there are numerous possible compromises between free-enterprise and socialist economic systems (which may or may not be workable), there is no middle way between freedom and slavery. This elementary fact rules out any serious consideration of proposals for federating the "two German states."

As the contributors to this book generally agreed, reunification with the Soviet Occupation Zone and settlement of the Eastern boundary question can be achieved only as part of a general European settlement in which a peace treaty with a united Germany would be a central feature. The challenge facing the West is to shift the economy of incentives so that the Soviets will see it in their own interest to relinquish political control of East-Central Europe.

Totalitarianism and Christian Obligation

The second section of the book, under the general heading "Christian Churches and Totalitarian Rule," is in essence a study of the anatomy of totalitarianism and of the moral problems it poses for practicing Christians. Professor Herberg's essay on "Christian Faith and Totalitarian Rule" is a fundamental study of political obligation, bringing into clear relief the moral principles pertinent to dealings with totalitarian regimes. The theological basis for Herberg's analysis is the distinction between the legitimate state contemplated in chapter 13 of Paul's Letter to the Romans and the so-called Beast described in Revelation 13. The legitimate state is not necessarily democratic or even humanitarian but it has certain functions as a necessary guardian of order and, above all, its functions are limited. In terms of contemporary political categories the line dividing legitimate from illegitimate governments is that between mere authoritarianism and totalitarianism. The essential issue is that of the limitation or totality of power, or, conversely, it is the issue of the private sphere of the individual. The Anglo-Saxon Protestant tradition includes religion in the private sphere; the function of the state is to employ its power to assure the freedom within which the voluntary "life of grace" can unfold. It might be observed, however, that the early Christians who carried on the Hebrew theocratic tradition became excited only when the Roman Emperor decreed worship of the "wrong" gods.

The proper sphere of politics and hence of legitimacy and obligation was stated by Thomas Aquinas in his *Summa Theologica* in two theses: first, every individual person is related to the community as a part of the whole; second, man is not ordained to the body politic according to all that he has and is. The Thomist view is that the ruler should keep order, dispense justice, and maintain law, which he can make only to a limited degree. He must not violate the divine law or exceed his proper powers. If he deliberately, systematically, and incorrigibly violates divine law and tramples upon the basic human rights to life, liberty, and property, he then becomes an illegitimate ruler, a tyrant, or, in Locke's words, "he ceases in that to be a magistrate." This doctrine was passed on via Wycliffe, Hooker, Locke, and Burke and has become the center of the Anglo-Saxon and American political traditions as well as taking root elsewhere, including the European continent. The totalitarian state, a state which claims the whole man, which wants to remodel him, is, however, essentially illegitimate. A Christian owes such a state no obligation, even though he may cooperate in putting out fires, obeying traffic regulations, and other practical matters. Since the totalitarian state is at war with mankind, there can be no peace with it, and Christians should not be confused by a misapplication of Romans 13 to cases it was never intended to cover. The actual course of action or, more precisely, the choice of methods of struggle against totalitarianism then becomes a matter of prudence.

Drawing on his experience in the "underground" Church of Slovakia, Bishop Hnilica gives a moving account of the sufferings of the clergy, members of religious orders, and Catholic laymen under communist persecution. It is evident from the statistics he cites that the communist regime has reduced radically the operational scope of the Church by removing its material and organizational substance, by permitting, for instance, the education of only a fraction of the number of priests needed to replace those who die or retire. The shortage of books is such that graves are opened to recover missals buried with the deceased. It is equally evident, however, that persecution awakens individual resources of faith and courage that recall the martyrdom of the early Christians.

The ensuing discussion brought out both the totality of the communist war against religion and the failure of Western Christians to help their fellow-believers east of the Iron Curtain. Sir Arnold Lunn commented on the double standard prevalent among modern Christians, who are quick to protest against apartheid in South Africa or Rhodesia but remain silent in the face of communist terrorism. This and the negative attitude of the Church in questions involving human freedom are, he feels, results of penetration of both the Catholic and Protestant churches by secularism and materialism. Christians who are serious about their beliefs, however, face serious questions of moral obligation. One of these, mentioned by Professor Walker, is whether Christians outside totalitarian states should aid anticommunist revolts such as those that have taken place in Soviet Zone Germany, Hungary, Czechoslovakia, and, more recently, Tibet. While Professor Herberg's essay deals specifically with the situation of individuals *within* such states, the obligations for men of goodwill outside them are implicit in his argument. It is pertinent in this connection that the traditional, and in this writer's opinion valid, concept of international law is that of the rules of intercourse within a family of *civilized* nations. The obligations of states to one another are mutual obligations, and if a state outlaws itself by violating the canons of civilized behavior, the external obligation to it ceases with the internal obligation. Under this criterion the United States has no obligation to respect the sovereignty of the Castro regime in Cuba.

While the mutual obligations of human beings—singly or in groups, and regardless of political systems—are matters of morals (though not necessarily of pacifist morality), the question of what to do about dictatorial regimes *as distinguished from the people under their sway* is strictly a matter of prudence. The Allies, for instance, had no obligation to the Hitler regime during World War II. They did have, and violated, an obligation to the people of Dresden and to the refugees in that city. It is necessary to make the same distinction in developing policies for dealing with communist regimes and the people under them.

THE LIMITATIONS OF EVOLUTION

The final section of the book deals with processes of change in the individual countries of Eastern Europe, with the recent evolution of Marxism-Leninism and its recognition by younger Communists as

ideology rather than science, and, in Mr. Davidson's essay, with the
need for a longer-range historical perspective as a point of departure
for contemporary policy. While varying degrees of liberalization have
been observed, it seems evident that its scope and degree, except
possibly and to a very limited extent in the case of Yugoslavia, have
remained within the range of totalitarianism. Such liberalization,
which is currently retrograde in Poland despite the loudly heralded
"Polish October," is not sufficient to create any political obligation
in the terms outlined by Professor Herberg. This suggests that the
cooperation of so-called progressive Marxists and revisionists, the
younger intellectuals whose ideas and activities Professor Lemberg
describes in such interesting detail, is essentially a matter of expediency. Perhaps it would be more accurate to say that their behavior
should be a matter of expediency if the commitment to human values
they claim has any substance.

In contacts and discussions with these Marxists of the younger
generation Westerners should always make their feelings on basic
issues quite clear. East European scholars who aspire to any sort of
humanism, whether derived from the young Marx or from other
sources, should be given to understand that their integrity as human
beings, however paradoxical it may sound, depends on their having
their tongues in their cheeks, at least so far as the Leninist side of
Marxism-Leninism is concerned.

The potential value of contacts with young Marxists is suggested
by a remark during the discussion about the death of ideology. The
goal of transition to communism, which even in the Soviet Union
never emerged fully from the mists of ideology, has been postponed
ad calendas graecas: in Hungary the utopian view has given way to
a concern with practical problems, while in Yugoslavia the search for
greater freedom continues and the party has abandoned its totalitarian claims. There is an opportunity, which must be grasped tactfully
but nonetheless definitely, deriving from the unadmitted but ines-
capable fact that revisionist Marxists are on their way to conversion
away from Marxism altogether. Stalin was the authentic successor of
Lenin because Stalinist totalitarianism—which rules out any humanist inhibitions against revolutionary *raison d'état*—is the only kind
capable of survival in the face of long-range evolution and the
natural desire of human beings for freedom. The history of communism in America shows that the Trotskyist heresy—as in the cases
of John Dos Passos, Max Eastman, and many other intellectuals—is

but a way station to outright apostasy. Although Trotskyism was dogmatic in its own way, the step away from Stalinism was usually the
first step toward a rejection of communism altogether—a fact of basic
importance. But fundamental evolution must still be cultivated;
relapses into Stalinism are entirely within the range of possibility.

The limited evolution that has taken place gives rise to a number
of questions, such as the extent to which a self-regulating market can
be combined with a planned economy. Nor can we be sure that
economic decentralization will always lead to political liberalization
or serve as a preventative against retrogression toward greater totalitarianism. The precedent of Lenin's New Economic Policy in Russia
indicates that at least a temporary and limited relaxation of economic controls is fully compatible with the suppression and liquidation of political opposition. In any case economic liberalization
within communist countries is likely to be hampered by Parkinson's
Law: the *apparatchiks* and planners must find themselves something
to do. Yugoslavia seems to have progressed furthest in the direction
of liberalization, but it still has its political prisons. The two-party
system is a long way in the future, if it is in the future at all. All
these facts indicate that the evolution currently witnessed in East-
Central Europe must be viewed with considerable skepticism.

The very limited degree to which internal evolution in Eastern
Europe has affected the political orientation of communist governments is illustrated by a problem that figures in several of the essays:
the issue of the Oder-Neisse boundary. There is a popular theory,
mentioned by several of the authors, that self-determination should
be granted to all nations except the Germans, who are invited to
make an advance concession in the interest of European pacification,
receiving nothing in return—particularly not the reunification with
Middle Germany that is the initial objective of West German and
Allied policy. Polish exiles, in particular, are fond of arguing that
Western recognition of the Oder-Neisse Line as permanent would in
some mysterious way weaken the Soviet position, and that it helps
the Kremlin to deny such recognition.

It is, however, unreasonable to suppose that not only Poland but
all the other satellites, including even "independent" Rumania,
would unanimously demand a measure that conflicts with Kremlin
policy. The fact that the Soviets have not offered to pay for recognition of the Oder-Neisse Line does not mean that they do not want
it. It simply means that they want it as cheaply as possible, and that

they are encouraged to think it available at a bargain price. Insofar as West German and Western policies are predicated on a sober assessment of interests, a proposal for recognition of the Oder-Neisse Line is worthy of consideration only if accompanied by direct and positive assurance by the Soviet government that such recognition will be compensated by immediate and unconditional withdrawal of Soviet troops from Middle Germany. Otherwise, such a suggestion is devoid of substance.

The Potsdam Agreement, frequently cited in discussions on Germany's eastern boundaries, provided only for provisional administration of German territories east of the Oder and Neisse, pending a peace treaty—presumably with a united Germany. But if Potsdam is suddenly to be resurrected, should this not include the all-German agencies provided therein, the treatment of Germany as an economic unit, and the freedom of movement between all parts of Germany that is implicit in the Potsdam Agreement? The Oder-Neisse Line is analogous to a dependent variable in mathematics: it is a state of affairs depending on some other fact—in this case Soviet hegemony in Eastern Europe. It is evident from the analyses of Soviet policy that the Kremlin will not make a peace treaty with a united Germany until the constellation of power and interests has changed and it is no longer in a position to maintain its East European hegemony. At that point, however, when the Soviet Union or perhaps a noncommunist Russian government is ready to make a stable peace to restore Europe to its natural structure, the Oder-Neisse Line will be obsolete.

There is a statute of limitations in international custom—a statute of limitations on the disabilities that a defeated state has to suffer after a war. It is conceivable that Germany might have accepted the Oder-Neisse Line in a treaty, if it had been signed in 1946—especially before Secretary Byrnes' speech in Stuttgart. But World War II is long since over: the period since the close of hostilities is already longer than the interval between the two world wars. The era of moral excommunication by the Allies and self-abasement on the part of the Germans, the period when a draconic peace seemed plausible not only to Western nations but to the Germans themselves came to an end with the integration of Germany into the Atlantic defense system and the European Community. It would be poor advice to the Germans to recommend that they accept a permanent territorial disability or a limitation of their freedom to negotiate when the moral justification for such discrimination is a thing of the past.

As Dr. Kuhn explains in his contribution to the symposium, the highest priority diplomatic objective of the Prague government is not the repeal of "Munich" but West German recognition of the "German Democratic Republic" as a second German state. There is a curious inconsistency in the fact that those who call for such recognition also demand West German acceptance of the Oder-Neisse Line—which in this case would be a boundary between two states foreign to the German Federal Republic. This insistence on having the Bonn government recognize a boundary after first having agreed that this boundary is not its concern seems to indicate that the Communists do not really believe their own two-state theory, and that they subconsciously accept what is obvious in the West: that the German Federal Republic is the only representative German government. Professor Mosely indicated the correct policy: the Soviet Zone should be treated for what it is, as a puppet without substance of its own.

The essence of a state—the first characteristic of any state recognized in international law—is sovereign independence. The so-called German Democratic Republic, however, exists only by virtue of its lack of sovereignty. The day on which the "GDR" became independent, it would cease to exist because its own inhabitants would abolish it. To find the most suitable descriptive term for Ulbricht's "Republic," it is necessary to borrow by analogy from American literary slang, which refers to a collection of meaningless noises between two covers as an "unbook." Extending this terminology to the "GDR," which exists precisely and exclusively because of its *lack of independence,* it is clear that the Soviet Zone government is to be classified as an unstate despite its superficial trappings.

In summary, while the changes reported in this book are in many ways both interesting and significant, they are changes within the totalitarian system. They do not justify any weakening or softening of Western policy. On the contrary, they call for a more energetic and consistent policy directed at the peaceful promotion of those genuine changes that will permit the final liquidation of World War II and the restoration of a European structure reflecting self-determination and justice.

Index

Index